W9-AQG-349

A HISTORY OF POLITICAL THEORIES
FROM ROUSSEAU TO SPENCER

THE MACMILLAN COMPANY
NEW YORK · BOSTON · CHICAGO · DALLAS
ATLANTA · SAN FRANCISCO

MACMILLAN & CO., LIMITED
LONDON · BOMBAY · CALCUTTA
MELBOURNE

THE MACMILLAN CO. OF CANADA, LTD.
TORONTO

A HISTORY OF POLITICAL THEORIES

FROM ROUSSEAU TO SPENCER

BY

WILLIAM ARCHIBALD DUNNING, LL.D., LITT.D.

LIEBER PROFESSOR OF HISTORY AND POLITICAL PHILOSOPHY
IN COLUMBIA UNIVERSITY

New York

THE MACMILLAN COMPANY

1920

Set up and electrotyped. Published November, 1920.

Norwood Press
J. S. Cushing Co. — Berwick & Smith Co.
Norwood, Mass., U.S.A.

PREFACE

The present work concludes the *History of Political Theories* of which two earlier volumes were published in 1902 and 1905 respectively. It is designed in this last volume to carry the subject through the first eight decades of the nineteenth century. Not that the year 1880 is a particularly logical stopping point. It in fact marks no era of importance in either general history or the special field which is the subject of treatment. The distinctive purpose served by the chosen date is to bring the history to an end while it is still history, and thus save the author from the temptation to deal with ideas that cannot, in the nature of things, be seen yet in their true perspective.

The first, fourth and seventh chapters of this volume have appeared in the *Political Science Quarterly* in substantially their present form. For suggestive comments upon various parts of the text I am indebted to Professor F. W. Coker, of the Ohio State University, and to my colleagues at Columbia, Professors Munroe Smith and Carlton J. H. Hayes. The greatest inspiration to me to continue the work to its completion has been the interest in the subject manifested by my students past and present, and to them I am privileged to offer here this grateful acknowledgment.

Columbia University,
September 6, 1920.

CONTENTS

CHAPTER I

JEAN JACQUES ROUSSEAU

CHAPTER II

THE RISE OF ECONOMIC AND JURISTIC SCIENCE

CHAPTER III

THE AMERICAN AND THE FRENCH REVOLUTION

CHAPTER IV

The German Idealists

CHAPTER V

Theories of Conservatism and Reaction

CHAPTER VI

The English Utilitarians

CHAPTER VII

Theories of Constitutional Government

POLITICAL THEORIES

CHAPTER I

JEAN JACQUES ROUSSEAU

1. *Source and Method of His Philosophy*

THE contributions of Jean Jacques Rousseau to political theory can be rightly understood only through a pretty clear idea of the man himself. He was no statesman, no scholar, no philosopher; and he gloried in the fact.[1] Though he claimed to be a man, he never developed morally beyond the stature of a spoiled child. He was, however, a child of genius. His mind was inordinately sensitive to certain types of impression, and his faculty for literary expression was remarkable. Upon any subject that engaged his errant and erratic fancy, he could concentrate a fervid and captivating eloquence, a wealth of seductive speculation and a plausible imitation of logical force. Certain problems of social and political life early attracted Rousseau's attention. Essays upon these topics revealed the vigor and grace of his style, and struck the dominant chord of public feeling. In 1750 he came

[1] "Lecteurs, souvenez-vous toujours que celui qui vous parle n'est ni un savant, ni un philosophe; mais un homme simple, ami de la vérité, sans parti, sans système, un solitaire, qui vivant peu avec les hommes a moins d'occasions de s'imboire de leurs préjugés . . ." *Émile*, liv. ii, in *Œuvres*, IV, 152.

suddenly to fame by an essay maintaining that the progress of the sciences and arts had tended to degrade the morals of men.[1] Four years later he further developed this general thesis in the famous *Discourse on the Origin and Basis of Inequality among Men.* From this time political and social themes formed the staple of his thinking till the culmination of his work in the *Social Contract* and the *Émile,* published in 1762.

It is rare in the history of political philosophy that the source of influential theory can be so precisely traced to individual personality as in the case of Rousseau. He was of a sensitive, emotional, self-conscious temperament, impatient of control, even of self-control, and resentful toward every institution or convention that suggested restriction or regularity. Of agreeable social relations with rational and cultivated men he was wholly incapable. Efforts of many such men, admirers of his genius and his theories, to establish and maintain cordial relations with Rousseau ended uniformly in failure, with a great access of bitterness and rancor on his part toward things in general. Only one human being seems to have possessed the power to induce more than a feeble flicker of the rudimentary social instinct in Rousseau, and this was the coarse and unlovely woman with whom for a third of a century he lived in squalid and irregular domestic relations.[2] Practically destitute of the qualities that

[1] This essay took the prize in a competition set by the Academy of Dijon on the subject: "Si les progrès des sciences et des arts a contribué à corrompre ou à épurer les mœurs." Dreyfus-Brissac, *Du Contrat Social,* p. iv.

[2] Morley, *Rousseau,* I, chap. iv.

make human society possible, his instinct was to disparage the conspicuous features of social life. His own incapacity for orderly and useful commerce with his kind he generalized into a characteristic of the race; and the protest of his vain and sensitive spirit against the restraints of law and custom became in his writings the universal truth of human freedom. He was himself the free and noble savage whom he pictured so pleasingly in his works. The *Confessions*, in which he presents himself with deliberate frankness, contain scarcely more of his intellectual autobiography than can be found in his *Discourses* and other political writings.

Such a temperament as Rousseau's could in no age and no place have found a more stimulating environment than the middle eighteenth century in France. The smouldering fire of protest that determined his restless and unhappy private life became a devouring flame when he attained publicity and turned his attention to the religion, morals, manners and politics of his day. Society on the continent, and more than elsewhere, perhaps, in France, abounded in conditions that were in the highest degree odious to thoughtful men. Feudal class distinctions, mediæval theology and divine-right monarchy were salient facts of the situation. The nobility still retained their privileges, though the justification for these had long disappeared with the loss of real political power; the clergy also retained their privileges, though their usefulness was waning through dissoluteness and dissensions within and scepticism without their circle. Louis XV, as an embodiment of God-given absolute power, was contributing all that his sodden and lustful nature could to destroy the sense of duty and respect on which the whole fabric of the monarchic system rested.

The reaction of rational philosophy against obscurantism and despotism was well under way when Rousseau appeared on the scene. Voltaire and Montesquieu had, in their widely different methods, roused the spirit of revolt. Diderot was just planning that *Encyclopædia* which in the scope and disconnectedness of its contents so well typified the genius of its projector, and in its reputation and fate so well expressed the antagonism between the established political system and the aspirations of current philosophy. Rousseau wrote his earliest political essays with the sympathetic coöperation of Diderot. Before the *Social Contract* appeared, however, the two men were wide asunder personally, and Rousseau had taken a course in his political speculation that put him far outside the Encyclopædist group. It was not in his nature to react mildly against a situation that galled him — as most facts of actual life did. He knew not how to stop short of the uttermost limit of protest. Liberal philosophers in Germany and France itself had for half a century waged vigorous war upon the oppressive and deadening principles and practices of the old régime.[1] The goal of their demands was, however, merely a tolerant and enlightened despotism. Even those who, like Montesquieu, conceived that salvation was to be found in the English system, looked for only some beneficent re-

[1] *Political Theories from Luther to Montesquieu*, pp. 373, 392.

arrangement of the organs of government. Rousseau, when he set about projecting political reform, never paused till he had provided for the total remodelling of government, state and society itself.

But the radical character of Rousseau's social and political theories was not due to any novelty in the ideas out of which they were made. He lighted up and magnified, but he did not create. Old and well-known concepts were played upon by his brilliant fancy till they were transfigured and made to appeal to men with an uncanny attractiveness. After the great success of his *Discourse on the Progress of the Sciences and Arts* he resolved to write a systematic work covering the whole field of political science. The *Social Contract* is a fragment of this work — the only part of it that ever took shape. In preparing for this enterprise, Rousseau familiarized himself with some of the chief writers on political philosophy. Pufendorf, Locke and Montesquieu found especial favor in his eyes, and their ideas were freely appropriated with and without acknowledgment. Grotius and Hobbes excited his wrath; protesting against the tendency of critics to praise Grotius while execrating Hobbes, Rousseau included both in the same condemnation. "The truth is," he said, "that their principles are exactly alike, distinguishable only in expression. They differ also in method. Hobbes supports himself on sophisms, Grotius on poets; in all else they are on common ground." [1]

Besides the influence of his rather superficial study

[1] *Émile*, liv. v, in *Œuvres*, V, 403.

of earlier philosophers, Rousseau's thought showed plainly the influence of his birthplace. It was with real pride that he described himself on the title-page of the *Social Contract* as a "citizen of Geneva." The Swiss city-state furnished him with many suggestions of a system in marked contrast to that which prevailed in France, and clearly strengthened his predilection for popular government. Even more important was the stimulus it gave to that unbounded admiration with which he, in common with all his contemporaries, regarded the Greek and Roman republics. He had no deep or scholarly acquaintance with the history of the ancient city-states, but he was full of the literary tradition that clothed their institutions with the perfection of wisdom and their heroes with the perfection of virtue. Not Machiavelli nor Montesquieu was more satisfied than he to clinch a demonstration with a reference to these overworked commonwealths. Rousseau's nimble logic could use them to prove a rule either by their conformity to it or by their deviation from it. Thus, he maintained that every state is bound to die; for "if Sparta and Rome have perished, what state can hope to endure forever?"[1] On the other hand, his contention that a system of public education was an essential feature of every good state was confronted by the fact that Rome knew nothing of it. That, he explained, signified nothing; since "Rome was for five centuries a continuous miracle, such as the world must never hope to see again."[2]

[1] *Contrat Social*, III, xi.
[2] *Économie Politique*, in *Œuvres* (1782), I, p. 391.

It was at times an amiable delusion of Rousseau's that his philosophy was fundamentally a series of inductions from the observation of ordinarily neglected facts.[1] In some measure this was true of his ideas about education, as expressed in the *Émile;* it was wholly untrue of his theoretical politics, in the *Discourse on Inequality* and the *Social Contract.* After his reputation was made, he was applied to for suggestions on the very concrete political situation in two troubled lands, Corsica and Poland. His responses embodied many shrewd and striking comments on the actual facts involved.[2] But more important here were the persistency and adroitness with which he applied, at whatever effort of twisting and straining, the dogmas of his earlier speculation; and these were no inductions from his own observation of facts or reading of history, but merely the product of judicious selection among the accumulated doctrines and traditions of *a priori* political science.

2. *Nature and Society*

Rousseau approached political theory by the well-worn pathway of the "state of nature." As to what precisely this term signified, he was not clear and consistent. He used it in practically all the various senses that had been attached to it in its long and

[1] "Mes raisonnements sont moins fondés sur les principes que sur des faits." *Émile*, ii, in *Œuvres*, IV, 152. ". . . je donne le moins qu'il est possible au raisonnement, et ne me fie qu'à l'observation." *Ibid.*, iv, in *Œuvres*, IV, 446.

[2] For his Corsican thoughts see Morley, *Rousseau*, II, 99 *et seq.*, and references. On Poland see his *Considérations sur le gouvernement de Pologne*, in *Œuvres* (1782), I, 417.

notable career. Throughout the fluctuations of his usage, one idea alone appeared unmistakable, namely, that the natural state of man was vastly preferable to the social or civil state, and must furnish the norm by which to test and correct it.

In the *Discourse on Inequality* the natural man appears first as the solitary savage, living the happy, care-free life of the brute, without fixed abode, without articulate speech, with no needs or desires that cannot be satisfied through the merest instinct. Rousseau's handling of this conception compares favorably with that of the best among the long line of literary artists who have used it. More apparent than in most of them, however, are his admiration and sympathy for the savage. The steps by which men emerge from their primitive state are depicted with fascinating art, but the author's regret at their success pervades the picture. In the natural man are to be found the elements of perfect happiness. He is independent, contented, self-sufficing. For others of his own species he has no need, and he regards them with the same indifference that he feels toward other animals. Save for the casual and momentary union that perpetuates the race, nothing draws him to commerce with his kind. He is not, however, the timid, cowering creature that Montesquieu described, fearful of every force around him. Nor on the other hand is he the energetic, aggressive monster of Hobbes, ceaselessly driven by his passions to war upon his fellows. Only through society does man become unbalanced by either fear or ambition; the "simple, regular (*uniforme*) and solitary" life of nature involves none of the evils of either.

The natural state, as thus conceived, is a state of substantial equality. No baneful distinction is to be seen among the individuals who pursue in isolation the placid routine of satisfying their physical needs. But the deadly seeds of a different order are ready to germinate. With no necessary ground for it in his description of the savage state, Rousseau assumes that the human race becomes increasingly numerous; divergencies of soil, climate and season then cause differences in manner of life among men. On the shores of the seas and the rivers they catch fish and invent the hook and line. In the forests they become hunters and invent the bow and arrow. Fire is discovered by some accident, and the fortunate discoverers develop its utilities. Stone and then metal tools are made. Economic progress moves apace, and rude huts instead of casual caves become places of abode. With the appearance of fixed homes, family and property are at hand, and the knell of human equality is sounded. Social organization has begun. Intercourse of individuals and families becomes common and through it the ideas of competition and preference are developed. Evils follow in their train, but this primitive society is not, to Rousseau, an intolerable state. Looked upon as a mean between the indolence of the savage state and the too intense activity of the later phase, it appears to him the happiest period in the life of humanity — "the least subject to revolutions, the best for man."

It is quite characteristic of Rousseau that while he is describing the savage state he is disposed to consider it as the happiest and best, and when he has moved on to the tribal and early social state, this in turn appeals to him as preferable. We shall see that in time he has kind words for even fully developed society, which in the *Discourse* is the summation of evil.

Man's emergence from the primitive social condition must have been due, Rousseau says, to some fatal chance. His exposition of the process reveals a number of catastrophes that contributed to the sad result. The arts of agriculture and metallurgy were discovered; and in the application of them men had need of one another's aid. Coöperation revealed and emphasized the diversity of men's talents and prepared thus the inevitable result. The stronger man did the greater amount of work; the craftier got more of the product. Thus appeared the difference of rich and poor — the prolific source of all the other forms of inequality. Property was doing its disastrous work. The climax came with the diabolical device of property in land.

"The first man who, after enclosing a piece of ground, bethought himself to say 'this is mine,' and found people simple enough to believe him, was the real founder of civil society."[1]

War, murder, wretchedness and horror without end followed this fatal proceeding. Rich and poor were ranged against each other in unrelenting hostility.

[1] *Discours sur l'Inégalité*, pt. ii, beginning.

Evils that had been unknown in the savage state, and but slightly manifested in primitive society, became now universal. To escape them, or at least to enable men to endure them, civil society was instituted. This was no recurrence to the natural order. It was, on the contrary, an enormous stride away from nature, and the introduction of still another mode of inequality among men. Its inevitable consequence was the final stage of inequality, the condition of master and slave.

Such was, in general outline, Rousseau's thought in the *Discourse on Inequality*. With proper allowance for the incoherence and inconsistencies of the work, it may be said that his state of nature is on the whole a historical rather than a psychological concept. Yet Rousseau, like Locke, who is strongly suggested by many points in the *Discourse*, refrains from insisting on the objective reality of the conditions he describes. The state he is considering is one, he says, "which no longer exists, which perhaps has not existed and which probably never will exist, but which must be accurately understood in order to get just notions as to contemporary society." [1] This view of his task would indicate that he, like Hobbes and Locke, was concerned merely with formulating the abstract qualities of human nature. But Rousseau's poetic faculty was too active and its pictures too vivid to leave room for the impression that his natural man was an abstraction or his state of nature a mere fancy. To one who does not read the warning of the preface, the *Discourse* can be nothing but an eloquent and moving

[1] *Discours*, Préface.

narrative of the actual descent of man from natural peace and blessedness to social servitude and woe.

Psychological analysis is not wholly wanting in the *Discourse*. Rousseau employs it, *suo more*, with little pretence to consistency, but sometimes with rather striking effect. He takes pains to repudiate at the outset the idea that man's life in the state of nature is regulated by reason. The truly natural man, *i.e.*, the savage, acts on two principles that are anterior to reason, namely, the feeling of interest in his own welfare and preservation, and the feeling of repugnance toward the sight of death or suffering in any animate creature, especially a human being. These emotions, rather than reason, determine the conduct of men throughout the various phases of the natural state and give way to reason only when degeneration has gone so far that civil society must be constituted. All the rules of natural right and natural law flow directly and exclusively from the operation of these primary sentiments — self-interest and pity.[1]

This curious theory, whatever other sources it had, was an obvious generalization of certain conspicuous traits of Rousseau's own character. He was extremely selfish and extremely sensitive to suffering in others — qualities that are notoriously quite compatible with each other. One immediate application of his theory was in refuting the dogma of Hobbes that the state of nature was a state of war. The innate repugnance to suffering in his kind would necessarily operate to limit the brutality of man to man.

[1] *Discours*, Préface.

It is in the *Émile* that Rousseau most elaborately develops his conception of the state of nature and the natural man as a philosophic ideal rather than a historical reality. The general theme of the work is the rearing and training of a child, and the unceasing exhortation of the author is to abandon methods that have their origin or justification in the real or fancied needs of social life. "Back to nature" is his cry. This does not mean that society must be destroyed and the savage state resumed. It means merely that nature must be the rule for men in society. The incoherence of Rousseau's definitions and explanations and rhapsodies about this matter is in his most characteristic style; and seeking to comprehend clearly his conception of "nature" is like trying to visualize the fauna of the Apocalypse.

His purpose is in a general way intelligible; it is to strip the human mind of all the attributes that are in origin or manifestation ascribable to social life. The residue is the mental equipment of the natural man. At birth the human being is, through his senses, susceptible to impressions from without. Toward the objects that create the impressions he has a feeling of attraction or repulsion according as they are agreeable or disagreeable, and, as his mind develops, according to the rational judgment he forms about their effect upon his happiness. But meanwhile he develops and falls under the constraint of habits and opinions, and through these his dispositions toward things are modified. "Prior to that modification they constitute what I call nature in us."[1]

[1] *Émile*, liv. i, *ad init.*

Such is the nearest approach to precise definition that Rousseau gives his readers. Despite its doubtful psychology it might, if adhered to, serve a useful philosophic purpose. But he does not adhere to it. One clear feature of the natural man as defined above is the use of his reason in judging his surroundings. Elsewhere Rousseau declares it characteristic of the natural man "that he be . . . subject to no government save that of his own reason." [1] With the rational faculty thus emphasized, it is discouraging to find pervading all Rousseau's philosophy, and often reiterated in set terms, the idea that reason and nature are antithetic and incompatible with each other. Reflection and its practical results he proclaims to be the pernicious product of society and its artificialities. "By nature man scarcely thinks." [2] "The man who reflects is a corrupt creature." [3] Our natural feelings (*passions*) alone give us peace and true liberty. So soon as we begin to reason and to project ourselves by induction and analogy into times and places and relations unknown to our original condition, oppression and misery crowd upon us. Thus, for example, man afflicts himself through unhappy foresight with the torture of anticipating death, while to unreflecting creatures it comes without distress.

In no small measure the vagaries and inconsistencies

[1] *Émile*, iv, in *Œuvres*, IV, 447.

[2] "Naturellement l'homme ne pense guère." *Ibid.*, v, in *Œuvres*, V, 302.

[3] "Si [la nature] vous a destinés à être sains, j'ose presque assurer que l'état de réflexion est un état contre nature, et que l'homme qui médite est un animal dépravé." *Discours sur l'Inégalité*, pt. i.

of Rousseau's views about nature and reason are due to the phrase-making instinct of the literary artist. He never thought of logic when the opportunity for a pretty turn of expression was at hand. "Forgive me my paradoxes," he wrote: "I like better to be a man of paradoxes than to be a man of prejudices."[1] Nor did he suspect that he was a man of both. The fixed and ever present, if not always conscious, motive of his thinking was to disparage those features of social life that were distasteful to himself. The violence of his protest was as excessive in dealing with the natural man in society as it had been in dealing with the natural man prior to society; the one, like the other, became an inhuman fantasy.

In stressing the emotions and minimizing the reason as the basis of the state of nature, Rousseau dissociated his doctrine from the whole philosophical tradition on this point. Reason had been always the characteristic ingredient of the pre-social or pre-civil order. Grotius, Hobbes, Pufendorf, Locke, and all their predecessors, great and small, had found man in the state of nature endowed with reason, and enabled by means of it to rise into social and political organization. Rousseau, with whatever vacillation and inconsistency, strove in general to represent reason and all philosophy as a calamitous aberration, deluding men with visions that brought them to ruin.

[1] *Émile*, liv. ii, in *Œuvres*, IV, 116.

3. *The Social Contract*

The most pestilential reasoning and philosophy was, in Rousseau's opinion, that which sustained existing forms of political and social inequality. "Nothing can be farther from the law of nature, however we define it, than that a child give orders to an old man, an imbecile direct a sage, and a handful of people be gorged with luxuries while the starving multitude lacks the necessities of life." [1] Yet society and government, though deplorable, were, he admitted, inevitable. It was necessary therefore to find some rational form through which their existence might be justified. In his *Social Contract*, Rousseau assumed the rôle of constructive philosopher and presented a theory of the state.

The precise problem that he undertakes in this work to solve is characteristically formulated in the famous phrases:

> Man is born free and everywhere he is in chains. One who believes himself the master of the rest is only more of a slave than they.[2] How does that change come about? I do not know. What can render it legitimate (*légitime*)? That question I think I can answer.[3]

[1] *Discours sur l'Inégalité*, end.

[2] This paradox is the topic of an eloquent passage elsewhere: ". . . ta liberté, ton pouvoir, ne s'étendent qu'aussi loin que tes forces naturelles et pas au delà; tout le reste n'est qu'esclavage, illusion, prestige. . . . Jamais ton autorité réelle n'ira plus loin que tes facultés réelles. Sitôt qu'il faut voir par les yeux des autres, il faut vouloir par leurs volontés. Mes peuples sont mes sujets, dis-tu fièrement. Soit. Mais toi, qu'es-tu? Le sujet de tes ministres. Et tes ministres, à leur tour, que sont ils? les sujets de leurs commis, de leurs maîtresses, les valets de leurs valets . . . Vous direz toujours: Nous voulons; et vous ferez toujours ce que voudront les autres." *Émile*, liv. ii, in *Œuvres*, IV, 95.

[3] *Contrat Social*, I, i.

That is to say, the liberty and equality that characterize the state of nature, in whatever sense the term is used, are in the civil state gone. He will justify their disappearance. And he does it, in his usual way, by proving that they are not gone at all, but subsist as fully after, as before, the institution of government. Nature and political society, liberty and authority, are absolute logical contradictories in the *Discourse* and the *Émile;* they become in the *Social Contract* inseparable and indistinguishable concepts. Such, at least, is the consequence of the theorizing in his earlier chapters. The author would not be Rousseau, however, if he did not later revert from time to time to the idea of a preëminent excellence in the non-political condition; and the typical climax of his method is to be seen in a rapturous glorification, at one point, of the political as compared with the natural state.[1]

The device that he hit upon for solving the problem of his work was the social pact. Authority of man over man can have no rational basis, he holds, save agreement and consent. And there is but one species of agreement conceivable in which liberty is retained while authority is instituted. This single species is the pact through which a multitude of individuals become a collective unity — a society. Rousseau's thought here shows the very strong influence of both

[1] ". . . ses facultés s'exercent et se développent, ses idées s'étendent, ses sentiments s'ennoblissent, son âme tout entière s'élève à tel point que, si les abus de cette nouvelle condition ne le dégradaient souvent au-dessous de celle dont il est sorti, il devrait bénir sans cesse l'instant heureux qui l'en arracha pour jamais, et qui, d'un animal, stupide et borné, fit un être intelligent et un homme." *Contrat Social*, I, viii.

Hobbes and Locke. It is the latter, however, whom he follows to the end — and beyond. From the ingenious reasoning by which Hobbes made absolute monarchy a logical corollary of the social pact, Rousseau turns with strong denunciation. But the Hobbesian precision in defining the terms of the pact obviously appealed to him, and his own treatment of the subject is but the substance of Locke developed by the method of Hobbes.

The formula on which civil society rests is, according to Rousseau, this: "Each of us puts into a single mass (*met en commun*) his person and all his power under the supreme direction of the general will; and we receive as a body each member as an indivisible part of the whole."[1] Through the act of a group of individuals in pronouncing, tacitly or expressly, together or in succession, this formula a moral body is constituted, with an identity, a life and a will of its own distinct from those of any of its component members. It is a public person — a body politic. From various points of view it is known as state, sovereign, power; and in the same way its members are known variously as the people, citizens, subjects.[2]

Rousseau's exposition of the spirit and effects of his contract is an amazing medley of bad logic and utter puerility. Equality, he declares, is insured, because each individual makes complete alienation of himself and all his rights to the community. That is to say, the individuals, reducing themselves to zeros, are as such equal. By the same reasoning the union

[1] *Contrat Social*, I, vi. [2] *Ibid.*

is, he explains, absolutely perfect, and no individual can claim anything. This would seem to mean as thorough submergence of the individual in the state as Plato ever conceived. But Rousseau finds the fullest liberty. For, he continues, "since each gives himself up to all, he gives himself up to no one; and as there is acquired over every associate the same right that is given up by himself, there is gained the equivalent of what is lost, with greater power to preserve what is left."[1]

This demonstration of liberty contains as many fallacies as clauses, and finds a fitting climax in the reference to "what is left" to the individual after the pact, following repeated declarations that the individual by the pact gives up everything. It is hardly strange that controversy has continued active as to whether Rousseau stood for absolute sovereignty or for a sphere of inalienable rights in the citizen.[2] He clearly stood for both, relying upon the simple device of maintaining each of two logical contradictories.[3]

His analysis and exposition of the contract are of like fabric. By the terms of this formula the act of association is clearly conceived as merely the expression of an identical purpose by each of a group of individuals. The purpose is to recognize henceforth

[1] ". . . . et plus de force pour conserver ce qu'on a." *Ibid.*

[2] *Cf. Political Science Quarterly*, XXII, 698.

[3] James Russell Lowell never more conspicuously nodded than in declaring that Rousseau "could not fail to be a good logician. He had the fortitude to follow his logic wherever it led him." (*Among My Books*, 1882, I, 340.) Of Rousseau's fortitude there can be no doubt. But the courage of his readers often falters when his logic leads in opposite directions at the same time.

a social or general authority as a substitute for the varying and conflicting authorities of the individual wills. Locke and Sydney, and others who set forth this same idea, did not undertake to analyze it into the elements and categories of a contract in private law. Hobbes, more rigid and inexorable in his method, applied the conceptions of the jurists to the social pact, and showed who were the parties to it, what precise obligation they respectively took upon themselves, and what penalty was incurred when the obligation was repudiated.[1] Rousseau seeks to imitate the method of Hobbes; but the result is ridiculous. The parties to the pact are declared to be on the one side the individuals and on the other the community,[2] and this though the community comes into existence only by virtue of the pact. The engagement made by the community appears at once, however, to be made in reality by the individuals. For, "each individual contracting, so to speak, with himself, finds himself engaged under a double relation, namely, as member of the sovereign toward the individuals, and as member of the state toward the sovereign." And Rousseau, after this sapient exposition, proceeds gravely to explain that there is no real opening here to apply the principle of the civil law according to which no one is bound by engagements made with himself; "for to be bound to one's self and to be bound to a whole of which one forms a part, are very different things." [3]

[1] *Political Theories from Luther to Montesquieu*, p. 278.

[2] ". . . l'acte d'association renferme un engagement réciproque du public avec les particuliers." *Contrat Social*, I, vii.

[3] *Ibid.*, I, vii.

If Rousseau could have remained certainly faithful through a whole section of his work to the truth embodied in this last sentence, his theory of the state would have been important. But his grasp on the distinction between the collective and the distributive aspect of an aggregate was very uncertain. Nothing better illustrates this fact than his easy assumption, noted above, that a promise by a society is the same as a promise by each member of the society. The same confusion appears again and again in his treatise. He glimpses often the fruitful concept of a beneficent and all-determining force in the social organism; but he lacks the dialectic power to disentangle it from the mass of individualistic prejudice that obscures it. He is nearest success in the attempt in his detailed discussion of the notion of sovereignty.

4. *Sovereignty and Law*

Rousseau's doctrine on this subject combined elements that had previously been considered incompatible with each other. The definition and development of sovereignty, as a concept of political science, had been almost entirely the work of those who, like Bodin and Hobbes, were defending absolute monarchy. By the liberalizing school of Locke and Montesquieu the idea of sovereignty was evaded as unnecessary in theory and dangerous in practice — a mortal foe to liberty. Rousseau, with characteristic boldness, proceeded to reconcile the absolutist with the liberal doctrine. He defined sovereignty with the fulness and precision of Hobbes, and gave it an abode and an operation that satisfied the feeling of Locke.

The social contract, Rousseau maintains, furnishes the solution of all questions about sovereignty. The body politic that is created by this contract is itself the only conceivable possessor of supreme power.[1] By the free act of those who enter into the pact all their rights and powers are resigned to the community, and their respective wills are merged into and superseded by the general will (*volonté générale*). By no possible process of reasoning or of fact, Rousseau holds, can sovereignty be traced to any other possessor than the body politic as a whole, or be identified in any other manifestation than that of the general will. He seizes with especial zest the idea of sovereignty as will, and uses it in many fantastic feats of pseudo-dialectic. His often absurd manipulation does not conceal, however, the real value of the idea. Hobbes had already exposed many of its possibilities as a clarifying agency in political speculation; but Rousseau gave the great impulse to that particular development which has centred about the idea of the social or group will.

The basis of will, Rousseau holds, is interest. The individual wills always what is for his interest. His interests conflict at many points with the interests of others; but at some point the interest of all is the same. This common interest is what makes the state possible.

[1] Althusius presented a doctrine of sovereignty in 1610 that was substantially the same as Rousseau's. *Cf. Political Theories from Luther to Montesquieu*, p. 63.

The general will is but the expression of what the common interest requires. The two ideas are inseparable in thought and in fact. If the interests of the individuals composing the state are at no point identical, a general will is inconceivable and society cannot exist. If an expression of will does not correspond to the common interest, it is not an expression of the general will and it lacks the quality of sovereignty. Only an act of the general will is properly called law (*loi*). Perfect generality is of the essence of it. Thus law can have no other source than the sovereign, that is, the community as a body politic. A rule or command prescribed by any other authority lacks the essential quality of law; and, conversely, a rule or command emanating formally from the sovereign body lacks the quality of law if its content or effect touches interests that are not general.

Sovereignty, conceived in such a way, is readily proved by Rousseau to be inalienable, indivisible and inerrant. It is inalienable, because the will cannot be bound by promises. "The sovereign can indeed say: I will now what such-and-such a man wills, or at least what he says he wills; but it cannot say: What that man shall will to-morrow, I shall still will." It can say: What that man shall will, I will do; but this is the formula of slavery, and pledges acts not conformed to the interest of the promisor. Since will in any true sense is inseparable from interest, the servile formula implies the dissolution *ipso facto* of the body politic that enacts it. "The instant there is a master, there is no longer a sovereign."[1] Such is the argument by which Rousseau disposes of the ancient dogma that the people may transfer sovereignty to a prince.

That sovereignty is indivisible is equally clear to Rousseau.

The will either is or is not general, is that of the whole people or that of part of the people. In the first case the expression of the will is a sovereign act and makes law; in the second case it is merely a particular will or an act of the magistrate — at most a decree.[2]

All the distinctions so much debated by philosophers between the different kinds of public acts are unwarranted, Rousseau holds, so far as they imply a division of sovereignty. That there is legislative power and executive power; that taxation and judicature and the affairs of war and peace are variously administered — affects not at all the unity of the sovereign. An act of the whole people for the whole people is, regardless of any other feature of the act, a manifestation of sovereignty.

To prove that the sovereign cannot err is a task that evokes the best effort of Rousseau both as reasoner and as rhetorician.[3] He is required to meet the familiar charge that a democracy is peculiarly apt to stray from expediency and justice. He meets it ingeniously if not conclusively thus:

It follows from the foregoing that the general will is always right and tends always to the public advantage (*utilité publique*); but it does not follow that the judgments (*délibérations*) of the people always have the same rectitude.

[1] *Contrat Social*, II, i. [2] *Ibid.*, II, ii. [3] *Ibid.*, II, iii.

A man always wills his own good, but he does not always see it; the people is never corrupted, but it is often deceived, and only then does it appear to will what is wrong.

Thus the virtue of the sovereign people is saved at the expense of its intelligence; and the inerrancy of the general will is established by the simple process of ascribing all wrong-doing to some other source. It is indeed not hard to see that by its very definition Rousseau's sovereign always wills the public good. Sovereignty is only another name for a generalized collective volition of that content. Difficulty arises, however, when the question changes from the abstract conception of sovereignty to its concrete manifestation. Rousseau's doctrine implies that a resolution adopted unanimously by a community is not necessarily an expression of the sovereign will. He distinguishes the general will from the will of all (*volonté de tous*). This latter is but the sum of all the particular volitions of the individuals about their private interests. The general will is the aggregate of such of these volitions as are common to all the individuals — such as concern interests that are common to all. With this distinction in mind, it is easy to see that a resolution of the whole people lacks the quality of sovereign law if it deals with any matter that does not involve the true interest of every citizen.

One important source of the mistakes often made by the people is to be found, Rousseau says, in the partial societies, or parties, that spring up in the state. When a party is constituted, a new corporate interest appears, coming between the individual interest and the general interest. There is no longer possible that comparison of individual wills through which alone the general will is determined. Party interest intervenes and misleads the people, with the result that the will of the party is mistaken for that of the sovereign. Rousseau's conclusion is, like that of many earlier thinkers, that if parties exist at all in a state, there should be many of them. Where two great parties divide the people, the will of one or the other of them habitually supersedes the general will, and the state ceases in fact to exist.

Rousseau is at some pains to exhibit the limits of sovereignty.[1] They are manifest chiefly, we have just seen, as immediate inferences from the definition of the term: the sovereign cannot do what is not for the general welfare, and cannot intrude therefore into the field of purely individual interest. Is there, then, a sphere of individual rights secure against invasion by the state? In answering this crucial question Rousseau fairly bristles with paradox and contradiction. He declares that "as nature gives to every man an absolute power over all his members, the social pact gives to the body politic absolute power over all its members." This proposition is followed by reference to the distinction between the duties of the individual as a subject and his natural right as man. In point-blank contradiction of what was earlier said as to the terms of the social contract, Rousseau now observes: "It is agreed (*on convient*) that what each alienates by the social pact is only that part of his power, his

[1] *Contrat Social*, IV, iv.

property and his liberty which may be used with advantage by the community." This clearly points to a reserved sphere of individual rights. But the next sentence turns the tables decisively against the individual: "It must also be agreed that the sovereign alone is judge of that advantage."

Formally, thus, there are no limits to sovereign power. Substantially, however, there are, Rousseau insists, the very real limits inherent in the nature of sovereignty. The relation of the individual will to the general will insures at the least the equality of all citizens before the law, and the rule of justice and equity. The sovereign community is limited to prescriptions that are for general, not for any particular utility, and it can impose no burden that is not alike for all. Rousseau's rhetoric in sustaining these amiable ideals is admirable; but his reasoning, while often very specious, never wholly disguises the vitiating assumption that an aggregate cannot possess attributes distinct from those of its component parts.

The most clear and self-consistent feature of his speculation on this general subject is that which deals with the idea of law. Even on this point his predilection for contract leads him into some cloudy quibblings about law as essentially a convention, to which the parties are respectively the community and its individual members.[1] But his central conception is made very distinct and suggestive. As has been stated above,[2] a law is a resolution of the whole

[1] *Contrat Social*, II, iv. [2] *Ante*, p. 23.

people for the whole people, touching a matter that concerns all.

> The law regards the subjects as a whole and actions as abstract, never a man as an individual nor a concrete (*particulière*) act. Thus the law can determine that there shall be privileges, but it cannot give them to anybody by name; the law can establish a classification of the citizens and describe the qualifications for the various classes, but it cannot assign certain men to specific classes; it can establish a royal government and hereditary succession, but it cannot choose a king nor name a royal family . . .[1]

From this conception of law Rousseau concludes that

> it is no longer necessary to ask whose function it is to make laws, since they are acts of the general will; nor whether the prince is above the laws, since he is a member of the state; nor whether the law can be unjust, since no one is unjust to himself; nor how one is at the same time free and subject to the laws, since they are merely registers of our own wills.[2]

No state is legitimate, according to Rousseau, unless it is ruled by laws, as thus defined; and every state so ruled, whatever the form of its government, is a republic.[3] The lucid interval in which he sets forth these fresh and striking conceptions is followed at once by a lapse into dreaming and rhetoric. For the practical realization of the republican state, as he has defined it, he has no suggestion save recourse to a "legislator,"[4] a superhuman or divinely inspired being, to impose upon a people the institutional order

[1] *Contrat Social*, II, vi.
[2] *Ibid.*
[3] "J'appelle donc république tout État régi par des lois, sous quelque forme d'administration que ce puisse être." *Ibid.*
[4] *Contrat Social*, II, vii.

that they are not qualified to discover for themselves — to enact that general will which they share but know not. In this recurrence to a useless and very much shop-worn device of political theory,[1] Rousseau exposes the purely idealizing tendency of his whole speculation. His brave undertaking to show the rational conciliation of liberty and authority ends in a trite glorification of Numa, Lycurgus and John Calvin, with a few practical suggestions, drawn largely from Montesquieu, as to the course most desirable for the next "legislator" that may descend upon mankind.[2]

5. *Government*

The distinction between state or sovereign and government is developed by Rousseau with the utmost exactness and consistency.[3] While "state" denotes the community as a whole, created by the social pact and manifesting itself in the supreme general will, "government" denotes merely the individual or group of individuals that is designated by the community to carry into effect the sovereign will. The government is created not by any contract but by a decree of the sovereign; and its function is in no sense to make, but

[1] The "legislator" was still doing hard service in philosophy; so sensible and practical a thinker as Montesquieu used him.

[2] Rousseau, in common with many intelligent contemporaries (notably Frederick the Great), was much impressed by the political spirit of the Corsicans, then just freeing themselves from Genoa. He says that the Corsicans are the one European people capable of legislating for themselves, and expresses a presentiment that "some day that little island will astonish Europe." (*Contrat Social*, II, x.) Napoleon Bonaparte was born less than ten years after this was written.

[3] *Contrat Social*, III, i.

only to administer law. Government, to Rousseau, means executive power. The individuals to whom this power is assigned are the officers or the agents of the sovereign. Collectively they may be called "prince" or "magistracy." Whatever their titles — kings, senators, governors — their function and their relation to the sovereign are the same. Their power is merely what is intrusted to them by their superior, and may be modified, curtailed or entirely withdrawn at the discretion of that superior.

This doctrine is substantially that of the whole anti-monarchic philosophy of the two centuries preceding Rousseau. His own contribution consists not in any new emphasis on the subordination of the prince to the people, but in the conclusions derivable from his definition of the people as sovereign. He indulges in a good deal of superfluous metaphysics over his conception of sovereignty as will, aiming apparently to clear up problems that would be as well solved without it. Thus he sets forth with great gravity the rather distressing condition of a citizen who is a member of the government.[1] Such a one embodies three distinct wills: first, the will that rests upon his interest as a mere private individual; second, the will corresponding to the corporate interest of the magistracy; third, the will of the community as a whole — the sovereign general will. "In the order of nature" these wills are respectively the more active as they are the more concentrated: that is, the individual will prevails over the general. But the social

[1] *Contrat Social*, III, ii.

order requires the domination of the general will. From this unfortunate contradiction Rousseau draws various inferences about the relative efficiency and desirability of different governmental arrangements — inferences that coincide with the commonplaces of earlier theory and observation.[1]

His classification of governmental forms follows the ancient and familiar categories — monarchy, aristocracy, democracy, and mixed. Democracy is that in which the sovereign assembly itself exercises the function of administrator. Such a union of functions does not appeal to Rousseau as a practicable system save possibly in a small and simple community. Sovereignty is necessarily democratic, in the most exclusive sense, in his theory, but democratic government is not suited to mankind.[2] Rousseau expresses indeed no definite judgment as to what form of government is best. He follows on this question the thought of the most judicious of his predecessors, and finds that each form may be peculiarly adapted to some particular set of conditions.[3] His discussion of the subject manifests a creditable knowledge and appreciation of the work of Montesquieu, in emphasizing the effect of varieties in economic and social conditions. But while the question as to what government is absolutely the best defies a categorical answer, Rousseau

[1] *E.g.*, that monarchic government is more energetic than that of an assembly.

[2] "S'il y avait un peuple de dieux, il se gouvernerait démocratiquement. Un gouvernement si parfait ne convient pas à des hommes." *Contrat Social*, III, iv, end.

[3] *Ibid.*, III, viii.

finds a single simple and conclusive test by which to determine whether a given nation is well or ill governed. This is the census.

Other things being equal, that government is infallibly the better under which, without extraneous measures, without naturalization, without colonies, the citizens show the greater increase in numbers. That under which a people is decreasing and dying out is the worst. Statisticians, the matter is in your hands: count, measure, compare.[1]

Both the establishment and the extinction of governments subject Rousseau's principles to rather severe tests; but his assurance carries him over the gaps that his reasoning fails to bridge. To set a government in operation would seem to be impossible under the conceptions of sovereignty and law that he so carefully defines; for while the sovereign may declare what the form of government shall be — a general act and hence appropriate to the sovereign, it cannot name the persons who are to man the offices, since that, Rousseau explicitly declares, is a particular act, wholly beyond the competence of the general will. Naming the magistrates is distinctively an act of government, not of sovereignty; and there is a difficulty, as Rousseau justly remarks, in understanding how there can be an act of government before the government comes

[1] *Contrat Social*, III, ix. In an interesting note at the end of this chapter, Rousseau develops the idea that neither general tranquillity nor a high state of intellectual and artistic culture is to be taken as a sign of good government. "Un peu d'agitation donne du ressort aux âmes, et ce qui fait vraiment prospérer l'espèce est moins la paix que la liberté." Which suggests the sapient observation of Thomas Jefferson, that a little revolution about once in twenty years is a good thing.

into existence.[1] To one who has achieved the delicate feat of creating a state by a contract to which the state itself is one of the parties,[2] this later problem proves a matter, however, of no real concern. We perceive here, Rousseau says, "one of those astonishing properties of the body politic by which it reconciles operations that appear wholly contradictory." There takes place a sudden conversion of the sovereignty into government, so that with no perceptible change and merely by a new relation of all to all, the citizens, becoming magistrates, pass from general acts to particular acts, and from the law to its execution. That is to say, the sovereign people, assembled to institute a government, vote that a certain form shall be established, and vote that certain men shall fill the offices thus created. The first vote expresses the general will and is in the strictest sense law; the second vote is not an expression of the general will, and is not law, but a mere governmental decree. Between the two votes the assembly changes its character, just as a parliamentary body changes its character when it goes into committee of the whole.[3] The people act in one instance as sovereign and in the other as a democratic government. Since the process here described is inevitable in the establishment of monarchy, aristocracy and all other forms, it follows that, in Rousseau's thought, every government must be considered as originating in democracy.

[1] *Contrat Social*, III, xvii. [2] *Ante*, p. 20.

[3] Rousseau refers to the House of Commons going into "grand committee."

Such being the method by which the inception of government is reconciled with Rousseau's first principles, let us examine their bearing on its normal operation. Law-making, in the strict sense, is of course a function not of the government but of the sovereign. It can be performed only by an assembly of the whole people. Representation is wholly out of the question in this matter. The general will can no more be represented than it can be alienated. The vaunted modern device of representative assemblies Rousseau regards as but an evidence of political decay. "Because of indolence and wealth they at last have soldiers to enslave the country and representatives to sell it."[1] Deputies may be chosen by the people for the despatch of certain duties; but they are merely agents, and have no final authority. "The English people thinks itself free; but it is greatly mistaken; it is free only during the elections for members of Parliament; so soon as they are elected the people is enslaved and becomes a zero." Whatever may be the inconvenience in large states, the whole people must be looked to as the sole legislator.

The question at once presents itself: shall the voice of the majority prevail as the general will? If so, how shall it appear that the minority, constrained by superior numbers, follows its own will and is free? Rousseau answers: only one political act requires unanimity, and that is the social pact.[2] No one is a member of the community except in consequence of his own deliberate volition. Within the state once

[1] *Contrat Social,* III, xv. [2] *Ibid.,* IV, ii.

formed both sovereign and governmental acts are determined by the majority. That the minority seems no longer free, because subject to laws to which they have not given their consent, is an illusion, due to a wrong way of looking at the question. When a project of law is laid before the assembly of the people, they are asked, not whether they approve or reject it, but whether it is or is not conformed to the general will. The vote of each is merely his opinion on that question: "When, therefore, the opinion contrary to mine prevails, it is merely proved that I was mistaken, and that the general will was not what I thought it was. If my opinion had prevailed, I should have done what I did not will; then indeed I should not have been free."[1]

Such is the burlesque of reasoning by which Rousseau seems to think that he actually clears up one of the most troublesome difficulties in ultimate political theory. A deliberation of the sovereign people appears as a guessing match and the law by which men are free is fixed by a majority of guesses. The citizen who is in the minority is not a slave but only a poor guesser. Rousseau characteristically follows this word-juggling with a frank admission that he has begged the question at issue: "This assumes, it is true, that all the elements of the general will are in the majority; when they cease to be there, whichever side prevails, there is no longer any liberty."[2]

The decline and death of the body politic are inevitable, Rousseau holds,[3] and his analysis of the

[1] *Contrat Social*, IV, ii. [2] *Ibid.* [3] *Ibid.*, III, x, xi.

causes turns still on his doctrine of will. The government tends incessantly to invade the sphere of sovereignty; that is, to substitute the will of the magistrates for the general will. The greater intensity of volition in the smaller body accounts for this. At the same time there is a ceaseless tendency of government to contract itself from democracy to aristocracy and thence to monarchy — and thus to increase the intensity of its volitions, as compared with those of the growing community. Only in small nations, amid simple conditions, does the general will have any assured operation. As a society grows and conditions become complex, not only the government, but also the numerous rival groups of private citizens strive to advance their special interests instead of the public advantage, and to substitute a particular for the general will. Because civilization, however deplorable, is inevitable, this process is certain. "The body politic, as well as the human body, begins to die at its birth and carries within itself the causes of its destruction."[1]

Something indeed may be done to retard decay and to preserve as long as possible liberty, equality and legitimate authority. Rousseau prides himself, and with some justification, on his suggestions in this respect.[2] They concern only the usurpatory tendency of the government; the vices of human nature that bring the other evils are beyond correction by political

[1] *Contrat Social*, III, xi.

[2] *Ibid*, III, xii, xviii. "Il est bien singulier qu'avant le Contrat Social, où je le donne, personne ne s'en fût avisé." *Gouvernement de Pologne*, ch. viii.

devices. There must be, he says, periodical assemblies of the sovereign people, for the purpose of maintaining the social pact. The meetings must be spontaneous — wholly independent of the government in summons and action. To the people thus assembled, two questions must be submitted: "First, is it the pleasure of the sovereign to preserve the existing form of government; second, is it the pleasure of the people to leave the administration to those who at present have it in charge."[1] So long as a free expression of the people's will on these two points is obtainable at regular and not too long intervals, the usurpations of the government will be reduced to a minimum. As an additional guarantee of this result Rousseau lays down the principle that when the sovereign is assembled the functions of the government are *ipso facto* suspended.[2]

The great political objection to Rousseau's scheme of legislation by a general assembly of the people was, of course, the apparent impossibility of its application to large states. Rousseau admitted that where population was great and the territory extensive, there would be grave inconvenience. Not for a moment on that account would he concede that representatives should be allowed to constitute the legislature. "Where right and liberty are everything inconveniences are nothing."[3] In a large country the assemblies could

[1] *Contrat Social*, III, xviii.

[2] "A l'instant que le peuple est légitimement assemblé en corps souverain, toute juridiction du gouvernement cesse, la puissance exécutive est suspendue . . . parce qu'où se trouve le représenté il n'y a plus de représentant." *Ibid.*, III, xiv.

[3] *Ibid.*, III, xv.

be held at different places in turn, and thus distribute the inconvenience among all the citizens alike. But at all hazards the principle must be maintained that every citizen should be entitled to participate on equal terms in the supreme function of law-making.

Despite all the tiresome metaphysics with which Rousseau surrounds his device for maintaining the state, it is easy to see that he foreshadows two very familiar institutions of nineteenth-century democracy, namely, the periodical popular vote on the question of revising the constitution and the periodical election of officers. Whether Rousseau would approve the manner in which his device is applied in many states of the American Union may be doubtful; but there is no room to doubt that the spirit of our constitutional provisions is very closely akin to the spirit in which his propositions were conceived.

6. *Strength and Influence of Rousseau's Work*

In the field of politics Rousseau's teaching was suggestive rather than conclusive; but the stimulating force of his suggestions long remained a cardinal fact of literature and history. His fancies, fallacies and quibbles often appealed more strongly than the sober observation and balanced reasoning of Montesquieu to the *Zeitgeist* of the later eighteenth century. Both the pure philosophy of politics and the practical statesmanship of the time clearly illustrate this. His spirit and his dogmas, however disguised and transformed, are seen everywhere both in the speculative systems and in the governmental reorganizations of the stirring era that followed his death.[1]

On the side of pure theory the most distinctive service of Rousseau was that due to his doctrine of sovereignty. The common interest and the general will assumed, through his manipulation, a greater definiteness and importance than philosophy had hitherto ascribed to them. They became the central features of almost every theory of the state. Through those concepts a way was opened by which the unity and solidarity of a population became the necessary presupposition of scientific politics. Rousseau thus contributed largely to promote the theory of the national state. His main purpose, however, was apart from this. Consciously he aimed only to devise a theory of sovereignty through which liberty and authority should be reconciled. His metaphysics and psychology, however ingenious, were not, as we have seen, equal to the task. He could offer no self-consistent reasoning by which it should appear that an individual's will was certain to be expressed in the general will, except in the same sense in which the individual's will was certain to be expressed in the will of a monarch to whom he had submitted himself. Rousseau failed, in short, to prove that the sovereignty of the community was any more compatible with individual liberty than the sovereignty of a monarch or an oligarchy. But his earnest and confident declamation about the virtues of the general will and the significance of the general interest brought those concepts into the foreground of

[1] He died in 1778.

political theory and evoked from more subtle reasoners than Rousseau more refined and self-consistent solutions of the problem he propounded. If their results were ultimately no more successful than his, that was due rather to the *a priori* conceptions of liberty and authority that were the common basis of this whole school of speculation than to any flaw in the logic by which the deductions from these conceptions were made. The assumption that true and perfect liberty could be predicated of only the non-social man, was fatal to any theory of political authority. Nothing could come out of this assumption save the empty paradoxes of Rousseau, the paralyzing transcendentalism of Kant, Fichte and Hegel, Rousseau's legitimate successors, or anarchy pure and simple. Making a state out of a group of perfectly free and independent individuals is like making a statue out of a heap of sand: some cohesive principle is necessary that it is beyond the art of the "legislator" or the sculptor to supply.[1] Aristotle furnished such a principle in his dictum that the social and political element is as strong and fundamental as the individualistic in man — that dependence on his kind is to be presumed of the normal human being. But in the eighteenth century the Aristotelian way of approaching politics made small appeal to intellectual men, and least of all to Rousseau.

Where Rousseau's theorizing touched government in its more practical aspects, his ideas were in some

[1] "Eine Summe von Individuen ist niemals und kann gar nicht eine Einheit sein, so wenig als aus dem Haufen Sandkörner eine Statue wird." Bluntschli, *Geschichte der neueren Staatswissenschaft*, 3te Aufl., 348.

cases singularly fruitful. His sharp distinction between the sovereign and the government was chiefly responsible for this. He has been criticised for his doctrine that only the sovereign can make law. But his theory here was perfectly self-consistent, and it moreover proved adaptable to the explanation of certain concrete institutions of a novel kind that soon after Rousseau's death became the subject of knowledge and interest to intellectual men in France. Law (*loi*) in Rousseau's thought was a term that could designate properly only a rule of perfect generality both in content and in application. Such being the case, his sovereign community was logically the only law-maker. The enactments of any so-called legislature that formed a part of the government could have only the character of decrees for carrying into effect the superior mandates of the true legislature. Rousseau's requirements for law in the strict sense were, we have seen, very exacting. The assignment of a citizen to an office, or the assessment of a tax upon specific citizens could not be effected, he held, by law; for such acts were not general but particular in their application, and hence involved not the general, but some particular interest. It is hard to accept Rousseau's reasoning in this detail; for he holds that the filling of an office must be treated as a matter rather of private than of public concern, and this is scarcely a tenable proposition. But apart from this minor point it is easy to see that Rousseau's "law" is substantially what came to be called fundamental law or constitution. Thus conceived, his doctrine of law-making is merely that now familiar dogma of political science, that the constitution is made by the sovereign people, and the government must conform its acts to this supreme law.

During the decade succeeding the death of Rousseau the interest of Frenchmen became by the course of events deeply enlisted in the affairs and institutions of the American states just freed from Great Britain. The political systems of these states presented in concrete realization principles of sovereignty and law that strongly suggested the doctrine in the *Contrat Social.* The formal written constitutions in which the organization and action of government were prescribed satisfied very well the requirements that Rousseau laid down for law in the strict sense. They were on their face the expression of the people's will; they dealt with only the fundamental questions of the political order; and they were clearly distinguished, both by their formal source and by their superior authority, from the mandates of the governments that they set up. Through these constitutions, thus, the sovereignty of the people and its relation to government were exemplified in actual institutions on lines that ran closely parallel to Rousseau's theory. This coincidence, fortuitous though it was,[1] did not fail of far-reaching influence on theory and on practice in the revolutionary movement that was impending.

We have now completed the tale of political doctrines put forth by Rousseau that were in any large measure

[1] A trace of common lineage may be discerned in the indebtedness of both Rousseau and the Americans to the theories and institutions of seventeenth-century England.

both original and important. His prolific literary genius gave great vogue and fleeting influence to various dogmas that lacked one or both of these qualities. A pretentious theory of a civil religion [1] formulated the creed to which every citizen must subscribe in order to escape banishment from the state. The articles, fixed by the sovereign "not exactly as dogmas of religion but as sentiments of sociability without which it is impossible to be a good citizen or a faithful subject," declared belief in God, in a future life of happiness for the good and punishment for the wicked, in the sanctity of the social contract and the laws, and in no toleration for intolerance. This creed, with its characteristic concluding paradox, is but Rousseau's adaptation of a device that had been more soundly if less flashily exploited by Spinoza [2] and others. None of his predecessors, however, had ventured to denounce the Catholics as incapacitated by their purely religious belief for good citizenship — and this in a plea for toleration.[3]

Besides this and other excursions into the theologico-political field, which always had a great attraction for him, Rousseau delivered many resounding judgments on the economic and fiscal problems that were uppermost in the political discussion of his day. Most of what was theoretically significant in his views was taken bodily from Montesquieu, and derived no force

[1] *Contrat Social*, IV, viii, "De la religion civile."

[2] *Tract. Theol. Polit.*, xx, 21; *Cf. Political Theories from Luther to Montesquieu*, 315.

[3] ". . . quiconque ose dire: 'Hors de l'Église point de salut,' doit être chassé de l'État. . . ." *Contrat Social*, IV, viii.

from Rousseau's adaptation.[1] It was for other thinkers, already making themselves felt when the *Contrat Social* was written, to develop an effective doctrine on these topics. The Physiocrats, in this economic field, a notable group of theorists in moral and political science proper, and a multitude of seekers after practical reform in the French government, filled France with earnest debate, growing hot and fierce as the cataclysm of 1789 approached. In none of these classes was Rousseau's political theory accepted in its entirety. In all of them, however, his dogmas and his phrases were in some measure current coin, and in all was manifested the confidence so eloquently preached by him, that the way to human welfare could always be easily found by getting back to nature.

SELECT REFERENCES

Atger, *Essai sur l'histoire du contrat social*, pp. 253–304. Bosanquet, Philosophical Theory of the State, pp. 11–16, 79–117. Bluntschli, *Geschichte*, pp. 334–362. Caird, Essays on Literature and Philosophy, I, pp. 105–146. Dreyfus-Brissac, *Du Contrat Social*, especially Introduction. Franck, *Réformateurs et Publicistes, dix-huitième siècle*, pp. 285–379. Janet, *Histoire*, II, pp. 415–477. Lincoln, "Rousseau and the French Revolution," in *Annals of the American Academy of Social and Political Science*, Vol. X, pp. 54–72. Lowell, "Rousseau and the Sentimentalists," in Among my Books (1870), Vol. I. Morley, Rousseau, especially Vol. I, chap. v, and Vol. II, chaps. iii and iv; "Rousseau's Influence on European Thought," in *Fortnightly Review*, 1872. Rousseau, The Social Contract, translated by Tozer.

[1] *E.g.*, *Contrat Social*, III, viii.

CHAPTER II

THE RISE OF ECONOMIC AND JURISTIC SCIENCE

1. *European Politics and World Politics*

THE year in which Rousseau's *Social Contract* was published, 1762, saw the practical end of the world-wide conflict known as the Seven Years' War. Three of the most conspicuous results of this desperate and protracted struggle were (1) the definite consolidation of the Prussian monarchy under Frederick the Great, (2) the deep humiliation and exhaustion of France, and (3) the enormous expansion of Great Britain's colonial empire. Each of these facts had a close relation to the salient features of the history of political philosophy during the next three decades. Frederick the Great, feared and hated by all his brother monarchs, furnished them, nevertheless, with the type and example of that enlightened despotism in which contemporary speculation found so much to approve and admire. Humbled and exhausted France, seeking and in some measure gaining revenge upon her ruthless despoiler, became at the same time more and more involved in economic and social troubles; and out of her necessities arose the philosophy that led straight to revolution. Finally Great Britain, undertaking to administer imperially her imperial dominion, alienated the Americans, who in proclaiming and establishing their independence, exhibited to the world for the first time in history the theory and practice of a democratic state under a written constitution.

The various phases of practical politics in Europe during this period were accompanied by a very great activity in theory. France was the centre of the literary speculation, but all Western Europe, from Italy to Scotland, contributed to the movement. In a general way the political philosophy of the time may be divided into two classes: first, that which was concerned primarily with problems of amelioration in the social, economic and administrative activities of governments; second, that which dealt with the more strictly political problems touching the form, organization and limits of governmental authority itself. Both species of speculation manifested the characteristic optimism of eighteenth-century philosophy. Both manifested for the most part an abiding confidence that a sure remedy for any social or political ill lay close at hand in "nature," awaiting the grasp of human reason, and that the ultimate principles governing any group of human phenomena could be readily cast into precise and absolutely conclusive formulas. Thus the Physiocrats furnished an enchantingly easy and simple solution for vexatious problems of finance and industry; the moral and legal philosophers resolved with a sentence the world-old obscurities in the conceptions of liberty and law.

The decades that we are considering were signalized in practical politics by the remarkable group of contemporary monarchs known as the "enlightened despots." Frederick the Great of Prussia (1740–86) was easily the chief of this distinguished collection, and his example notoriously inspired the policies of others, like Catherine II of Russia (1762–96) and the Emperor Joseph II (1765–90). In international and dynastic affairs these rulers were far more despotic than in any modern sense enlightened. Where opportunity was presented to strengthen his own position or weaken that of a rival none of these monarchs felt restrained by respect for God or man. The adepts of the law of nature and of nations strove with pathetic patience to discover in the practice of the eighteenth century any of the noble principles that were supposed to lie at the basis of their science. It was otherwise, however, in the internal administration of the various governments. Here the rulers displayed a serious and apparently not a purely selfish interest in promoting the welfare of their subjects. Far-reaching reforms were effected in taxation and in judicial procedure. Commerce and industry were relieved of restrictions that hampered their development. The throttling grip of ecclesiastical authority on intellectual life was relaxed. In every way the princes gave sympathy and support to the intelligent and progressive middle class as against the stagnating clergy and nobility.

The reforming activity of the monarchs was in many notable instances directly aided by the philosophers of the day. It became something of a fad to have the royal projects viséd by the thinkers whose theories were embodied in them. Frederick the Great was too hard-headed a statesman to be carried away by this idea: he could and did supply both the theory and the practice of his policies. Yet his relations with Voltaire were significant of the spirit that prevailed in royal courts. The politically absolute ruler craved the companionship of the intellectually absolute subject. It is not strange that theories about state and government multiplied in number and audacity, when the most clamorous critics of existing institutions were so conspicuously honored by princes. There was in this practice something, indeed, of mere patronage; but that was not the whole of the matter. A deliberate alliance was struck between political practice and political theory, with results that were not always discouraging. Rousseau's exploits in constitution-making [1] were not very useful, and the colossal self-consciousness of Mercier de la Rivière failed to civilize at command the Russian Empire and its imperious mistress; [2] but Turgot in France, Beccaria in Milan and Filangieri in Naples are shining examples of theorists who were no less serviceable in practice.

The theories and the reforms that met with favor in the European monarchies at this time were in very large measure the outcome of Montesquieu's economic and social suggestions and doctrines. It would be

[1] *Supra*, p. 7.

[2] Catherine summoned the philosopher to advise as to a proposed code for her dominions. She was not favorably impressed with his manner, writing to Voltaire: "He thought we were still going on all fours and he very politely took the trouble to come and show us how to stand on our hind legs." For the whole incident see *Physiocrates*, II, 431–433.

hard to over-estimate the respect and deference that were shown to him by the philosophers of the day. Under the circumstances there might reasonably be expected some tendency toward adoption of his more strictly political dogmas. His conception of a representative body as essential to a rational monarchy, and his doctrine of the separation of powers as indispensable to liberty [1] were very generally accepted in theory, but the attempts to put them into practice were few and feeble. The princes who effectively promoted reforms in administration, judicature and education found it easiest to do so without entering upon the difficult task of governmental reorganization. Only in France and Great Britain did this latter issue become prominent. The French *parlements* manifested aspirations to assume the rôle of defenders of political liberty against the king, and they were summarily suppressed by Louis XV in 1771, leaving the Bourbon monarch for the remainder of his reign unquestionably despotic, but as unquestionably free from any taint of enlightenment. In England George III devoted himself to the purpose of rescuing the royal authority from the degradation to which, as he considered, it had been reduced by Parliament. For a time he was successful. His methods, however, as illuminated by the controversies of the English parties, caused thoughtful observers on the Continent to question the accuracy of Montesquieu's analysis of the constitutional system, or the justification for his

[1] *Political Theories from Luther to Montesquieu*, pp. 403–404, 409 *et seq.*

eulogy of it. Then came the discontent and revolt of the Americans. Their cause and its eventual success brought to the forefront of speculative interest the fundamental principles of sovereignty, liberty and popular self-government. When, a few years after the achievement of American independence, a crisis was reached in French politics, hundreds of influential Frenchmen were familiar with the institutions and the ideas suggested by the names of Washington, Jefferson and Franklin.

The concrete problems of the situation in France included much that was unknown to America. But in the fundamental philosophy of the French movement there was a steady tendency to conform to the lines of the transatlantic debate; and the principles of 1789 in the one land are closely parallel to the principles of 1776 in the other.

2. *French Social and Moral Philosophy*

Prior to the crisis in French practical politics that produced the revolution the basic doctrines of political theory were influentially debated by a group of thinkers whose chief interest was social and ethical rather than strictly political.

Without attempting any full enumeration or classification of these philosophers we may notice briefly a few of the most conspicuous. Their views diverged very widely at many points. All voiced, however, the feeling of Montesquieu and Rousseau, that the civilized society of their day was corrupt and ill-adapted to the requirements of rational beings. "Nature," all believed, had decreed for enlightened men social and political institutions quite different from those that actually existed. Mankind had gone astray and philosophy must point out the way to return to the "natural" and rightful order of things. As to what was the chief source of corruption and error, the philosophers differed much from one another. Some found it in private property, especially in the ownership of land, and set forth projects of communism and socialism. Others found it in a perverted conception of morals and a degrading religious belief, and preached Hobbesian ethics and atheism. All the systems of proposed reform involved suggestions of political improvement, and few of these suggestions failed to reveal the indebtedness of their sponsors to the comprehensive genius of Montesquieu.

The chief exponent of the communistic idea was the Abbé Mably (1709–85).[1] He found, with Rousseau, that inequality of possessions was the fountain-head of social and political evil; and he believed with Plato that, as unwise legislation had produced, so wise legislation alone could remove, the vicious conditions that burdened the peoples. By nature men were not, indeed, endowed all with equal faculties; but the differences were insignificant in comparison with the inequalities sanctioned by the existing social order.[2] In recognizing and promoting private property mankind had strayed from the path of perfect development.

[1] Morelly, in his *Code de la Nature*, 1755, set forth a very complete and coherent system of communism. This was never so well known and influential as Mably's works.

[2] Mably, *De la Législation*, I, ii.

Lust for possessions and for power had supplanted the natural deference to virtue and talent. The need of the times, Mably argued, was far-reaching reform in the direction of equality. The task was one for a law-giver of the ancient type, who should by a drastic code correct the aberrations of a nation's life and set the people on the straight course of right and virtue. Lycurgus and Solon figured frequently in Mably's philosophy, and their treatment of questions of property made a strong appeal to him. They were his types of the legislator who is guided by pure reason and justice rather than selfish class interest. It was because so much power had been usurped by the wealthy and ambitious that the sad and demoralizing class conflicts persisted in society.

Mably was wholly Rousseauish in his development of social and political doctrine. With more logic and less literary brilliancy he laboriously expanded the suggestions of Jean Jacques into a coherent system.[1] Helvetius and Holbach, the other two thinkers whom we shall consider in this section, were ostentatiously hostile to Rousseau at many points, especially in respect to religion. While he passed from the deism of his day over into a sentimentalism that left little distinction between him and the more mystic devotees of the orthodox cult, his philosophic *confrères* took the opposite direction and reached almost unqualified atheism. Their moral and political doctrine showed

[1] "In his [Mably's] most important work . . . we see Rousseau's notions developed, with a logic from which their first author shrunk, either from fear, or more probably from want of firmness and consistency as a reasoner." Morley, *Rousseau*, I, 185.

much of the quality of Hobbes, diluted by the less virile dogmas of Locke and Bolingbroke.

Helvetius, in his works *De l'Esprit* (1758) and *De l'Homme* (1772) was pronouncedly Hobbesian in his ethics. Men, he held, are born with substantially equal powers and capacities, and their conduct is determined solely by self-interest. The maximum happiness, that is, satisfaction of desires, is the motive of all their actions. To this end societies and governments are constituted, wherein the happiness of the greatest number becomes the test of excellence. The varying degrees in which happiness is realized and diffused in different peoples is not due to varieties in the form of government, or to original divergencies in the spirit and character of the races. Every form of government operates on the same principle, namely, the love of power, and every government is essentially despotic. Democracy and aristocracy possess the same power and act on the same motives as monarchy. Only by the measure of enlightenment displayed by those in authority is one government better than another. Where there is the discernment to detect and the wisdom to apply the true principles by which nature regulates human affairs (that is, of course, the principles of Helvetius), there will be good government, whatever the particular form. The character of a people does not determine the nature of their government, but contrariwise the character of a government has an enormous influence on the spirit and manners of a people. This latter dogma is reiterated in many variations by Helvetius and is fundamental in his teaching. "The vices and virtues of a people are always a necessary effect of their legislation."[1] On this principle he based his contribution to the general chorus of philosophy demanding far-reaching reforms in the social and political system of his day, especially in France. For despotism *per se* he had no dislike, but for unintelligent despotism his contempt was unmeasured.[2]

More specific and systematic than Helvetius in strictly political doctrine was his associate in the fraternity of *les philosophes*, the Baron d'Holbach. The *Système de la Nature* (1770) and *Système Social* (1773)[3] presented as to politics a Gallicized version of Locke, purged of the errors introduced by Rousseau. Man's natural state, according to Holbach, is that of rational association with his kind under the law of nature. The glorification of the savage as the really natural man is dismissed as the fancy of a morbid imagination.[4] From natural to civil society the transition is made by contract, express or tacit, and the effect of this contract is to establish the rule of law. By law is meant only the will of the society as a whole. Thus conceived it is the absolute norm for social and political life. Its end is the end for which society is instituted, viz., the maximum welfare of the

[1] *De l'Esprit*, III, xxii.

[2] *Cf.* the preface of the *De l'Homme*, where he is hopeless of France's future, but sees great promise in the dominions of Frederick the Great, Catherine II and Joseph II.

[3] See also his *Politique Naturelle* (1773) and *L'Ethocratie* (1776).

[4] Holbach designates the theorists who glorify the *bon sauvage* as "*spéculateurs atrabiliaires*" — which is sufficiently crushing. *Cf. Système Social*, I, xvi.

greatest number of the citizens. Specifically this welfare means the guarantee of liberty, property and security [1] — a modification, not particularly happy, of Locke's trinity, life, liberty and property.

Government, Holbach conceived, is but the group of citizens chosen by the rest to promote the ends of the society. There is a contract between government and subjects, and the bond ceases to hold when those in authority fail to promote the welfare of the whole body. This general welfare Holbach interprets in the individualistic spirit. It means the happiness of every man so far as his own efforts can achieve it. Therefore the duty of the government is to enable every man to work out his own good. Where this duty is performed liberty exists; for liberty is but the power to get what is essential to well-being.[2] Not that every man must have the same content to his life as every other man in order to be free. Liberty does not mean equality. Nature makes men unequal, in physical and in mental strength. The law that insures liberty guarantees to every man the product of his endowment, protecting equally the rich and the poor, the great and the small, sovereigns and subjects.[3]

As to forms of government, Holbach finds all alike defective and void of promise for permanent good. Even the English constitution, so highly eulogized by

[1] La liberté, la propriété, la sûreté. *Système de la Nature*, I, ix.

[2] "La liberté est le pouvoir de prendre les moyens nécessaires pour se procurer le bien-être." *Système Social*, II, iii.

[3] "La vraie liberté consiste à se conformer à des lois qui remédient à l'inégalité naturelle des hommes, c'est-a-dire, qui protégent également le riche et le pauvre, les grands et les petits, les souverains et les sujets." *Système Social*, II, iii.

philosophers, he thinks scarcely more promising than the rest.[1] His survey of the contemporary situation leads to the despairing reflection that there is not on earth a well-ordered political constitution.[2] Chance, unreason and violence have determined the establishment and the reform of governments. It is time, he urges, for a radical change of method. In the full spirit of all contemporary philosophy he calls for a return to the natural order of things under the lead of enlightened opinion. Intelligent men must cast off their indolence and their blind veneration for institutions whose age is their only virtue. The welfare of the people and the imprescriptible rights of men must triumph over the antiquated systems of the past.[3] Government must be made conformable to the clear demands of reason and justice; the laws must be reduced to a short and simple code, based on natural good sense.[4] With such initial changes in institutions and laws, the character of the peoples, now sadly astray from virtue and uprightness, will be brought back to its true mould.

Holbach is acute and audacious in his criticism of political as of moral theories and practices. He is vehement and stirring in his exhortations to reform. But the general effect of his work is much more to create the conviction that everything is wrong than to make clear the way of reformation.

Holbach, and in general the group of thinkers to

[1] *Système Social*, II, vi. [2] *Ibid.*, II, ii. [3] *Ibid.*, III, iii.

[4] "Un code simple et court, conforme au bon sens naturel." *Ibid.*

which he belonged, became wholly concrete and definite at only two points in their demands for reform — tolerance as to religious creed and freedom of the press. These they held, on grounds that had become commonplaces of philosophy,[1] to be fundamental in any rational conception of freedom. The peculiar force and clarity with which these dogmas were presented were testimony to the strenuous conflict of the day between the rationalistic writers and the ecclesiastics who used the governmental machinery to harass them.[2] Philosophy put at the forefront of human rights those that should insure the comfort and happiness of the intellectual class.

3. *Physiocrats and Economists*

Quite a different class of society was the centre of interest to the famous group of French thinkers known as the Physiocrats. The problems which they sought to solve concerned the material more than the intellectual life of the nations, and the theme of their discussions was the functions, relations and prosperity of those classes that were economically productive — farmers, manufacturers and merchants. "Political economy" in its strict etymological sense — the household management of the state — was the original field of physiocratic speculation. It was sought to determine, from the governmental point of view, the

[1] *Political Theories from Luther to Montesquieu*, Index *sub voc.* "Expression," "Toleration."

[2] Helvetius left his *De l'Homme* for posthumous publication in order to escape the persecution it would bring upon him. See Preface to *De l'Homme*.

most effective methods of assuring an adequate revenue to the state. This opened up the whole wide subject of taxation — its objects, operation and effects. From this the transition was easy into questions as to the sources of the wealth of which taxes were the government's share, as to the methods of its production and distribution, as to its relations to the general welfare, and to the particular character and size of a given population.

With the more purely economic developments of physiocratic doctrine, interesting and important as they were, we are precluded by the scope of this work from detailed concern. The foundation of political theory, however, which was carefully placed under the economic doctrines, is significant and well worth some attention. Its importance is not that of innovation, but rather of support from a new standpoint to a familiar philosophy.[1]

The two concrete policies that engaged the chief interest of the Physiocrats were the introduction of the single tax (*impôt unique*) on land and the abolition of the internal duties on the grain trade in France. It was not hard to show that these policies promised much in the way of easy revenue to the government and prosperity to the people in general. Such utilitarian argument made no conclusive appeal, however, to the spirit of the time, and it was necessary to prove that the single tax and free trade were required by

[1] An excellent summary of physiocratic doctrine is embodied in the short work by the youngest of the school, Dupont de Nemours, *Origine et Progrès d'une Science Nouvelle*, reprinted in *Physiocrates*, Par. I, p. 335.

nature and by nature's law. Dr. Quesnay, in his *Natural Right*,[1] and Mercier de la Rivière, in *The Natural and Essential Order of Political Societies*,[2] furnished this requisite theory, which was summarily as follows:

Justice is the very first condition of all society, and indeed a condition of human life prior to society. Justice consists essentially in regard for two rights that belong by nature to every man, namely, liberty and property. In forming the body politic men do not renounce any of their natural rights. On the contrary, the whole end of association is to extend the enjoyment of these rights.

Laws (*les lois*) are rules of justice and morality, the supreme reason that governs the universe. They are never made, but merely discovered, by men, who may be *législateurs*, but never *législfacteurs*. Only ordinances can be made by human authority, and these have for their end the execution of the laws.

Three species of property are included in the natural rights of every individual. First, the property of his person, which includes the right to use all his faculties, and hence the right to labor. Second, the movable property, which consists of the results of his labor. Third, landed property (*propriété foncière*). All property is limited by the other properties surrounding it, as all liberty is limited by the other liberties.

[1] *Le Droit Naturel* (1765), in *Physiocrates*, Par. I, p. 41.

[2] *L'Ordre Naturel et Essential des Sociétés Politiques* (1767), reprinted in *Physiocrates*, Par. II, p. 445.

Society is organized to provide a mutual guarantee of these various individual properties. For this end a guardian authority is necessary, which must centre in a sovereign armed with a force sufficient to overcome all obstacles. The sovereign must be a unity. There can be no division of sovereign powers. The sovereign authority is not instituted to make laws, for laws are already made by the Supreme Being who creates rights and duties. Positive enactments by sovereigns can be only declaratory of the essential laws of the social order (*lois essentielles de l'ordre social*), the laws namely of liberty and property. Ordinances contrary to these essential laws are null.[1]

It is the great duty of sovereigns to promulgate through their positive ordinances the natural and essential laws of the social order. The legislative, or more strictly the law-declaring, power and the executive power belong exclusively to the sovereign. On the other hand, the function of judging the citizens is incompatible with sovereignty; for the judicial function requires the investigation of minute details and the judgment of special cases, which would be foreign to the whole end of sovereignty.

Magistrates, that is, judges, must compare the positive ordinances with the laws of justice, and apply the ordinances only so far as they conform with these laws. It follows from this duty of judges that a very high degree of training is indispensable to them in

[1] "Il y a donc un juge naturel et irrécusable des ordonnances mêmes des souverains et ce juge est l'évidence de leur conformité ou de leur opposition aux lois naturelles de l'ordre social." Dupont de Nemours, *Origine et Progrès*, sec. viii.

order that they may know well the "natural and essential laws of the social order."

As to the best form of government physiocratic doctrine stood stoutly for hereditary monarchy. No danger from despotism need be feared so long as the philosophers' system should be faithfully maintained. Under this system the protection of liberty and property would be the sole function of the monarch; his ordinances for this purpose would be subject to the judgment of enlightened magistrates in cases where particular citizens were concerned; and the chief source of oppression upon the whole community would be removed by the fiscal system based upon the single tax on land, whereby an adequate revenue for the crown would automatically accompany the maximum of well-being for all the subjects.

The foregoing résumé of physiocratic doctrine shows clearly enough the relation of the political theory it involves both to Locke and Montesquieu and to the contemporary French thought. Where Helvetius and Holbach found the beneficent "nature" that must restore human happiness in psychological truths and moral virtues, the Physiocrats found it in the conditions determining the production and use of material wealth. On the one hand there was a refurbishing of dogmas and formulas as old as literature and philosophy; on the other there was a systematic and comprehensive marshalling, for the first time in history, of vital principles of social life. The reforms demanded by the Physiocrats tended as a whole to trench deeply on the hitherto recognized field of state activity.

Gournay, the earliest of the school, made the world familiar with the famous formula for the government's most effective promotion of commerce and industry, *laissez faire, laissez passer.* Abolition of the ancient restrictions on French trade and manufactures was a central feature of the Physiocrats' programme of practical reform, and their theory included among the natural rights of men freedom of labor, freedom of exchange, and in general freedom from all restraints upon the use of their faculties and their property. Economic law might be depended upon to bring about the best good of men and nations if governments kept their hands off. In one respect, however, the Physiocrats demanded the positive and powerful application of the sovereign's authority, and that was in education. Public instruction must be maintained in order that citizens, magistrates and majesty itself might never lose sight of the unvarying laws of social order, that is, of the great truths of Physiocratic philosophy.[1]

The eminent Turgot, though too broad in his philosophy to be called strictly one of the Physiocrats, gave great support, nevertheless, to their system both in his public career and in his writings. As Intendant at Limoges he applied physiocratic principles in a remarkable effort to improve the desperate condition of agriculture and industry in that region. Called to the ministry of finance in 1774, he entered vigorously upon projects for a general reform of the royal administration and revenue, but fell before the resistance

[1] Dupont de Nemours, *Origine et Progrès*, sec. xxi.

of the privileged classes and established interests.[1] Turgot's proposals, though unsuccessful, profoundly influenced the thought of the time. His policy included the general freedom of commerce in grain, sweeping reforms of the land tax, the removal of many antiquated restrictions on manufactures and the abolition of the guildlike monopolies called *jurandes*. Every proposal was accompanied by a philosophical explanation and defence of the measure; and the general tenor of these justifying pieces, together with his earlier *Eulogy of Gournay* (1760) and *Reflections on the Production and Distribution of Wealth* (1766), rightly gave the support of his great name to the theories of governmental functions held by the Physiocrats. Like them he sustained enlightened monarchy as the best form of government. Like them he placed the economic freedom of the individual high among the natural rights. His philosophy was not bounded, however, by the narrower economic interest; and his assertion of the rights of labor and trade was no more vigorous than his defence of that less novel item of liberal political theory, the right of religious freedom.[2]

As the course of events in France tended steadily to subordinate all other speculation to that bearing on constitutional issues, the tradition of purely economic doctrine crossed the Channel to the calmer atmosphere of Great Britain and found an exponent and promoter

[1] For a summary view of his administration see Morley, *Miscellanies*, II, 150 *et seq.*; fuller account in Tissot, *Turgot*, 133 *et seq.*

[2] *Cf.* Memoir to the king on Toleration, June, 1775. Also Tissot, *op. cit.*, 348 *et seq.*

in Adam Smith. His *Wealth of Nations*, first published in 1776, determined the type of political economy as an independent science. The close relation of this work to physiocratic doctrine on the economic side is obvious. On the side of political theory Smith discarded the formal elaboration of the doctrines on which Quesnay and La Rivière built up their science; but the tacit assumption of these doctrines appears frequently throughout the *Wealth of Nations*. Thus it repeatedly appears in that work that it is no function of government to determine how capitalists shall employ their resources; that it is the natural right of His Majesty's subjects to exercise what species of industry they please.[1] Industrial and commercial freedom thus is the premise of Smith's economic teaching. The theoretical development of this premise in his own mind is revealed in the recently discovered notes on his lectures as university professor in 1763.[2] These lectures were not published, however, and their influence was thus limited to the relatively small circle of his students. Smith's political thought as here revealed is interesting in some respects; but when summed up, so far as is possible from the mere student's notes that have come down to us, it appears to be an ingenious but hardly fertile blend

[1] *Wealth of Nations*, IV, ii. *Cf.* the famous passage referring to restrictions upon American manufacturers: "To prohibit a great people . . . from making all that they can of every part of their products, or from employing their stock and industry in the way that they judge most advantageous to themselves, is a manifest violation of the most sacred rights of mankind." *Ibid.*, IV, vii.

[2] *Adam Smith's Lectures, Police, Revenue and Arms.* Edited by Edwin Cannan, 1896.

of what had already been enunciated by Locke, Montesquieu and Hume.[1]

4. *Adam Ferguson*

Another Scot, Adam Ferguson (1723–1816), the contemporary and friend of Adam Smith, and scarcely less famous than Smith during their lives, developed doctrines of social and political philosophy that are for our purpose more significant than those in the *Wealth of Nations.* The critical spirit of Hume and the historical spirit of Montesquieu were most attractively combined in Ferguson. He stood quite apart from the fervid a-priorism of the French thinkers of his day. While they, and with them Adam Smith, set up absolute standards by which to realize the social ends discussed in the *Spirit of the Laws*, Ferguson, more faithful to the author's innermost feeling, discarded all ready-made systems of what is "natural," and studied society and its institutions as "going" concerns, beyond hope of control by even the wisest philosophers. His interest was to determine by the light of history whither society was moving, not by superhuman wisdom to fix its course. The problems that thus appealed to him had been more or less discussed by Hume, and the incisive scepticism of this philosopher, in assailing pretentious dogmas and long-current beliefs, was abundantly reflected, though much softened in form, throughout Ferguson's work.

His most influential treatise was his *Essay on Civil*

[1] For a suggestive estimate see Hasbach, in *Political Science Quarterly*, XII, 684.

Society, published in 1765. More systematic but of less attractive literary form was his *Principles of Moral and Political Science* (1792), embodying his lectures as professor in the University of Edinburgh.[1] Fundamental in both these works was Ferguson's emphasis on the unforeseen and unwilled elements determining social and political growth. He had none of the enthusiasm of the French reformers for remodelling institutions on principles of *a priori* science. The origin, the policy and the governmental order of a state are determined, he held, by circumstances, quite without reference to the speculations of philosophers. "No constitution is formed by concert, no government is copied from a plan."[2] It is in vain that statesmen seek ingenious devices for promoting the arts and commerce by political means. Not positive legislation, but the uncontrollable operation of the principles on which social life rests, fixes the course of progress in civilization.[3]

This fundamental divergence from the dominant philosophy of his time is further developed in Ferguson's views about "nature." None of the long current concepts denoted by this term appeals to him. In his view whatever is, is natural. "All the actions of men are equally the result of nature."[4] Art and refined society are as truly natural to man as

[1] Like Hume, Ferguson was historian as well as philosopher. His work on the *Progress and Termination of the Roman Republic* (1783) was famous and popular.

[2] *Essay on Civil Society*, Pt. III, sec. 2.

[3] *Ibid.*, III, 7, 8; IV, 1.

[4] *Ibid.*, I, 1. *Cf. Principles of Moral and Political Science*, I, 3, 1.

barbarism. Neither Rousseau's gentle savage nor Hobbes's warlike savage nor the sublimated being in whom the idealists have concentrated pure reason is in any peculiar sense the natural man. The state of nature is neither a condition of listless contentment nor one of ruthless strife for mastery nor yet the serene emotionless contemplation of the sage. Man is a complex being and the one truth that history certainly reveals is that no single faculty is more characteristic than any other. He is a being destined to progress, and no single stage in his progress is more distinctively human than any other.

What especially repelled Ferguson from the Rousseauish and Hobbesian and Stoic conceptions of the natural state of man was the implication in all of them that peace and stability constituted the goal of social and political science. He, on the contrary, regarded opposition and strife among men and communities as not only inevitable, but also beneficent.[1] Effort was the necessary concomitant of progress. The strenuous life was the normal life of man. Competition in politics, industry and commerce and war in international relations were merely expressions of this truth and could never be exorcised by speculation from human affairs. This thought recurs very often in Ferguson's works and gives to his philosophy much of its most characteristic quality.[2] Civil liberty and

[1] "Without the rivalship of nations and the practice of war, civil society itself could scarcely have found an object or a form. . . . He who has never struggled with his fellow-creatures is a stranger to half the sentiments of mankind." *Civil Society*, I, 4.

[2] *Cf. Civil Society*, I, 9; III, 1, 2, 4; IV, 2, 3, 4.

economic prosperity he finds to be in large measure the unforeseen products of political and military strife.

The application of the principles just described is the distinctive feature of Ferguson's doctrine as to the origin and growth of society and government. Instinct and habit, not reason and calculation, create social forms.[1] Men are equal only in the right to exist and employ their faculties. These faculties vary in quality and efficiency, and therefore gradation is of the essence of social grouping. The only natural right is that of using the faculties that one is endowed with and of resisting any obstruction to such use. Out of the blind efforts of the individual to secure his happiness, that is, his existence, arise the order and the authority of a society. Out of the efforts of societies, or nations, to secure their respective interests, that is, their existence, political institutions and authority take shape. The forms and powers of government are determined by the incidents of these struggles, not by the classification and speculations of philosophers. Ferguson is especially contemptuous towards those who would have political organizations adapted primarily to the promotion of culture and virtue. These are indeed, he concedes, most desirable ends; but nations do not consciously seek them. Interest and profit furnish the motives by which nations actually determine their organizations and policies; moral and intellectual uplift, when it comes, is but a by-product.[2]

[1] Men "pass on, like other animals, in the track of their nature, without perceiving its end." *Civil Society*, III, 2.

[2] *Civil Society*, III, 3. Ferguson does not, of course, use this term.

Despite his repudiation of conscious purpose and will in the origin and progress of society, Ferguson ultimately, in his lectures on political science, felt obliged to introduce contract as an element in the philosophy of government. While authority in society is a *de facto* attribute of superior persons or classes, it is limited in scope, he held, to the prevention of harm. The wider power of *de iure* government depends upon consent and compact of the parties concerned.[1] Not that government is actually instituted by formal compact. This idea he clearly rejects. The transition from instinctive society to conscious polity is gradual. Conventions and agreements that give rise to state forms and laws are made from time to time to correct or prevent abuse of the power that had its origin in unreflecting submission.[2] With advanced intellectual development, social institutions become largely consensual and thus political. Their original quality, however, never wholly disappears. Sovereignty, government and law have for their end the security of individuals or groups. The consent on which political organization and action rest never extends to violations of natural rights or natural law. Neither sovereign nor magistrate possesses an arbitrary and unlimited authority.

At this point Ferguson came fully into the current

[1] "It is a manifest principle of the law of nature that a right to command or an obligation to obey beyond what is required to the mere prevention of harm, can be founded in consent alone." *Mor. and Pol. Science*, Vol. II, p. 244.

[2] As *e.g.*, of the child to the parent, of the weak to the strong, the poor to the rich, *etc.* *Mor. and Pol. Science*, Vol. I, p. 262.

of Locke's political theory and was not distinguishable from the dominant doctrine of the day. Nature, he maintained, provided a limit that clearly marked the scope of sovereign governmental power. He was scarcely less sure than the French philosophers or Adam Smith that the natural rights of the individual could be marshalled in formulas that should fix for all times and places the bounds of political authority. His doctrines as to rights and liberty and law present little that is novel or striking.[1] He appears clearly enough as hostile to absolutism in state or government. The rigid demonstration by Hobbes of unlimited sovereignty Ferguson combats by denying Hobbes's premises.[2] Liberty, on the other hand, is carefully distinguished from license and is held not to imply equality.[3] The forms and functions of government are treated with little variation from the dogmas of Locke and Montesquieu.

These later views of Ferguson on politics proper appear little in keeping with the tone and spirit of his social doctrines. He exhibits a good deal of the a-priorism that his *Essay on Civil Society* so cleverly condemns. In this very fact, however, the innermost temper of the philosopher is revealed. His was a moderate, conservative, optimistic spirit, with an obvious touch of the cynicism that much study of history is likely to create. Extremes and extravagance in thought or action alienated him. Accordingly his work of 1765 was a protest based on history

[1] See his *Mor. and Pol. Science*, Part II, chaps. iii and vi.
[2] *Ibid.*, Pt. II, chap. iii, sec. 10.
[3] *Ibid.*, II, vi, 7.

against the philosophy of reform proposed; his work of 1792 was a protest, on the only ground that then could claim a hearing, against the facts of revolution achieved.

5. *The Legalists*

In addition to the social, moral and economic doctrine that influenced the form of political theory in the sixties and the following decades, noteworthy discussions of jurisprudence in one or another of its aspects contributed much to the same end. Under this head must be mentioned the influential essay of Cesare Beccaria, the Italian jurist, on *Crimes and Punishments*.[1] The substance of this little work was a plea for far-reaching reform in criminal law and procedure on the Continent. Protests against the barbarous practices that were in vogue in both the trial and the punishment of accused persons were a feature of all the programmes of social amelioration at this period. Montesquieu had sketched the ends toward which improvement should be directed.[2] Beccaria filled out the sketch with a force and clarity of presentation that won universal applause. The approval of his plea for rational methods in restraining crime naturally extended to the general principles on which the special plea was based. He became thus an influential promoter of the dogmas that the sole aim of legislation should be the greatest good of the greatest number;[3] that laws (*leggi*) are but the conditions under which

[1] *Dei Delitti e delle Pene*, first published in 1764.

[2] *Esprit des Lois*, liv. vi and xii.

[3] La massima felicità divisa nel maggior numero. *Delitti e Pene*, Introduzione, p. 30.

men, naturally independent, unite themselves into society; that individual self-interest is the supreme motive of human actions, both before and after entering into social bonds;[1] and that laws and punishments are just, therefore, only so far as they are indispensable to the maintenance of society. From these distinctly Hobbesian principles Beccaria reaches conclusions in favor of a clear, compact and explicit code of criminal law, intelligible to all, shaped by pure reason and secure against the influence of passion or prejudice in its application. This ideal illustrates again the trend of thinking that has been noted in the moral and economic field.[2]

Blackstone, whose *Commentaries*[3] also first appeared in that remarkable decade of the sixties, is significant in the history of political theory in the same incidental way as Beccaria. Montesquieu's eulogy had given so exalted a reputation to the constitution and laws of England that an analysis and exposition of them could not have failed to attract general attention even if the author had lacked the learning and literary faculty that Blackstone so conspicuously possessed. The main theme of his *Commentaries* is preceded by his views on law in general and on the nature of society and civil government.[4] In this are found dogmas and

[1] Nessun uomo ha fatto il dono gratuito di parte della propria libertà in vista del ben pubblico; questa chimera non esiste che ne' Romanzi. *Ibid.*, sec. ii.

From this it follows that the public good is merely the sum of individual goods, *i.e.*, the good of the majority.

[2] *Supra*, pp. 56, 60.

[3] *Commentaries on the Laws of England*, first ed. 1765.

[4] Introduction, sec. ii.

formulas that were made axiomatic in the thinking of all English-speaking people by the vogue attained by Blackstone as an authority on law.

There was little of novelty, however, in his principles. He summed up and elegantly expressed the ideas that were considered respectable by English gentlemen of his day. For such ideas his hospitality was perhaps too generous; for they were welcomed to a place in his system with small regard to scientific consistency. The most antique and venerable moral and religious proprieties were satisfied by the recognition of a law of nature, willed and partially revealed by God, and discoverable by human reason. More recent and fashionable ethics was then recognized by the dictum that self-love is the God-implanted principle of human action, and that the sole and sufficient precept of natural law is: "man should pursue his own true and substantial happiness." This Blackstone followed with the ancient dogma that human laws have no validity if contrary to the laws of nature.

In his distinctively political theories [1] Blackstone followed Locke and Montesquieu rather closely. He rejected, however, the idea that society could have originated in the deliberate agreement of previously isolated individuals.[2] Such a notion he believed "too wild to be seriously admitted," and, moreover, plainly contradictory to Revelation. Communities grew up gradually through the efforts of individuals to secure

[1] *Commentaries* (13th ed., 1800), Vol. I, pp. 46 *et seq.*

[2] For Locke on this point *cf. Political Theories from Luther to Montesquieu*, pp. 350 *et seq.*

their respective interests, and the "original compact of society" signifies only the arrangement through which the community protects the individual and the individual submits to the laws. Government is the agency through which the community performs its functions under this compact, and the essential attribute of every government is a "supreme, irresistible, absolute, uncontrolled authority in which the *iura summi imperii*, or rights of sovereignty, reside."

In taking up so rigorous and uncompromising a conception of sovereignty Blackstone separated from Locke and Montesquieu, who, as we have seen,[1] avoided the term. But the separation was only temporary. He defined sovereign as synonymous with law-maker and found it, for Great Britain, in Parliament. This brought him to the real goal of his analysis — a glorification of the British constitution as a perfect example of the mixed form of government, and as a system in which "political or civil" liberty falls "little short of perfection." Blackstone manifested no misgivings about the compatibility of perfect liberty with the "irresistible, absolute, uncontrolled authority" of the sovereign. He insisted no less strenuously on the paramount natural rights of the individual than on the paramount legislative will of the government.[2]

[1] *Political Theories from Luther to Montesquieu*, pp. 352, 411; *cf.* also p. 381. Blackstone may have been under the influence of Bolingbroke at this point. "There must be an absolute, unlimited and uncontrollable power lodged somewhere in every government." Bolingbroke, *Works*, IV, 244. But Bolingbroke elsewhere expresses ideas quite inconsistent with this.

[2] "Society," "government" and "sovereign" are used without discrimination by Blackstone.

> The principal aim of society is to protect individuals in the enjoyment of those absolute rights which are vested in them by the immutable laws of nature; . . . the first and primary end of human laws is to maintain and regulate these absolute rights of individuals.[1]

These absolute rights Blackstone defined, however, as constituting "natural liberty," that is, the "power of acting as one thinks fit"; and as being a "wild and savage liberty" such as every reflecting man seeks to get rid of by entering society. This explanation gives the surprising result that while the chief aim of society is to protect men's natural rights, the aim of men in entering society is to get rid of those rights. There appears in Blackstone's exposition also a plain implication of a pre-social and savage state of nature, which he elsewhere rejects as a wild and impious idea.

Such ramshackle logic pervades all Blackstone's preliminary philosophy. Yet there emerges from the incoherence now and then a suggestive and forceful formula destined to a useful career. Such, for example, is his definition of civil liberty,[2] namely, "natural liberty so far restrained by human laws (and no farther) as is necessary and expedient for the general advantage of the public."[3] The content of this liberty in England, where it attains substantial perfection, is indicated by Blackstone in the familiar phrase, personal security, personal liberty and private property. What the precise relation of these rights is to the state of

[1] *Commentaries*, book i, chap. i.
[2] He calls it "political or civil."
[3] *Commentaries*, book i, chap. i.

nature or to the irresistible, absolute and uncontrolled sovereign law-maker, does not clearly appear. The subject is entangled in an appalling jumble of incoherencies concerning sovereignty. Having declared that term convertible with "legislature,"[1] and fundamental in any conception of a state, Blackstone gravely proceeded to demonstrate the *right* and the *duty* of the sovereign, that is, the legislature, to legislate. This absurd proceeding, analogous to proving the right and duty of a man to be a man, had importance in serious political philosophy only through the scorching criticism that it received from Jeremy Bentham in his *Fragment on Government.*[2]

Another panegyric of the English constitution, nearly contemporary with that of Blackstone, supplemented on the Continent the influence of Montesquieu's ideas and became in Great Britain itself a power for the promotion of the national self-satisfaction. De Lolme, a native of Geneva, published the original French version of his *Constitution of England* in Holland in 1770, and five years later the English translation. In this treatise the excellencies of the English system were found at just the points indicated by Montesquieu and Blackstone — the separation of powers, the check and balance among the various branches of the legislature, the representative system, the jury and the writ of *habeas corpus.* While De Lolme was rather more discriminating in his eulogies, and gave more attention to some of the qualifications with which the theoretical advantages must be judged, yet in the

[1] *Commentaries* (1800), Vol. I, p. 46. [2] *Infra*, p. 214.

general summing up he found the best guarantees of liberty in the constitution of England.

The acuteness of De Lolme's analysis is well illustrated by his discussion of the question whether liberty is guaranteed through direct popular legislation.[1] Liberty, he declares, consists simply in this: "That every man, while he respects the persons of others and allows them quietly to enjoy the products of their industry, be certain himself likewise to enjoy the products of his own industry, and that his person be also secure." In other words: "To live in a state where the laws are equal for all and sure to be executed (whatever may be the means by which these advantages are attained), is to be free." Thus conceived, individual liberty is not assured by the privilege of voting on a project of law, or indeed on the choice of a representative. The "silent, powerful and ever-active conspiracy of those who govern" cannot be greatly affected by the unorganized and unintelligent suffrages of the multitude. What passes for the will of the people is really the will of the politicians and the great interests. They wake while the people sleep; and they alone know the times and methods for gaining their ends regardless of the public welfare. Through their manipulation popular voting becomes a mere agency for the prosecution of their projects. As compared with the results of such legislation, the advantage of the public would be better promoted if laws "were to be made by drawing lots or casting dice." [2]

[1] *Constitution of England*, book ii, chap. v.
[2] *Constitution of England*, p. 177.

This vigorous polemic against Rousseau's doctrine is wholly characteristic of De Lolme's philosophy, and reveals with distinctness his fundamental sympathy with the view that the way to true liberty lies rather through a happily contrived practical correlation of governmental organs than through devotion to a metaphysical ideal.

The most comprehensive attempt in these pre-revolutionary decades to apply the general spirit and method of Montesquieu to the requirements of social and political reform is to be found in the work of the Neapolitan Filangieri, *The Science of Legislation*, that appeared in 1780. It may readily be conceded — what Janet and other French critics have laboriously striven to prove [1] — that Filangieri owed most of his leading doctrines to Montesquieu. Yet the Italian developed and applied them in a new spirit. He was very sensitive to the intellectual influences making for far-reaching reform. In his enthusiasm he conceived that the human mind had reached a stage in its grasp of social phenomena that warranted a definitive code of laws covering all the larger aspects of politics and government. As Montesquieu had revealed the *spirit* of the laws, Filangieri would set forth the specific *content* of the laws,[2] as reason and experience dictated. Mankind, at least in Western Europe, had reached, he believed, a condition of permanent peace and stability. The wars, conquests, ambitions and downfall

[1] See Janet, *Histoire de la Science Politique*, II, 529, citing Villemain.

[2] "Montesquieu cerca in questi rapporti lo spirito delle leggi, ed io vi cerco le regole." *Scienza della Legislazione*, Vol. I, p. 17.

of strong men would no longer vex the race and shape its institutions.[1] Industry, commerce and the arts, once a source of weakness to a nation ("perhaps rendering Tyre the prey of Alexander and Carthage that of Scipio"), were henceforth to be the chief supports of its prosperity. Liberty, once the plaything of conquerors and their rivals, was now fixed on generous and inspiring foundations. In view of these happy conditions Filangieri believed the time ripe for a science of legislation suited to the fully-developed race.

The details of his system we need not follow. They were but the familiar ideals of contemporary liberalism, illuminated, however, by a winning optimism and enthusiasm that were Filangieri's own. In criminal jurisprudence his principles were those of Beccaria. In economic doctrine he reflected the ideas of the Physiocrats. His theory of the nature and principles of government followed Montesquieu closely. In respect to the English constitution,[2] however, his attitude was more critical than that of Montesquieu and Blackstone, and more akin to that of De Lolme. The working of party government in England and the revolt of the Americans caused Filangieri to feel that the theoretical merit of the constitutional system was hardly an adequate guarantee of practical merit. He thought that results would have been better in late

[1] "Il tempo della fondazione e del rovesciamento degl' imperi è passato; . . . non si ritrova piu l'uomo innanzi al quale la terra taceva." *Ibid.*, p. 23. In view of what happened in the three decades beginning with 1789, this is an interesting prophecy.

[2] *Scienza della Legislazione*, lib. I, cap. xi.

years if a Locke or a Penn had been at the head of the government.[1] These Englishmen, in their capacity as lawgivers for colonies in America, were greatly admired by the Italian philosopher. Penn, in particular, was glorified as the virtuous legislator who would have overshadowed the fame of Lycurgus and Solon, if he had been born twenty centuries earlier, and who had "made Pennsylvania the fatherland of heroes, the asylum of liberty and the admiration of the universe." [2]

Whatever may be thought of the soundness of this estimate, the fact that Filangieri made it is significant. It illustrates the entrance of American conditions and institutions as an influential element in political philosophy. The winning of independence by the colonies diverted to the victors some of the interest and respect that had hitherto been concentrated upon the constitution of the mother-country. In the search for principles adapted to political liberty the American systems were studied by many European thinkers. It was appreciated that the economic and social conditions were quite different on the two sides of the Atlantic. Filangieri, in a strain of prophetic eloquence,

[1] ". . . se alla testa del Governo Britannico ci fossero stati in questi ultimi tempi un Lock (*sic*) o un Pen (*sic*)." *Scienza della Legislazione*, Vol. I, p. 64.

[2] *Ibid.*, p. 148. Filangieri's particular enthusiasm for "Pensilvania" probably reflects contemporary feeling in Paris, where the *Mercure de France* said, in June, 1778: "Les législateurs de la Pennsylvanie doivent être au dessus de Lycurge et de Solon comme notre siècle est au dessus de celui de Solon et de Lycurge." Quoted in Rosenthal, *America and France*, p. 68, note. Some expressions of Filangieri suggest that he may have supposed Penn to be the author of the Pennsylvania constitution of 1777. Montesquieu had eulogized Penn. *Esprit des Lois*, IV, vi.

voiced America's defiance of Europe based on the potential wealth, resources and character of the newborn nation.[1] Many other philosophers saw in the simplicity and crudeness of American life a semblance of that "nature" from which Europe had gone far astray, and to which it must return. In the decade preceding the outbreak of revolution in France, therefore, America was much studied by political philosophers and its governmental system in particular was analyzed with care. That it is easy to exaggerate the influence of this study on the course of events and of theory in France, may be admitted. But it would be an even more serious error to neglect this influence. Our account of the trend of political philosophy at the time of the French revolution must be accompanied, therefore, by some account of the ideas that came into prominence through the revolution in America.

SELECT REFERENCES

Blackstone, Commentaries, Introduction, sec. ii; Bk. I, chap. i. Bluntschli, *Geschichte*, pp. 328–333 (Filangieri). Dupont de Nemours, in *Physiocrates*, II, pp. 335–366. Ferguson, Essay on Civil Society, Part I; Part III, secs. 2, 3, 7. Filangieri, *Scienza della Legislazione*, Vol. I, pp. 15–47. Helvetius, *De l'Esprit*, Essay II, chaps. xv–xvii; Essay III, chaps. xvi–xxviii. Higgs, The Physiocrats. Holbach, *Système Social*, Part I, chap. xvi; Part II. Janet, *Histoire*, II, pp. 478–508; 520–572; 635–682. John Morley, Miscellanies, II, pp. 111–162 (Turgot). Sorel, *L'Europe et la Révolution Française*, Vol. I, pp. 100–124. Stephen, English Thought in the Eighteenth Century, II, pp. 209–217; 305–328. Tocqueville, *L'Ancien Régime*, liv. iii, chaps. i–iii.

[1] *Scienza della Legislazione*, I, p. 163 *et seq.*

CHAPTER III

THE AMERICAN AND THE FRENCH REVOLUTION

1. *General Trend of Events*

THE question of property and taxation, the traditional source of political agitation in England, kindled in America the flame of revolution that was destined to sweep over the whole civilized world. *A priori* the Stamp Act of 1765 was a fair and reasonable measure of policy. Its mischievous bearings were at first unperceived by many experienced politicians on both sides of the ocean. To the British leaders the omnipotence of Parliament was the sole principle upon which the unity of the vast empire could be securely established. The suspicious and high-spirited Americans were quick to discover, however, that the omnipotence of Parliament meant in this particular aspect the right of the English aristocracy to divest the colonists of their property at will. It meant taxation without representation. That such a principle was in the English constitution, the Americans would not believe. The liberties traditionally insured by that body of law were as highly revered a heritage in Massachusetts and Virginia as in England itself. Hence the colonists joined issue first in a hot constitutional and legal debate. Against the pretensions of Parliament they appealed to the king, to their charters, to the long recognition of their autonomy in taxation, and to their rights as Englishmen. Behind all this appeared now and again, even from the outset, the ominous reference to the natural rights of men.

In this initial phase of the controversy the practical victory, as well as a pretty clear triumph in the argument, fell to the colonists. The English government did not, however, relinquish its claims or its purpose. By taxes laid upon imports rather than upon internal business Parliament flanked the strongest legal position of the colonists and obliged them to sustain even more openly the doctrine that not even revenue for clearly imperial purposes could be raised in America save through the colonial assemblies. For this doctrine support had to be sought more and more in the law and rights of nature rather than in English law. For all the principles and precedents of legislation touching trade and navigation contradicted point-blank the idea that acts of Parliament were subject to any restriction whatever.

Finally, for the purpose of enforcing its laws against the increasingly violent opposition in America the British government resorted to the despatch of several bodies of troops to the colonies, and enacted very stringent laws for the enforcement of its trade and revenue acts. In opposing these last measures and denying their validity the Americans had to take the ground that without representation legislation in general, no less than taxation, was tyranny. At the same time no demand was made for delegates to the Parliament at

Westminster, but through concerted action among the various colonies measures of hostility to both royal and Parliamentary authority were devised. The debate now showed small attention to constitutional and legal questions, but was animated chiefly by a spirit of resistance to oppression. Nature rather than the English constitution became the great tribunal of appeal. For union as an expedient in sustaining legal rights was substituted the profounder conception of an inherent national unity. A Continental Congress devising policies of common defence and general welfare gave very concrete expression to this idea. To the dogged royal self-consciousness of George III, as well as to the legalistic spirit of many broader-minded Englishmen, the attitude of the Americans was simply rebellion, to be crushed by force. Force was applied; but it encountered a spirit no less dogged and tenacious than the king's own, and the event was the disruption of the British empire and the independence of the United States.

The course of events in America was followed from the outset with close attention by the thinking men of continental Europe, especially in France. Practical statesmen were moved chiefly by a malicious joy in contemplating and multiplying the troubles of the British government. Philosophers, on the other hand, found in the work of the Americans, both destructive and constructive, abundant food for speculation. To a generation permeated by the feeling that a radical reform of political and social institutions on purely rational lines was sorely needed, the revolution in

America appeared as a practical realization of the idea. A primitive people, unspoiled by the vices of civilization and near to the simplicity and purity of nature, had deliberately, on ground of natural right, cast aside one government, and with like deliberation and like respect for the light of nature and pure reason, had installed for themselves another. Such tended to be the interpretation put by French philosophy on the events in America. It was confirmed by the very remarkable series of state papers in which the principles of the revolution were formulated as well as by the constitutions that embodied the details of the new political order. The representatives who were sent to care for American interests in France contributed much also to support the current views about the revolution. Franklin, John Adams and later Jefferson, warmly welcomed by the intellectual leaders of France, all shrewdly kept their republican simplicity well to the front, while holding their own in all forms of philosophical discussion. Thus the natural man, as exemplified by these presumably typical Americans, exhibited precisely the traits that respectable philosophy (though not the Rousseauish school) demanded.

The French government, in 1778, formally took up the cause of the Americans, and its aid was very influential, if not absolutely decisive, in bringing the war to a successful conclusion. France had thus effectively avenged the humiliation that Great Britain had put upon her in the Seven Years' War. Such was the reflection that gave comfort to the French king and his advisers. It was, according to the traditional standards, a most satisfactory reflection. But events tended speedily to moderate the complacency of the court. Assisting the Americans and humbling Great Britain had been very expensive and the long impending bankruptcy of the royal treasury began to seem very near. The attention of the government was therefore diverted from its triumphs abroad to its perils at home.

Louis XVI had assumed the crown in 1774. He was as far as possible from the stuff of which an absolute monarch should be made. His natural endowments would have qualified him for the career of a mechanic, but would hardly have guaranteed him a good living from the wages he could earn. He was temperamentally good-natured, and intellectually dull. At his accession he manifested sympathy with the reforming philosophy that was current, and summoned Turgot to take charge of the finances. The projects of this eminent minister were far-reaching and might have been efficacious; but they trenched on the privileges of the nobility and clergy and on the interests of powerful industrial corporations, and the king was influenced to dismiss him. Necker, an experienced and successful banker, took up the task of fiscal administration, but abandoned it in 1781 when the effect of the intervention in America rendered his plans hopeless. A series of little politicians of the old school carried business along with no effort at reform till the insolvency of the treasury became a fact.

The ultimate causes of this disastrous situation lay deep in the outworn economic and administrative conditions of the old régime. Most conspicuous of the obstacles to all serious projects of reform was the resistance of the nobles and clergy to any infringement of their ancient privileges under which they were exempt from many taxes. The discussion of the royal finances accordingly shaped itself into a struggle between the privileged classes and the common people. It gave fresh fuel to the smouldering discontent that was kindled by other causes. The literary and intellectual classes, the men of professions and of business and the great mass of peasants, all had their grievances against the aristocracy, and all were stirred to air them by the struggle over taxation. Political agitation and debate of a scope and intensity unknown to France since the sixteenth century developed throughout the land as the successive ministers failed to relieve the embarrassments of the government. There was in this agitation little hostility to the person or office of the king. Louis XVI was regarded as a benevolent ruler, anxious to do what was best for France, but prevented by the malign influence of his court from seeing the true way. All manner of schemes were proposed by which the wishes of the French nation, rather than those of the old ruling clique, should have an effective place in the counsels of the monarch. By the "French nation" and the "French people" was meant, of course, the commons, *bourgeoisie* or Third Estate. The demand was, in short, for some modification of the absolute monarchy in the sense of popular government.

The strength and volume of the agitation tended steadily to paralyze all the activities of the administration. After a futile attempt to solve the problem by an Assembly of Notables, which served only to exhibit again the blind obstinacy of the privileged classes, the king resorted to the Estates General — the long-disused organ of old-time communication between the crown and all classes of its subjects. This body met May 5, 1789, and within six weeks revolution in France was an accomplished fact. From the outset the representatives of the Third Estate disregarded the character which ancient law and custom gave to the Estates General. They refused to recognize the royal command that the three orders — clergy, nobility and commons — should deliberate and vote separate from one another. They proclaimed themselves, June 17th, a "national assembly," empowered to interpret and express the general will of the nation, irrespective of any veto by the king. Three days later, in the famous oath of the tennis court, they swore that they would never separate till they had performed the duty to which they believed themselves called, namely, "to determine (*fixer*) the constitution of the kingdom, effect the reformation of the public order, and maintain the true principles of the monarchy." [1]

With this action of the assembly the old order in France passed away.[2] To the assumption of supreme power in the state by this body, lacking though it did all sanction in law, the king did not — doubtless could not — oppose any serious resistance. Of the privileged classes the same was true. A considerable number of

[1] Hélie, *Constitutions de la France*, I, p. 22.

[2] *Cf.* Robinson, "The Oath of the Tennis Court," in *Political Science Quarterly*, X, 460.

the representatives of the nobility and a clear majority of those of the clergy joined voluntarily with the assembly, which soon, with full recognition by the king, settled down to its self-appointed task. The "reformation of the public order" was effected by the abolition of privileges, and of the nobility itself, the civil constitution of the clergy, and the whole series of drastic decrees in the spirit of liberty and equality. The "constitution was determined" by the promulgation, in September, 1791, of an elaborate document, preceded by a "Declaration of the Rights of Man and of Citizen," and embodying in its provisions the governmental frame of a limited — very much limited — monarchy.

Long before this end was reached, however, the revolutionary impulse, penetrating to the lowest strata of society, had produced anarchic conditions, and had strengthened the influence of the most radical theorists and agitators. The king's assent to the new constitution was given under obvious duress, and the hapless monarch's longing to escape from the grasp of his loving subjects and their constitution was more than suspected. Brother monarchs undertook to rescue him, and under the added strain of foreign war and invasion the vaunted constitution collapsed in 1792 as utterly as the *ancien régime* in 1789. A National Convention, summoned with some color of legality, assumed all governmental as well as constituent functions. The king was deposed and executed, monarchy was abolished, the republic proclaimed, and amid the hideous orgies of the Terror and the fantastic experiments of Girondists, Jacobins and the Directory France moved deliriously back to order under the "enlightened despotism" of Napoleon Bonaparte.[1]

It was a much mooted question prior to 1789 — and authorities differ on it to the present day[2] — whether France under the *ancien régime* had a constitution. However this may be answered, by the end of the Napoleonic period the fundamental public law of the nation had been so often and so variously formulated and proclaimed as to make it certain that there was a constitution, while leaving in obscurity at any given time only the question as to what its content was. The idea that some formal code, making intelligible to all men the organization and powers of government, was indispensable in a free state, survived all the vicissitudes of the revolutionary era in France, and was carried into all the lands that were reached by French influence.[3] The written constitution thus became one of the foremost topics in the theories of philosophers who were concerned with politics. Questions as to the true source and sanction of its provisions, the scope of its authority, the method of its establishment and amendment, added a novel element to political theory. But this was only one element. The heated discussions of this agitated period embraced every aspect of political and social life, and solved anew, in the modes and phrases of the day, the problems that had been

[1] Sorel, *L'Europe et la Révolution Française*, I, p. 548.

[2] Hélie, writing in 1875, declared roundly that France had a constitution (*Les Constitutions de la France*, I, p. 3); Sorel, in 1887, held the contrary (*op. cit.*, I, 189).

[3] Borgeaud, *Adoption and Amendment of Constitutions*, pp. 23–55.

solved so often in other modes and phrases since the dawn of man's self-consciousness.

2. *American Ideas and Influence*

On its destructive side the American revolution was sustained almost exclusively by dogmas that were familiar and undisputed in Great Britain in the middle of the eighteenth century. The influential men among the colonists were saturated with the spirit of English political literature and of English law. The postulates of their theories of government were those that were transmitted in the history of the revolutions in England during the seventeenth century and in the writings of Harrington, Sydney, Locke and the lesser and later expounders of the successful system. Among the ardent asserters of American rights during the time of hottest controversy were many who reproduced, in manner and in matter, the Levellers of the previous century.[1] The effective control of affairs was exercised, however, by men of relatively conservative spirit and balanced judgment, and the convincing evidence of their strength and poise is to be found in the admirable state papers in which they proclaimed the principles of their policies. For the substance of the political philosophy of the American Revolution it is not necessary to look beyond the Declaration of Independence and the earliest constitutions, state and federal. The assemblies in which these documents took shape included men as gifted in power of expression as in thought. Jefferson, Mason and John Adams, the

[1] *Cf. Political Theories from Luther to Montesquieu*, pp. 236 *et seq.*

draughtsmen respectively of the Declaration of Independence, the Virginia Declaration of Rights and the Massachusetts Constitution of 1780, all blended admirably in their phrasing the spirit of the doctrines inherited from the Old World with the spirit that was peculiar to the New. Probably, however, it was not so much the specific content of these state papers as the mere fact of their publication, that is significant in the history of political theory; for they gave the impulse to the practice, soon to become universal, of justifying revolution by appealing to the general sentiment of mankind and of basing government on a written code of public law.

Summarily stated the ideas of the Americans were these: an original, pre-political state of nature, in which men are free and equal; a contractual procedure by which the free and equal individuals establish government for their joint and several welfare; a body of rights in every individual secure under all circumstances from denial by the government; the indefeasible sovereignty of the people, expressed ultimately in the right of revolution; the restriction of all governmental organs by reciprocal checks and balances and by the careful prescriptions of a written constitution.

The state of nature, as conceived by the Americans, was that of Locke, and had in it no suggestion of Rousseau's "*bon sauvage.*" It was very like Braintree, Massachusetts, or Westmoreland County, Virginia, when politics was dull. The natural man was the decent, well-to-do farmer or townsman, respecting his neighbors, respected by them, gladly concerting with them projects for peace and comfort, but suspicious and resentful toward regulations transmitted from any remote source. Whatever authority was necessary must spring naturally and simply from "the people," as constituted by the social compact. This familiar concept had in America the same variety and vagueness of meaning that it had elsewhere. Most explicit was the definition in the preamble to the constitution of Massachusetts:

> The body-politic is formed by a voluntary association of individuals: it is a social compact by which the whole people covenants with each citizen and each citizen with the whole people that all shall be governed by certain laws for the common good.[1]

The thought here obviously is that only political association is formed by the contract. In the Virginia Declaration of Rights, on the other hand, "men . . . by nature equally free and independent" appear to "enter into a state of society" by compact. Despite variation in the forms of expression, however, the general feeling of the American Fathers was, as Locke had so clearly held, that political, not social, organization was the subject-matter of the contractual procedure.

It is even more clear that the natural rights of individuals survived the compact and were guaranteed by it. Jefferson's famous phrase in the Declaration of Independence, that men are "endowed by their Creator with certain unalienable rights," to secure which governments are instituted, appears substantially in

[1] This and all following quotations from American documents are taken from Poore's collection of federal and state constitutions.

all the discussion of the years before as well as after 1776. Most of the states prefaced their early constitutions with "Declarations of Rights," in which an enumeration of these unalienable, inherent natural rights was undertaken, together often with the principles and institutions of government deemed essential to secure them. These lists show clearly the advance in the conception of liberty since the revolutions of the seventeenth century.

In the Declaration of Independence the unalienable rights were summed up in a variant of a centuries-old formula of English law and agitation,[1] "life, liberty and the pursuit of happiness." More specific reference to property appeared in the state Declarations. Virginia's included among the inherent rights "the means of acquiring and possessing property" and Massachusetts employed substantially the same words. The two rights for which the English Independents had struggled[2] received now most explicit recognition — freedom of worship and freedom of expression. In the same category of indestructible rights were incorporated the familiar ingredients of English judicial process — arrest by warrant, detention for cause shown and trial by jury. The democratic spirit of the Americans gave now the character of law to the principle for which the extremists of the Puritan Revolution had striven in vain — equality among citizens. The Virginia Declaration expressed the doctrine thus:

[1] *Political Theories from Luther to Montesquieu*, Index *sub voc.* "Natural Rights."

[2] *Ibid.*, p. 245, *et passim.*

That no man, or set of men, are entitled to exclusive or separate emoluments or privileges from the community, but in consideration of public services; which, not being descendible, neither ought the offices of magistrate, legislator or judge to be hereditary.

And with this extinction of privilege was united the ascription of the right to vote and hold office to every man "having sufficient evidence of permanent common interest with, and attachment to, the community."[1] Other additions to the list of natural rights were of less immediate significance, though destined to a distinguished future. Thus Massachusetts included the right of reunion — to assemble and consult upon the common good; and Pennsylvania proclaimed the inherent right to emigrate from one state to another, or "to form a new state in vacant countries." While there were variations among the states in some of these minor points, there was uniformity and uncompromising clearness in announcing the sovereignty of the people and the right of cashiering governments. The Declaration of Independence naturally made this doctrine particularly conspicuous. Governments, it affirmed, are instituted to secure the unalienable rights of men; their powers are derived from the consent of the governed; and when any form of government becomes destructive of the ends for which it was established, "it is the right of the people to alter or abolish it and to institute new government," based on such principles as seem best

[1] Virginia Declaration of Rights, vi. The Massachusetts Declaration was less explicit, assuring the suffrage and eligibility to all inhabitants "having such qualifications as they shall establish by their frame of government."

adapted to effect their safety and happiness. The state Declarations of Rights were no less explicit. Virginia assigned to "a majority of the community" the "indubitable, unalienable and indefeasible right to reform, alter, or abolish" an inadequate or offending government; and Massachusetts characterized this right "of the people" as "incontestable, unalienable and indefeasible."

As to the principles and powers through which governments could best realize their true end, the promotion of the general weal, there was naturally much diversity among the various states, as revealed in their respective constitutions. A study of these documents furnishes, however, a few doctrines that sum up the theory of the time on this subject.[1] The powers delegated to the government should be narrowly restricted; they should be divided among the legislative, executive and judicial departments in such manner as to insure the checking of each by the others; executive and legislative functionaries at least should all be elective and for short terms, in order that abuse of power might be promptly corrected by the people. These were obviously the doctrines of a democracy in government as well as in sovereignty. They sprang less from the long traditions of speculative philosophy than from the practical conditions of life and administration in the colonies. The interesting fact, from our point of view, is that the Americans were the first people in history to frame consciously and deliberately a system of government in

[1] Merriam's treatment of the topic is excellent. *Op. cit.*, pp. 74 *et seq.*

which leading dogmas of philosophy received the form and sanction of law.

On one fundamental question the formal pronouncements of the Americans were hardly more coherent and logical than the multitude of democratic theories that had preceded them. They furnished no precise conception of "the people" or "a people." The term was used indiscriminately in the collective and in the distributive sense. No criterion was afforded by which the possessor of sovereignty or of rights could be identified. It was made clear by the Declaration of Independence that those in whose name it was published conceived themselves as a distinct people so far as concerned all other communities of men. The occasion of the document was that it had become "necessary for one people to dissolve the political bands which have connected them with another and to assume among the powers of the earth the separate and equal station to which the laws of nature and of nature's God entitle them." These glowing and exalted phrases of Jefferson expressed a conception of "people" that was rarely discernible in the early state or federal constitutions. In these the unity and solidarity made so conspicuous in the Declaration disappeared and thirteen peoples were displayed instead of one. The "original, explicit and solemn compact" on which the constitution of Massachusetts was based, united the people of that state, not the American people; and the "sovereignty, freedom and independence" that inhered by nature in every people were declared by the Articles of Confederation to belong to each of the thirteen states. In fine, the democratic theory of America in the eighteenth century, somewhat like that of the Dutch and the French in the sixteenth and seventeenth, was permeated with the idea that a sovereign people of any considerable size must be a group of groups rather than a group of individuals.[1]

In the primary group, however, the particular commonwealth, the Americans manifested in one respect a very great clarity of democratic analysis. The framing of their constitutions they insisted should be the particular function of a special organ, distinct from the government and immediately representative of the people. Thus the constitutional convention came into the field of law and of philosophy. Where circumstances prevented the assembling of a special delegate body for the making of the constitution, a draught was prepared by the legislature, but was not recognized as in force until formally ratified by the people. The first constitution of Massachusetts was rejected at the polls for the reason, among others, that it had been framed by the legislature rather than by a special convention.[2] In its dread of oppression by government, even when the officials were their own agents, the American democracy added a new check upon its power by the device of a constituent and revising assembly. Thus the written constitution was made an expression of the deliberate popular will not only in content but also in origin.

The political pronouncements and experiments of

[1] *Political Theories from Luther to Montesquieu*, pp. 62–63, 78–79.

[2] *Cf.* Cushing, *From Provincial to Commonwealth Government in Massachusetts*, p. 193. On the transition in general see Jameson, *Const. Convention*, ch. iv, secs, 126 *et seq.*

the United States were closely studied by European philosophers, especially in France and England. That the republican form of government could succeed in so extensive a territory and so large a population, was contradictory of a dogma of political theory that had become almost axiomatic. The devices by which the Americans sought to maintain their system were therefore closely scrutinized. A collection of the state constitutions was published by order of Congress in 1781, and was through Franklin's influence soon translated into French.[1] That it contributed something to the flood of revolutionary doctrine then rising in France cannot be doubted.[2] Turgot, Mably and Condorcet all made the American system the subject of more or less elaborate criticism and commentary. Their strictures evoked the works [3] in which John Adams' spirit and learning were revealed to the intellectual world. As events moved on to the cataclysm of 1789 the American influence blended indistinguishably in the general agitation for political reform. That a new constitution for the United States had to be framed in 1787 was a fact not lost sight of by the French and English theorists, and the work of the Philadelphia convention, with the splendid sagacity of its exposition and defence in the *Federalist*, were familiar to many of the busy spirits that promoted the assembling of the Estates General.

[1] A French translation of the state constitutions, dedicated to Franklin, was published in Switzerland as early as 1778. Jellinek, *Declaration of Rights*, p. 18.

[2] For the evidence see Rosenthal, *France and America, passim. Cf.* Scherger, *Evolution of Modern Liberty*, chap. x.

[3] *Defence of the Constitutions . . . of the United States* (1787–88) and *Discourses on Davila* (1790). *Cf.* Merriam, *op. cit.*, p. 123.

3. *Siéyès*

When we recur to the specific theories that dominated the earliest practical proceedings of the French Revolution we are confronted by a mass of material that defies analysis in the scope of this work.[1] The general principles we have already seen in the systems treated in the preceding chapters. To what extent the reforming ideas of Montesquieu, Rousseau, *les philosophes*, the Physiocrats and the great foreign thinkers had permeated the French spirit, is best revealed by the *cahiers*, in which the electoral districts of the whole kingdom formulated their grievances and suggestions at the meeting of the Estates General. Along with the complaints of concrete oppression, inequality, over-taxation and maladministration in general, these *cahiers* embody every abstract principle of politics that was to play a part in the coming years. Rights of man, rights of citizen, social contract, popular sovereignty, with every conceivable dogma as to origin, end and form of government — all were in the *cahiers*, an impressive revelation of the political ferment throughout the nation. In addition to this a prodigious mass of pamphlets, brochures and more pretentious treatises on current topics accompanied every phase of the revolutionary movement. Without attempting any résumé of this we will consider only the ideas of that writer who by the agreement of both contemporaries and historians made most precisely the sparking contact

[1] For a very useful bibliography see Robinson and Beard, *Readings in Modern European History*, I, 403.

between popular feeling and literary expression at the beginning of 1789.

The famous essay: *What is the Third Estate?* contains substantially the whole of the Abbé Siéyès' theory of the state.[1] It was written as a contribution to the hot debate over the method of procedure that should obtain in the approaching Estates General. Its author claimed that he wrote it not as a statesman but as a philosopher, concerned with propounding the truths of political science, but not with the task of adapting them to immediate practical needs. As a matter of fact the course of events by which the Estates General was transformed into a constituent assembly followed exactly the line that he indicated.

The familiar triad of questions that introduced the plan of his work shows sufficiently its general trend: "What is the Third Estate? Everything. What has it been hitherto in the political order? Nothing. What does it demand? To become something in that order." Much of his fundamental doctrine turned upon the assault on the privileged classes that he and many others had previously developed.[2] Privilege, he argued, is exemption from the law; but law is the general will of the nation; therefore those who are not under the law are not in the nation. The unprivileged — the third estate — embracing nineteen-twentieths of the population, satisfying by their varied toil and activity all the needs of social life, and constituting in fact the real

[1] *Qu'est-ce que le Tiers État?* Précédé de *l'Essai sur les Privilèges.* Paris, 1888.

[2] *Cf.* his *Essai sur les Privilèges.*

strength of the community, has in itself the essentials of a complete nation.[1]

To settle the controversies then current in France Siéyès contended in his fifth chapter that a few simple principles of pure reason would serve better than the delicate and complex devices of great statesmen. Such principles he proceeded to set forth. They were the principles of Rousseau's *Contrat Social*, with the addition of representative government, which Rousseau repudiated.[2] Individuals will to unite into a community; *ipso facto* the nation exists. A general will thereupon takes the place of all the individual wills. When the number and dispersion of the individuals become so great as to make difficult the expression of the general will, that part of the national will and power necessary to provide for public needs is confided to certain of the people. Such is the origin of representative government.

The organization thus instituted is limited in its powers. Its will is not the "real" general will (*volonté commune*), but a "representative general will." The forms and laws that determine how the government shall fulfil its function are prescribed by the nation and, taken as a whole, they make up the constitution. But this is the constitution of the government, not of the nation. "The nation is before everything; it is the origin of everything. Its will is always legal; it is the

[1] Note the menace in chap. iii: "On ne doit point se le dissimuler; le garant de la liberté publique ne peut être que là où est la force réelle. Nous ne pouvons être libres qu'avec le peuple et par lui." *Op. cit.*, p. 54.

[2] *Supra*, p. 34.

law itself." On this point, that the nation is above and independent of the constitution, Siéyès was very strong and insistent.[1] The constitution binds the government, and any contravention of constitutional prescriptions by the ordinary legislature is illegal and void. But nothing binds the nation. It makes the constitution: in terms that at once became fixed in political science Siéyès declared: "The constitution is the work not of the constituted but of the constituent power."[2] His argument largely reproduced that of Rousseau on sovereignty.[3] The will of the nation cannot be alienated or bound; it ought not to be alienated or bound. It is like any other will, free and self-determined. No particular mode need be followed. "In whatever way a nation wills, it is enough that it wills; all modes are good, and its will is always the supreme law."

But if the mode (*manière*) in which the nation wills is a matter of indifference, the same is not true of the organ through which the supreme national power is exercised. There is but a single body conceivable that is capable of this function, when circumstances render it impossible for all the individuals forming the nation to assemble. This body is an assembly of extraordinary representatives (*représentants extraordinaires*) to which the nation shall have intrusted the

[1] The point had a great importance in the practical problem of the time. It furnished the ground on which the Estates General was turned into a constituent body.

[2] " . . . la constitution n'est pas l'ouvrage du pouvoir constitué mais du pouvoir constituant."—P. 67.

[3] *Contrat Social*, liv. ii, chaps. i–iv. *Cf. supra*, p. 22.

authority. Neither the ordinary legislature nor any other organ of the government is qualified to determine what is the constitution — to make it or to mend it. These governmental bodies are mere creatures of the constitution, circumscribed by its provisions. To make a constitution, or at any point to define its content, is the task of a representative assembly especially designated for the purpose by the nation.

Such is Siéyès' conception of a national constituent assembly. It signalizes a distinct advance in the theory of popular sovereignty. We have seen how again and again in the history of this theory promising systems became inconsistent and vague at the point where it became necessary to say precisely how the will of the sovereign people was to be ascertained. The Monarchomachs of the sixteenth century conceived that the various organs of provincial and municipal government could voice the people's will; the revolutionists in England in the next century clung to their ordinary Parliament, however mutilated, as adequate to the purpose; Rousseau insisted that the whole mass of individuals who constituted the sovereign people must be consulted; Siéyès developed the idea of a special representative assembly for every constitution-making function.

The immediate practical purpose that shaped Siéyès' conception was easy to see. The king and the privileged estates — clergy and nobility — claimed a decisive share in determining the solution of the crisis in France. They based their claim on the ancient constitution of the kingdom. Siéyès sought to put the solution in the hands of the Third Estate exclusively. To the king he conceded the quality of "first citizen," by virtue of which he might take the initiative in seeking the will of the nation. The expression of that will could be only by a majority of the representatives of the people chosen for the purpose. That a minority, like the privileged estates, should have a share out of proportion to its exact number, he insisted was a proposition that lay outside the field of rationality.[1] The deputies of the Third Estate represented twenty-five millions of people: those of the nobility and clergy represented two hundred thousand. It was for the former, therefore, if they could not by themselves make up the Estates General, to assume the functions of a "national assembly."[2] How precisely Siéyès spoke the spirit of the time appears in the famous declaration of the Third Estate at Versailles on June 17 by which it formally assumed the functions and the title that he had claimed for it.[3]

The power, precision and insight with which Siéyès worked out his conception of the constituent organ give him a prominent place in the history of formal political theory. Before he wrote, however, and without any paraphernalia of philosophic dogma, the framers of the American constitutions had realized the conception in the work of their constitutional conventions.

[1] "Si l'on abandonne un seul instant ce principe de première évidence, que la volonté commune est l'avis de la pluralité et non celui de la minorité, il est inutile de parler raison." — P. 74.

[2] "Le tiers seul, dira-t-on, ne peut pas former les États généraux. Eh! tant mieux! Il composera une Assemblée nationale." He had used this same term in an earlier essay. *Cf.* Zweig, *Pouvoir Constituant*, 121–122. In 1787 Lafayette had suggested the summoning of an "assemblée nationale." See his *Mémoires*, II, 177.

[3] Hélie, *Constitutions de la France*, I, p. 19.

4. *Condorcet*

Siéyès seems not to have been aware that his doctrine of the constituent power had been anticipated by the practice of the Americans.[1] Condorcet, on the other hand, who contributed much to clarify the doctrine, was well acquainted with American institutions. He criticised with earnestness some features of the governmental organization that prevailed; but for the written constitutions and the convention by which they were framed and revised he had only admiration. His approval sprang in no sense, however, from mere regard for the accomplished fact. As a political philosopher Condorcet expressed in a peculiarly marked way that eighteenth-century spirit which trusted in the power of pure reason to define and mould the form of institutions. A political system was in his eyes primarily good, not because it would work, but because it fitted the requirements of rational philosophy. The task of the French National Assembly was, he said, to frame

> a constitution which, based solely on the principles of reason and justice, should assure to the citizens the most complete enjoyment of their rights; to combine the parts of that constitution in such a way that the necessity of obedience to the laws, of submission of the individual wills to the general will, should leave intact both the sovereignty of the people, the equality among the citizens and the exercise of natural liberty.[2]

The making of a constitution was thus, to Condorcet, primarily a problem in deductive logic. From a few

[1] Lafayette, *Mémoires*, IV, 36.
[2] "Plan de Constitution," in *Œuvres*, XII, 335.

simple principles concerning sovereignty, liberty and rights — principles too axiomatic to require discussion, exact reasoning would inexorably deduce the fundamental law of a nation. This law, being the general will, could be formulated only by an assembly of the whole people, or of their representatives. On the nature, authority and action of the constituent assembly, or constitutional convention, Condorcet's theorizing was practically exhaustive.[1] This organ of the national will he found to be the absolute and uncontrollable source of public law. It could make and unmake governments and constitutions. It could and should preface a constitution with a declaration of inalienable rights and immutable principles; but it could later revoke the declaration. Changes in the fundamental law Condorcet believed to be inevitable, and for that reason he held that provision for making them through a convention should be a part of every constitution. To leave to the government, or any branch of it, any share in amending the constitution, would be illogical and perilous. The organic law itself, therefore, must prescribe the method of its own revision, and provide for the automatic assembling of a convention for this purpose. Only in such a way could the certainty and security of law be infused into the supreme law, and instability itself be subjected to rule.[2]

[1] "Für die Lehre vom pouvoir constituant hat Condorcet eine dialektische Arbeit von nicht zu unterschätzendem Werte geleistet. Theoretisch hat er das Problem erschöpft." Zweig, *Lehre vom Pouvoir Constituant*, p. 115.

[2] The origin and details of Condorcet's views on this general subject are treated at length by Zweig, *Lehre vom Pouvoir Constituant*, p. 97 *et seq*.

Condorcet's doctrines on this subject show clearly enough the influence of Rousseau's theory on the one side and American practice on the other.[1] Whatever the relative importance of these two factors, it is sufficient for our purpose to note that at this early period in the history of the written constitution all the bearings had been investigated of that complex and trouble-making question of later days: How can an unchangeable constitution be amended? Condorcet was a radical republican. He could see no higher authority on any constitutional question than the "immediate majority of the people, the first of the political powers"; and his preoccupation was to insure that the action of this authority, although above law, should be regulated by the law.[2]

The most famous of Condorcet's works was doubtless his *Outlines of an Historical View of the Progress of the Human Mind*,[3] written while he was in concealment from the proscription of the Jacobins and very shortly before his death. Though this essay owed something of its reputation to the circumstances under which it was written, it was from every point of view a monument to its author's genius. His philosophy of history was in striking contrast to that of the earlier

[1] *Cf. supra*, pp. 37–38. Of the original state constitutions, those of Mass., Penna., Md., S. C., and Ga., contained provisions for amendment, those of Penna. and Ga. approaching most nearly to Condorcet's idea.

[2] See his interesting explanation in "Plan de Constitution," *Œuvres*, XII, 365–366.

[3] I have used an anonymous translation published in London in 1795. For the French original, "Esquisse d'un tableau des progrès de l'esprit humain," see *Œuvres*, VI.

eighteenth century. Where his predecessors were in despair, because of the vices of civilization and the decay of rational institutions, he found all things making for progress. The formation of the French republic was to him the supreme triumph of reason in society and government, and the beginning of complete regeneration of the race. To the example of the American revolution he ascribed an important influence in the larger movement. But, he said, "it would be easy to show how much more pure, accurate and profound are the principles upon which the constitution and law of France have been formed than those which direct the Americans." Both alike realized the great and novel idea of distinguishing the constituent from the ordinary legislative power; and both provided by law for reforming their constitutions. The Americans, however, erred, he declared, in organizing their governments with reference to a "factitious identity of interests" rather than to an equality of rights, and in trusting for the proper working of the system rather to a complex balancing of powers than to the simple and unified action of the national will.

Condorcet's objections to the American system were directed at the points which in experience, as compared with France, seem to have proved most sound and useful. The protection of individual rights has been rather better secured by the check and balance system than by the simplified expression of the popular will in the plebiscite; and regard for work-a-day human interests has promoted equality no less at least than has the solemn reiteration of the rights of man. But if the philosopher's prevision failed somewhat at these points, it showed at others an amazing strength. His forecast of the general progress of the world reads to-day much like a history of the nineteenth century. He foretells the wide diffusion of constitutional liberty, the independence of European colonies and the vast increase of their populations, the abolition of government by chartered companies, the freeing of commerce from restrictions, and the extension to Asia and Africa of the uplifting influence of French and American institutions. Before the triumphant march of republican ideas all forms of inequality are doomed to disappear, as political inequality has already done. Wealth, social condition and culture will be equally distributed among citizens through the enlightened operation of free government.

Finally, Condorcet's confidence in the beneficent working of change was so great that he agreed with Jefferson in limiting the permanence of the social pact itself. No generation, he held, could bind its successor. Every generation must determine for itself the scope and form of its institutions. This is a logical result of the dogma that society rests upon the free action of the individual will; but Condorcet's acceptance of the conclusion was rendered easier by his conviction that each successive generation, in renewing the pact, would take a position in advance of its predecessor and contribute thus its share to the progress of mankind.

5. *Thomas Paine*

In the Abbé Siéyès were incarnate the spirit and philosophy that were distinctively French. Condorcet exhibited in some measure the qualifying influence of American ideas. A very remarkable blend of the two systems, where the separate ingredients are practically indistinguishable, is to be found in the works of Thomas Paine. Paine was indeed primarily and essentially an agitator and a pamphleteer rather than a detached and systematic philosopher; but he had a wonderful faculty of both thought and expression, and his keen wit and vivid phrases caught and fixed the doctrine of the revolutions often much more effectively than the weightier and deeper analysis of mightier intellects. A summary view of some leading aspects of Paine's work will be most useful for our present purpose.

The substance of his political philosophy is to be found in his famous pamphlets "Common Sense" and "The Rights of Man."[1] The former of these, as is well known, played a great part in the early days of the American Revolution; and the latter of them was no less conspicuous and influential in the critical period of the French cataclysm. Throughout both of these works Paine's facility in denunciation and invective was characteristically prominent. Monarchy, nobility, and all such incidents of hereditary government were systematically loaded with scorn and bitter reproach; but apart from this common practice of anti-monarchic agitation Paine presented from time to time in forceful terms the elementary principles of a constructive political philosophy.

At the very basis of his positive doctrine he puts a distinction between society and the state, or as he more

[1] In *Writings*, Conway's ed., Vols. I and II respectively.

commonly calls it, government. The opening passage of "Common Sense" is a classic in this respect.

Some writers have so confounded society with government, as to leave little or no distinction between them; whereas they are not only different, but have different origins. Society is produced by our wants, and government by our wickedness; the former promotes our happiness *positively*, by uniting our affections, the latter *negatively*, by restraining our vices. The one encourages intercourse, the other creates distinctions. The first is a patron, the last a punisher.

Society in every state is a blessing, but Government, even in its best state, is but a necessary evil; in its worst state, an intolerable one; for when we suffer, or are exposed to the same miseries *by a Government*, which we might expect in a country *without Government*, our calamity is heightened by reflecting that we furnish the means by which we suffer. Government, like dress, is the badge of lost innocence; the palaces of kings are built upon the ruins of the bowers of Paradise.[1]

The distinction here so strikingly expressed recurs again and again in his writings. His thinking on this point is very obviously derived from the philosophy transmitted by Locke. It lends itself readily to a further notion, exploited at length by Paine, namely, that the function of government is after all a narrowly limited and relatively subsidiary one. Paine exhibits clearly the influence of the *laissez-faire* dogma that pervaded his time. To him, as to very many others of the revolutionists, the rights of man inevitably suggest the limitations of government.

Paine's classification of governments was reminiscent of Montesquieu and Rousseau. His especial problem

[1] *Writings*, I, 69.

was to find a place for the category "republic"; for Paine was in the fullest sense a republican, as opposed to the monarchists. With the natural tendency of the controversialist, he gave to the term republican the meaning of supreme dignity. He adopted substantially the doctrine of Rousseau, that all legitimate government is republican.[1]

> What is called a *republic* is not any *particular form* of government. . . . It is a word of a good original referring to what ought to be the character and business of government. . . . Republican government is no other than government established and conducted for the interest of the public, as well individually as collectively.[2]

The distinct forms of government that he recognizes are the democratical, the aristocratical, the monarchical, and what he says is now called the "representative." Of these monarchy and aristocracy are corrupt, as incompatible with the true end of government; democracy is inadequate to the affairs of an extensive population; and representative government thus becomes the only logical and adequate system. The ideal, as he sees it, is representation engrafted upon democracy. The advantages of such a system are "as much superior to hereditary government as the republic of letters is to hereditary literature."

Another significant doctrine of Paine's is that as to the nature of a constitution. On this point he takes advanced ground for the scientific excellence of what America has produced. Burke's vague and mystic conceptions based upon the English constitution excite Paine's utmost irreverence.

[1] *Supra*, p. 28.

[2] *Writings*, II, 421.

> A constitution is not a thing in name only, but in fact. It has not an ideal, but a real existence; and wherever it cannot be produced in a visible form there is none. A constitution is a thing *antecedent* to a government; and a government is only the creature of a constitution. . . . Can, then, Mr. Burke produce the English Constitution? If he cannot, we may fairly conclude that though it has been so much talked about, no such thing as a constitution exists or ever did exist; and consequently that the people have yet a constitution to form.[1]

Whatever we may think of the ultimate soundness of Paine's argument on this point, it certainly does not lack clearness and a sort of rude vigor that must have appealed very strongly to the radical elements of his day. It is not surprising that he was looked upon in England as a dangerous man. Before such sharp and practical dogmas as those quoted, the mass of vague and antiquated traditions and practices that made up so much of the English constitution appeared ridiculous. After a satirical sketch of the various elements of the English constitution in their origin and history, Paine said:

> I cannot believe that any nation reasoning on its own rights would have thought of calling those things a constitution if the cry of constitution had not been set up by the government. It has got into circulation like the words 'bore' and 'quoz' [quiz] by being chalked up in the speeches of Parliament, as those words were on window-shutters and door-posts.[2]

On the form and content of the written constitution, to him the only constitution proper, Paine had much to say, based almost entirely on the constitutions of the

[1] *Writings*, II, 309–310. [2] *Ibid.*, II, 438.

United States with which he was so familiar. His confidence was strong that the work of the Americans had made an epoch in the history of political science. "The American constitutions," he said, "were to liberty what grammar is to language. They define its parts of speech and practically construct them into syntax."[1] On one very conspicuous feature of the American constitutions, namely, the threefold classification of the powers of government, Paine was at variance with the leaders of American thought. He perceived and pointed out that there were in fact but two kinds of power. The function of government, he held, was exhausted in, first the making, and second the executing, of laws. Everything pertaining to civil government could be classed under one or the other of these two divisions. In taking this position Paine, of course, merely developed what Montesquieu himself had casually remarked, that the judiciary is not in its essence distinct from, but is merely one aspect of, the executive power.[2]

A feature of the American system on which Paine dwelt with special approval was the provision made for revision and amendment of the constitution. It was not in the spirit of the man to recognize anything as permanent, or as entitled to special respect by virtue of its age. He was thoroughly at one with his time in expecting and providing for a continuing progress in political as in other human concerns.

Finally, it is worth while to notice the clearness of Paine's analysis in respect to the conception of law.

[1] *Writings*, p. 336. [2] *Esprit des Lois*, liv. xi, chap. vi.

Obviously influenced by the idea of law that Rousseau particularly emphasized, Paine took occasion to point out that by no means all the enactments of a legislature are entitled to the name and character of law. "All laws," he says, "are acts, but all acts are not laws." Much that has the form of legislation is in fact but business, contract, agency, negotiation — the normal procedure by which an association of men carries out certain purposes. Distinct from these administrative instructions, laws are only those acts of the assembly or commonwealth that have universal operation, or apply to every individual of the commonwealth.[1] This very useful distinction Paine employed in setting forth his own particular views as to the then troublesome affairs in America of the finances and the paper money.

6. *The French Constitutions*

Siéyès, Condorcet and Paine were all members of one or both of the assemblies in which the French constitutions of 1791 and 1793 were framed. The documents reflect clearly enough the doctrines conspicuous in these philosophers; but many minds no less strong and fertile than theirs influenced the form in which the constitutions were cast. The problems of statecraft in France during those years were as complex as any that ever vexed the human intellect. Practical politics pressed insistently upon the attention of the revolutionary leaders. To frame a constitution amid the turmoil of the time was a task for titans. The outcome has been the text for as virulent criticism as has

[1] *Writings*, II, 142.

ever been directed against a work of man. That mistakes were made may readily enough be admitted; that the adaptation of means to ends in the organization of the government lacked something of practical sagacity cannot be questioned; but taken as a whole and in view of all the difficulties with which the work was surrounded, the first written constitution of France was a remarkable monument of constructive power. It certainly does not suffer by comparison with the first attempts in England[1] and in the other nations of continental Europe. Nor indeed was its practical failure more complete than that of the first general constitution of the United States — the ill-fated Articles of Confederation.

The French constitution-makers, like the American, judged that the fundamental principles of their political philosophy ought to form a part of their positive law.[2] Hence the famous Declaration of the Rights of Man and of Citizen, first adopted on August 26, 1789, was made a part of the completed constitution of 1791, and appeared with more or less modification in those of 1793 and 1795. In most respects the content of the French Declaration was identical with that of the American Bills of Rights.[3] The same theory of the relations between the state and

[1] I refer to the abortive "Agreement of the People." *Political Theories from Luther to Montesquieu*, p. 238.

[2] Opinion on this point was by no means unanimous in the Constituent Assembly. *Cf.* Buchez and Roux, *Hist. Parlementaire*, II, 200.

[3] Jellinek found an American analogue for each article of the French Declaration. *Cf.* his *Declaration of the Rights of Man*, ch. v. His inference that the French merely copied from the Americans was attacked with vigor and some bitterness by Boutmy in *Annales de l'École Libre*, XVII, 415.

the individual was set forth, but with distinctly more precision in expression and logical coherence in arrangement than appeared in any of the American documents.

In its preamble the French Declaration states the reason for its existence — to enable anybody at any time to compare the acts of legislature or executive with the fundamental principles of government. Then follow these principles. Men are from birth free and equal in rights. The end of every political association is the maintenance of the natural and imprescriptible rights of man, which are summed up as "liberty, property, security and resistance to oppression." Liberty is defined: "the power to do anything that does not harm another"; it includes, therefore, such exercise of natural rights as is consistent with the like exercise by others. The limitation thus necessary upon the exercise of the natural rights can be fixed only by law (*loi*); and law in its turn is defined in the phrase made so familiar by Rousseau — "the expression of the general will (*volonté générale*)." In the formulation of the law it is the right of every citizen to participate either in person or by representative; and the prescriptions of the law must apply with precise equality to all.

The purpose to leave no ground for the ancient order of privilege and arbitrary rule is clear in all these elaborate dogmas about law. This purpose is achieved, however, at some cost of logical consistency. For while law, as the expression of the general will, should be deemed self-determining as to its content, we find the Declaration anxiously asserting that the law "has no right" to forbid what is not harmful to the society (art. 5) and that the law "ought to be the same for all" (art. 6). These locutions, if not the result of mere inadvertence, suggest something less than perfect confidence on the part of the Assembly in the practical working of the system that was being established.

As elements of the "security" that belongs of natural right to man, the Declaration enumerates the familiar safeguards of English and American practice in regard to arrest, detention and punishment. Freedom of opinion, "even religious," and of expression are specifically catalogued as natural rights, and in the main body of the constitution (Tit. I) the list is increased by freedom of movement, of peaceable assembling and of petitioning the authorities. The "sacred and inviolable" right of property is assured by provisions for equal taxation and for compensation when private possessions are taken for public use.

It was not alone by the formal recital of natural rights that the French constitution-makers sought to insure respect for them. An explicit positive guarantee of them was incorporated in the constitution. With like explicitness the abolition of all institutions incompatible with liberty and equality was decreed. Moreover, the principles of recent philosophy as to the source and organization of power in the government were announced and applied. Sovereignty was declared to reside exclusively in the nation,[1] and to be "one, indivisible, inalienable and imprescriptible."[2]

[1] "Le principe de tout souveraineté réside essentiellement dans la nation; nul corps, nul individu ne peut exercer d'autorité qui n'en émane expressément." Declaration, art. 3.

[2] Const., Tit. III.

The powers of the sovereign nation must be exercised by delegation, and accordingly the assignment of functions to legislative, executive and judicial organs was systematically prescribed.[1] In this matter the doctrine of Montesquieu, already adopted by the Americans, was applied by the French of 1791 in its fulness. The separation of powers, like the guarantee of individual rights, was roundly declared to be an indispensable evidence that any nation possessed a constitution.[2] The particular category to which the constitution of 1791 belonged was announced in these terms: "The French constitution is representative: the representatives are the *Corps Législatif* and the King." [3] Why the elected judges to whom the judicial power was formally delegated were not included among the "representatives" does not appear. The omission again illustrates the practice, started by Montesquieu himself, of attributing relative insignificance to the judiciary as compared with the other departments.

Having adopted advanced philosophy as to individual rights and governmental organization, the Constituent Assembly unflinchingly propounded the capital dogma of revolution: "The nation has the imprescriptible right to change its constitution." [4] Not by way of restricting this absolute right, but as a measure of expediency,[5] a method of amendment was incorporated

[1] Const., Tit. III.

[2] "Toute société dans laquelle la garantie des droits n'est pas assurée ni la séparation des pouvoirs determinée, n'a point de constitution." Declaration, art. 16.

[3] Tit. III, art. 2. [4] Tit. VII, art. 1.

[5] ". . . considérant qu'il est plus conformé à l'intérêt national d'user seulement, par les moyens pris dans la constitution même,

in the constitution. The process prescribed was long and complex, and it deviated much from the principle that the constituent power shall be entirely separate from that of ordinary legislation.[1] The labor expended in devising this process was wasted. Less than two years after the Constitution of 1791 went into effect it was summarily set aside, with scant regard for its own provisions, by decree of the *Corps Législatif*,[2] its own creature. This same body, assuming the historic name "National Assembly," but disclaiming the right to prescribe rules for the exercise of sovereignty, "invited" the citizens to choose in indicated ways delegates to a "National Convention."[3] The invitation was duly accepted and the famous Convention became for three anarchic years the titular wielder of all political authority, constituent and governmental, for the distracted French Republic.

Psychology and sociology, rather than political science, must explain the frenzied travesty of rational government that characterized the ascendency of the Jacobins. A passing glance only may be given to the evidence that the theory of individual rights endured and expanded even while the Terror was making it in practice a bloody mockery. The Girondists, during their brief control of the Convention, framed a constitution in which the influence of Condorcet and Paine was preëminent. Their draft shared in their fate when the Jacobins overwhelmed them, and in June, 1793, the

du droit d'en réformer les articles dont l'expérience aurait fait sentir les inconvénients. . . ." *Ibid.*

[1] *Cf. supra*, pp. 104, 107.

[2] Hélie, *op. cit.*, pp. 326 *et seq.*

[3] *Ibid.*, p. 329.

triumphant faction adopted its own version of the supreme law of the French Republic. This draft was duly ratified by the people in such an election as the conditions permitted, but it was never put into practical operation.

This abortive instrument begins with a Declaration of Rights that exceeds in fulness that of 1789. The end of "society" is asserted to be the general welfare (*le bonheur commun*) and the object of government to be the guarantee of man's natural and imprescriptible rights. To the list of these rights is made the significant addition of public assistance (*les secours publics*) to the unfortunate. "Society owes subsistence to unfortunate citizens either in procuring work for them or in insuring a livelihood to those who are unable to work."[1] Public education is also guaranteed to every Frenchman.[2] As to sovereignty, its depositary is declared to be "the French people"; and the sanction of this truth is proclaimed in the ancient dogma of tyrannicide: "Let every individual who would usurp the sovereignty be instantly put to death by free men."[3] In no less ambiguous terms the right of insurrection is proclaimed: "When the government violates the rights of the people, insurrection is for the people and for every part (*chaque portion*) of the people the most sacred of rights and the most indispensable of duties."[4]

The militant democracy that speaks in these drastic dogmas reveals itself with equal distinctness in the governmental organization in the constitution of 1793.

[1] Declaration, art. 21.
[2] Const., art. 122.
[3] Declaration, art. 27.
[4] *Ibid.*, art. 35.

The separation of powers, which two years before had been declared the *sine qua non* of a constitution, is utterly ignored. Not through the jealousy and strife of rival subordinate authorities, but through the direct and increasing activity and control of the sovereign people itself are guarantees sought for liberty and equality. A legislative assembly (*Corps Législatif*) is provided for, chosen annually by manhood suffrage; no law can have effect, however, until approved by the people in their primary assemblies.[1] The administration is put in the hands of an executive council of twenty-four, elected by the legislative assembly from a list of candidates named by electoral assemblies; of independence with respect to the legislature no vestige is possessed by this council.

Pending the putting in force of this Constitution of 1793 the French Republic, by proceedings that lacked the crudest elements of rational politics, achieved an astounding triumph over its foes both domestic and foreign. The driving force in this extraordinary exploit was a fury of patriotic emotion as primitive as the religious fanaticism that installed the Mohammedans upon the ruins of the Roman dominion. In 1795, with returning sanity, the Convention resumed its constituent activity, but discarding its earlier scheme, it put in force an entirely new constitution. This manifested a pronounced reaction from the extreme democracy of 1793. The Declaration of Rights omitted

[1] On certain enumerated subjects the *Corps Législatif* was empowered to issue "decrees" without submitting them to the people. Acte Constitutionnel, secs. 53, 54, 56–60. In Hélie, *op. cit.* I, 380.

tyrannicide and insurrection, public assistance and education,[1] and seriously qualified other provisions that had proved baneful in recent experience. Most significant of all, perhaps, was the appearance of a list of *duties* annexed to the *rights* of man and citizen. Nothing in this constitution more strikingly suggests the mental attitude of France at this time than the grave enumeration of the simplest maxims of morality in the fundamental law. "Do not to another what you would not have done to you. Do to others the good that you would like to receive." "No one is a good citizen who is not a good son, or father, or brother or friend or spouse." "No one is a good man (*homme de bien*) who does not freely and religiously obey the laws." It is hard to realize that such elementary moral doctrines should have been soberly enacted into law by an enlightened people.

In the organization of government there was in large measure a reversion to the principles of 1791. Sovereignty, which was in 1791 ascribed to the "nation" and in 1793 to the "French people," now was found in "the whole body (*l'universalité*) of French citizens." The separation of powers appeared again, as essential, however, not to a constitution, but to "the social guarantee."[2] The executive as an independent power was reconstituted after its three years of abeyance, but was put into commission and vested in a Directory of five members. A bicameral legislature was a new

[1] A system of public schools was provided for (Const. Tit. X), but without assertion that these were of natural right.

[2] "La garantie sociale ne peut exister si la division des pouvoirs n'est pas établie. . . ." — Declaration, art. 22.

feature in French practice. It was not constituted, however, on the English and American model, with chambers of largely identical powers. In the new *Corps Législatif* the Council of the Five Hundred had the sole power to propose laws and the Council of the Ancients the sole power to enact them.

With the Constitution of 1795 ended for nearly a score of years the formulation of the public law of France in the terms of political philosophy. Neither internal nor external conditions were such as to permit of popular government. With the revelation of genius in Napoleon Bonaparte the distracted people were well satisfied to acquiesce in his assumption of the right to govern in their name. Consulate and empire followed in due course. For these systems also there were written constitutions; but they contained nothing about natural rights, or the separation of powers, or the sovereignty of the people, or the right to cashier governments, or any other of the great dogmas of political philosophy. Substantially their whole content was a series of shrewdly planned regulations through which an efficient administration directed public affairs according to the will of the monarch. In the Napoleonic régime practically the only vestige of revolutionary principle was the dogma that the Emperor governed as the chosen representative of the French people, whose will was expressed in the plébiscite by which each step in the transformation of the government was ratified.

7. *Conclusion*

By the American and French revolutions the methods of political salvation that had appealed to the philosophy of the mid-eighteenth century were pretty thoroughly tested. The simple principles of a rational theory of state and government were embodied in constitutional codes, where every man might readily find clearly outlined the source and substance of the social and political order. Nature, universal and immutable, was the basis of these codes; liberty and equality for every individual were the imperative dictates of nature's organ, reason. Thus the ancient dogma of the Stoic jurist became at last effective positive law. The Declarations of Rights put adequate qualifications upon natural rights to convert them into workable civil rights, and the sovereignty of the people received an intelligible democratic interpretation in a wide manhood suffrage, acting through a distinct constituent organ, and assuring to a numerical majority of the citizens the effective expression of the sovereign will.

In neither America nor France were the dogmas of these democratic constitutions fully realized in practice. On the one side of the Atlantic Indians, negroes and loyalists found little security for life, liberty or property; on the other side even less was the lot of royalists, aristocrats and the minority factions in general. This condition was in large measure due, of course, especially in Europe, to the exigencies of flagrant war, during which philosophy, like law, is necessarily in abeyance. There was, however, a defect in fundamental theory that was manifest in the imperfect working of the new constitutions. The rights of man is *prima facie* a cosmopolitical dogma. Its application is to all men. To bring it into operation in any limited group requires first a most explicit definition of the group. The constitutions that bestowed and withheld rights in the name of France, or the Nation, or the French People, or the French Republic, failed to fix with philosophical precision the concept that each of these terms designated. The individual was ruthlessly overridden in maintaining the rights of the nation or the people; but no clear coherent declaration appeared cataloguing these rights and defining in logical formula the entity that possessed them. What was "France" or the "French Nation," from the point of view of nature and reason? Only the totality of those individuals, with their possessions, who willed to unite under that designation. Such would have been the logical answer of the revolutionist philosophy. But the obvious deductions from this dogma[1] were such as to repel the most fanatical devotee of theory. Hence the France that the republicans so effectively maintained against domestic and foreign foes was the France of heredity, of history and tradition. These were, however, sorry principles to be employed by the devotees of nature and abstract reason. Tradition and history were the capital supports for the claims of the Bourbons and the *émigrés*. When

[1] It would have excluded la Vendée, for example, from the Republic.

the French Republic turned from defence to aggression and began to annex territory on the Rhine and in Italy, all the specious paraphernalia of appeals to the oppressed and of plébiscites did not disguise the fact that the policy and theories of Louis XIV and his predecessor were again determining European politics. Nor was the evidence of this fact obscured when Napoleon Bonaparte assumed the leadership and systematically put into the foreground the ideas and institutions of Cæsar and of Charlemagne.[1] When a hereditary empire, with a hereditary nobility, was established in France, with dominion over all Western Europe, and these with the enthusiastic approval of a majority of the French people, it was obvious that the political philosophy of 1789 and 1793 had lost its hold on governmental affairs, and that the principles of the reaction were beginning to gain the upper hand.

Before examining these principles in detail, it is essential, however, to devote some attention to certain aspects of liberal thought that prevailed outside of France. At the end of the eighteenth century, while the typical philosophy of the century had run its course to desuetude in the practical politics of France, it was in Great Britain and Germany receiving a significant

[1] Sorel acutely discerns the spirit of the old régime continuously operating from the beginning of the revolution. Speaking of the common boasts of the French republicans that the spirit of other free peoples was manifest in themselves, he says: "On leur déclare successivement qu'ils sont des Anglais, des Américains, des Romains, des Spartiates: ils demeurent le lendemain ce qu'ils étaient la veille, des Français du dix-huitième siècle, et l'esprit de l'ancien gouvernement se retrouve jusque dans les institutions destinées à l'anéantir." *L'Europe et la Révolution française*, I, 223.

development in the speculations of certain powerful intellects. Jeremy Bentham, the chief of the English school, we shall leave for consideration in a later chapter.[1] The Germans, who were peculiarly expert in giving logical perfection to the system that the French politicians were reducing to a nullity, must receive our attention here.

SELECT REFERENCES

Annales de l'École libre de la science politique, July, 1902, p. 415. Borgeaud, Adoption and Amendment of Constitutions, chaps. iii, iv. Condorcet, "*Plan de Constitution,*" in *Œuvres*, Vol. XII. Jellinek, Declaration of the Rights of Man and of Citizens (translation). Merriam, History of American Political Theories, chap. ii. Michel, *Idée de l'État*, pp. 89–104. Paine, Common Sense; Rights of Man, Part II. Rosenthal, America and France. Scherger, Evolution of Modern Liberty, chaps. viii–xii. Siéyès, "What Is the Third Estate?" chap. v. Sorel, *L'Europe et la Révolution française*, Part I.

[1] *Infra*, chap. vi.

CHAPTER IV

THE GERMAN IDEALISTS

1. *Immanuel Kant*

When the storm of revolution broke over Europe Kant was the generally recognized leader of German philosophy. His *Critique of the Pure Reason*, published in 1781, was in the most literal sense an epoch-making work. It produced at once a profound impression on the intellectual life of Germany, and its influence, sustained and promoted by that of the other works that followed it, fixed the lines in which philosophy moved for a century. Yet Kant was not, in the substance of his thought, an innovator. His rôle was rather that of the harmonizer and systematizer of familiar but conflicting doctrines. In metaphysics he mediatized between the dogmatists and intuitionists on the one side, and the sceptics and empiricists on the other, who in their reciprocal antagonism had brought philosophy to an *impasse*. Fundamentally Kant was with the intuitionists. Ultimate truth and reality were for him as for them predicable of ideas that were independent of sense-perception and experience. Yet his analysis of the intellectual faculties, especially of reason itself, gave a new and fruitful aspect to this ancient idealism. At the same time Kant took the doctrines of the empiricists into his system by a dualism that got as near to formal unity as any like system in history. His *Critique of the Pure Reason* was followed in 1788 by a *Critique of the Practical Reason.* As the first presented the categories and formulas through which all phases of existence could be known in thought, the second presented the categories and formulas through which existence could be known in experience. What is thinkable was the subject of the one; what is observable, of the other. To use Kant's own expressions, the one deals with the noumenal, the other with the phenomenal.

Of these two fields of speculation, Kant's most distinctive work was done in the former. By temperament and training he was a closet philosopher, and his genius found most to attract it in what was remote from the thought and action of everyday life. Thus his political philosophy was far stronger in its analysis and definition of the ultimate concepts liberty, law, rights, state, than in its treatment of government and administration. Kant's proper field was obviously *Staatslehre* rather than *Staatsrecht* or *Politik.* In neither branch of the science, however, did he make any original contribution. His function was to cast the dominant ideas of the later eighteenth century into the categories and formulas of his critical philosophy. His doctrine as to the origin and nature of the state is merely Rousseau's, put into the garb of Kantian terminology and logic; his analysis of government follows Montesquieu in like manner. Kant's admiration for these two French writers [1] was deep and unconcealed, and his incorporation of their ideas into his system was destined to promote greatly the influence of liberalism when the Kantian system got a firm hold on intellectual Germany.

Kant's political philosophy was embodied chiefly in his *Metaphysical First Principles of the Theory of Law*, written in his old age and published in 1796.[2] A year earlier some phases of his doctrine were presented in his brochure *For Perpetual Peace.*[3] A brief summary of his leading ideas will show how far from novel they were.[4]

Men are naturally free and equal. A state is the product of a contract through which individuals put their inalienable rights under the guarantee of the people (*Volk*). The people only is the sovereign and the supreme law-maker; the general will is the ultimate source of law — is itself law. A constitution is an act of the general will through which a crowd (*Menge*) becomes a people (*Volk*). There are three powers in every state — the sovereign legislative (*Herrschergewalt; Souverainetät*), the executive and

[1] Especially Rousseau. See Paulsen, *Immanuel Kant*, translation, p. 39.

[2] Metaphysische Anfangsgründe der Rechtslehre. This constitutes Part I of the *Metaphysische Anfangsgründe der Sittenlehre*, of which Part II is Tugendlehre. The Rechtslehre, preceded by Kant's general *Einleitung* to the *Sittenlehre*, has been translated by W. Hastie with the title *The Philosophy of Law* (Edinburgh, 1887).

[3] *Zum ewigem Frieden.*

[4] A very systematic presentation of Kantian political theory in condensed form may be found in Levkovits, *Die Staatslehre auf Kantischer Grundlage* (*Berner Studien zur Philosophie*, Band XIV).

the judicial; the separation of the first two in exercise is indispensable to liberty. The forms of state are three in number — autocracy, aristocracy and democracy; the forms of government are two, republican and despotic, according as there is or is not a separation of the legislative and the executive powers. Any form of government (*Regierungsform*) that is not representative Kant declares to be out of rational consideration (*ist eine Unform*); but the function of representative may be vested in king or nobility as well as in elected deputies.

This body of doctrine is obviously an attempted blend of Rousseau and Montesquieu. If such a blend were logically possible, the subtle intellect of Kant might be expected to succeed in making it. But the difficulties are too great. Upon the dogma of sovereignty, absolute and indefeasible, in the general will of the community, not even Kant's compelling logic can base three forms of state. There is no room — and Rousseau makes this clear[1] — for any such concept as autocracy (monarchy) or aristocracy, when the general will is sovereign. Kant sought to evade Rousseau's conclusion by resort to the dual aspect of philosophy. The sovereign conceived as the general will was, he said, a concept of pure reason — an abstraction, a "*Gedankending.*" To give it objective, practical reality, it must be expressed in physical form, as one, or few or many persons.[2] Such an explanation, however, failed to sustain his case, in view of his repeated attribution of sovereignty to the people ex-

[1] *Supra*, pp. 22 *et seq.* [2] *Rechtslehre*, sec. 51.

clusively, whatever the form of the chief of the state (*Staatsoberhaupt*).[1]

Kant's inconsistency here is due not only to his respect for Montesquieu but also, probably, to the fact that he was an aged professor in a royal university of the kingdom of Prussia. It was hard in the days of Frederick the Great and his successors (as indeed it remained to the end of the monarchy) for a loyal subject of the Hohenzollerns to think of a king as merely a chief executive. Few philosophers were able to free themselves from the idea that something, at least, of sovereignty inhered in the monarch, no matter how peremptorily they preached the absolute supremacy of the people or the nation or the state.

Kant's weakness at this point leads him into rather pitiable confusion in several places. He asserts most explicitly that the legislative power pertains solely to the people, yet finds room for a ruler of the people (*Beherrscher des Volks*) who is legislator, not administrator, who has toward the people rights but no duties, and whose transgressions of the constitution are above any effective control.[2] Against this legislative chief of the state (*das gesetzgebende Oberhaupt des Staats*) there is no right of resistance; and Kant argues passionately against popular revolution. If a constitution is defective, changes must be made "only by the sovereign itself, through reform, not by the

[1] *Rechtslehre*, sec. 52.

[2] In the *Rechtslehre* compare sec. 46 with sec. 49A. Hastie's English version contains abundant evidence of hard labor by the translator in the effort to make the passages consistent. At some points rather daring liberties are taken with the original.

people, through revolution."[1] The people (*Volk*) ought not even to inquire too closely about the origin of the supreme power (*oberste Gewalt*), no matter how it came into being.

The inconsistency and incoherence of such doctrine, which so severely test the patience of reader and translator, sprang partly from the conservatism of age, and partly from the philosopher's natural antipathy toward turbulence and disorder. Kant's greatest influence was not due, however, to these features of his system, but rather to the exalted idealism of the psychology and ethics on which his politics immediately depended. His dogmas of the categorical imperative, the autonomous will and humanity as an end in itself, sustained a closely articulated system of principles that embodied the absolute truth at the basis of morals, law and politics.[2] A conclusion of the pure reason had for Kant the same unconditional validity that the "idea" had for Plato. The element of will, however, entered very largely into the German's conception and distinguished it from the Greek's. Man appeared, abstractly considered, as rational will, free and self-sufficing. Morality, law and politics were but various aspects of the logical process through which the coexistence of two or more free rational wills could be conceived. Thus a supreme maxim of Kant's practical morality was: "So act that thy will can regard itself as dictating universal laws";

[1] ". . . nur vom Souverän selbst durch Reform, aber nicht vom Volk, mithin durch Revolution." *Rechtslehre*, sec. 49A, end.

[2] Janet's analysis and criticism of Kant's ethics is admirable. *Hist. de la Science Politique*, II, 574 *et seq.*

that is, do only that which is consistent with the same action by every other. And law in general (*Recht*) he said, consisted in "the possibility of harmonizing a general and reciprocal constraint with the liberty of each." The state, therefore, as pure idea, is conceivable only through a formula in which the authority of the general will is consistent with the perfect freedom of the individual will. The formula is the social contract. Only through this is the jural state (*Rechtsstaat*) thinkable.

Kant thus came out where Rousseau did, but his route thither was far longer and not less thorny. Throughout his wanderings in the desert of metaphysical subtleties the pillar of cloud and fire that unfailingly guided him was the supreme worth and dignity of a rational being. Liberty and equality, as the necessary attributes of such beings, gleam brightly through the murkiest depths of his *Staatslehre*. And while he assigned proper weight and significance to society and state and people, as collective entities, it was the reason-endowed individual with the autonomous will that was salient in his philosophy. The whole trend of Kant's influence, in political speculation at least, was individualistic; and one of the entertaining episodes in a field that hardly abounds in amusement was the astonishment of the arch-individualist of the nineteenth century, Herbert Spencer, on discovering that one of his most laboriously worked-out dogmas had been anticipated by the (to him) unknown German philosopher.[1]

[1] Spencer, *Justice* (1891), Appendix A.

2. *Johann Gottlieb Fichte*

Fichte, the brilliant but short-lived (1762–1814) successor to Kant in philosophical preëminence in Germany, presented the same idealizing method as his master. The world of thought and the world of sense were distinct realms, and the former was in last analysis reality. Fichte's dialectic subtlety was, if possible, more refined than Kant's, and his criticism and modification of the latter's metaphysics made a sensation in the learned circles of Germany.[1] In social and political speculation Fichte's ideas were very greatly influenced by the events of external history. He was far less a closet philosopher than Kant, and his pen was very active in connection with the practical questions of the day. Because of the suspicion engendered by his views on religion and politics he was forced to leave his position at the University of Jena, in Saxony. Received into Prussian educational circles, he shared with his new people the disasters of the Napoleonic conquest, becoming eventually professor in the newly established University of Berlin. In the deep movement of national feeling that led to the overthrow of the French Fichte's influence was important;[2] his untimely death came with the triumph of the cause he had promoted.

The experiences of his personal career are readily traceable in their influence on his political theories. His earlier writings include a justification of the French

[1] Adamson, *Fichte, passim.*

[2] *Infra*, p. 145.

Revolution,[1] in popular style, and a systematic treatise on political science,[2] containing his whole theory of state and government. In these works his doctrines are substantially those of Rousseau, with less deviation than Kant made. Fichte's later works, however, show a notable shifting of interest. While the individual and his rights had been at first the central point of the theory, the people (*Volk*) and the nation now take that position. In Fichte's *Closed Commercial State* [3] and in his last lectures on the *Theory of the State* [4] there is set forth an elaborate theory of state-socialism and of a national state.[5]

Fichte's political science starts with the rational self-consciousness of the individual. He demonstrates that consciousness of self necessarily implies consciousness of other like beings and of a relation between the self and the others. This relation is the basis of *Recht*—a word that must be translated in this place rather "social regulation" than "law." It consists in the recognition by a free rational being that its freedom is limited by the idea (*Begriff*) of the freedom of others. This idea of social regulation (*Rechtsbegriff*) is not to be thought of, Fichte holds, as a product of experience or education; it is inherent in the consciousness of every rational being.[6]

[1] *Beiträge zur Berichtigung der Urteile des Publikums über die französische Revolution* (1793), in *Werke*, Band VI.

[2] *Grundlage des Naturrechts* (1796), in *Werke*, Band III.

[3] *Der geschlossene Handelsstaat* (1800), in *Werke*, Band III.

[4] *Die Staatslehre* (1813), in *Werke*, Band IV.

[5] For a clear and interesting account of the currents in Fichte's philosophy as disclosed in these works see Bluntschli, *Geschichte*, 414 *et seq.*

[6] "Deduction des Begriffes vom Rechte" is the subject of the Erstes Hauptstück of his *Grundlage des Naturrechts*.

Having deduced the relation of beings considered as merely intelligences, he proves with like formalism that material bodies are inevitable appurtenances of such beings, making them persons, and complicating the problem of their reciprocal freedom. This problem, reached after the philosopher's wide rambles in metaphysics, is the familiar one with which Rousseau opens his *Contrat Social*,[1] though the striking metaphor of the Genevese is not suggested in the cold phrase of the German: "How is a community of free beings as such possible?" The answer is Rousseau's: through a social contract, effecting a union of wills and maintaining the autonomy of each.

Fichte departs from the usual doctrine, however, in respect to natural rights and the state of nature. There is no presocial state of nature, he holds, in which men possess natural rights. "The state (*Staat*) itself is men's natural condition (*Naturstand*)." There is indeed no such thing as natural rights (*Urrechte*), in the plural. Only natural right (*Urrecht*), in the singular, is a rational concept; and this he defines as "the absolute right of the person to be in the world of sense only cause and never effect" — a conception which is identical, he explains, with that of an absolute will.[2]

Fichte's doctrine thus is, that personality necessarily implies the untrammelled activity of the rational will. Restriction of that activity is conceivable only as self-restriction. This is the dictum of pure thought.

[1] *Supra*, p. 16.

[2] ". . . das absolute Recht der Person, in der Sinnenwelt *nur Ursache* zu sein (schlechthin nie Bewirktes)." *Werke*, III, 113–119.

The realization of this idea in the world of sense requires a formula of action through which, as he expresses it, a will is produced "in which private will and general will are synthetically united." The terms of this synthesizing process are those of Rousseau's contract. But Fichte carries his analysis of the contract to a refinement that would have made Rousseau stare and gasp. Three distinct agreements are shown to be involved in the social pact. By a very bold and striking generalization Fichte includes the whole sphere of individual freedom under the concept "property," which he defines as "rights of free action in the world of sense."[1] The precise boundary to the property of each is fixed by a first contract of each with all. Each abandons his claim to what lies outside of a certain sphere, on condition that all abandon their claims to what lies within that sphere. This property contract (*Eigenthumsvertrag*) is followed by the protection contract (*Schutzvertrag*), by which each agrees to contribute his share of the force necessary to maintain the partitions established by the former agreement. Then comes a third pact by which each agrees with each to unite into a whole for the effective accomplishment of the ends involved in the prior contracts. This union contract (*Vereinigungsvertrag*) completes the social pact (*Staatsbürgervertrag*) and constitutes a sovereign. Fichte takes great pains to avoid the idea that the individual is merged entirely in the sovereign state.

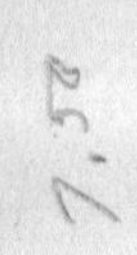

[1] "Rechte auf freie Handlungen in der Sinnenwelt." *Werke*, III, 195. For Locke's similar idea see *Political Theories from Luther to Montesquieu*, p. 346, note.

Rousseau's dictum that each gives up himself and all his possessions, is vigorously repudiated.[1] Protection of the rights that make up the individual is to Fichte the function of the state, and beyond what is given up as indispensable to the realization of this function the sphere of individuality remains intact.

To determine with some precision what, on grounds of pure reason, is included in the scope of the state's function, especially in the matter of trade (*Handel*), is the purpose of Fichte's *Closed Commercial State*. He rejects emphatically the idea that the end of the state is "to make men happy, rich, healthy, orthodox, virtuous and, God willing, saved eternally." On the other hand he likewise denies what he had earlier asserted, or appeared to assert, that it is the function of the state "merely to preserve and protect each in his personal rights and his property." His contention now is that individual property has no existence save through the state, and that the true formula for the function of the state is this: "To *give* to each for the first time his own, to *install* him for the first time in his property, and then first to *protect* him in it." [2]

What is meant by giving to each his own is elucidated in a curious theory of economic organization. In any society, Fichte declares, the division of productive activities among various classes — farmers, artisans, merchants — rests upon contract of each class with every other class, and within each class, of each

[1] *Werke*, III, 205.

[2] The *Geschlossene Handelsstaat* is in Werke, Bd. III, pp. 389–513. For the passages above see Buch i, Cap. i.

individual with his fellows. The substance of these various contracts is that the parties refrain from encroaching on one another's special field. As a result, the sphere of free activities is divided mong all the individuals, and the share that comes to each is his property, in the scientific sense of the term. These individual properties must for any particular occupation be precisely equal in value, as Fichte proves by elementary mathematics. The total value of any occupation is, he says, the sum of satisfactions (*Annehmlichkeit des Lebens*) resulting from it. Divide this sum by the number of individuals in that field, and the quotient is what belongs to each. The shares may be larger or smaller according to circumstances, but it is inconceivable that they ever under given circumstances differ from one another.[1]

By this reasoning Fichte establishes the meaning of his dogma that the state must give to each his own. It must secure to every individual that share of satisfactions which is his according to the principles above laid down. In the *Closed Commercial State* the philosopher deduces the industrial and commercial system through which alone, in the view of pure reason, this purpose can be fulfilled. The state must adjust in proper proportions the three chief classes of producers — (1) farmers, miners and the like, (2) artisans and (3) merchants, limiting each to a fixed number of individuals; must insure to each individual a proportionate share of all the raw and manufactured products of the country; must for this purpose fix

[1] *Handelsstaat*, I, i, 2.

and maintain the relative value and money price of all these commodities; and finally, as absolutely indispensable to the foregoing ends, must render impossible direct trade between citizens and the foreign world.[1] So far as commerce with other peoples may be deemed desirable, it must be carried on by the state itself.

These are astonishing conclusions to be derived from the strongly individualistic premises of Fichte's philosophy. He was turned in this unexpected direction not only by the idealizing spirit that produced a like doctrine in Plato, but also by a consciousness of the economic influences that underlay the developing idea of a national state. Indeed, though he did not cease to insist that his Closed Commercial State was a concept of the pure reason (*Vernunftstaat*), he set forth very clearly the concrete conditions, historical and contemporaneous, that bore upon its objective realization. To be economically exclusive and self-sufficing, he argued, was of precisely the same significance politically as to be exclusive and independent in legislation and judicature. Christian Europe was originally a political unit with a common government, a common law, and appropriately enough, general freedom of commerce. The modern states have arisen through the creation of separate governments and distinct systems of law; but the corresponding differentiation of commercial relations has not been reached. The idea that men shall freely trade with one another, regardless of their political allegiance, is

[1] *Werke*, III, 440.

a relic of an outgrown past.[1] What is suitable to the present, Fichte argues, is an economic solidarity and exclusiveness among fellow-citizens no less perfect than the governmental exclusiveness already attained.

The geographic basis of such a state, Fichte found indicated by nature herself. "Certain parts of the earth's surface, with their inhabitants, are evidently determined by nature to form political units." [2] Set off by seas, rivers or impassable mountains, and embracing diversities of soil adapted to produce all desirable varieties of goods, such a region should be the situs of a self-sufficing community. This, Fichte declared, was the point of view from which to perceive the true meaning of the term "natural boundaries," so common in modern politics. It means not, as commonly used, the line best adapted to military ends, but rather the line that marks the bounds of economic independence and self-sufficiency. Such boundaries a state must have — no more, no less. Shut up within them and rigidly excluding the poison of unregulated intercourse with citizens of other communities,[3] a people will realize the ends of a rational state (*Vernunftstaat*). Wars will cease. It has long been the privilege of philosophers, says Fichte, to sigh over war.

[1] "Alle Einrichtungen welche den unmittelbaren Verkehr eines Bürgers mit dem Bürger eines anderen Staates erlauben oder voraussetzen, betrachten im Grunde beide als Bürger eines Staats, und sind Ueberbleibsel und Resultate einer Verfassung die längst aufgehoben ist, sind in unsere Welt nicht passende Theile einer vergangenen Welt." — *Werke*, III, 453–4.

[2] *Handelsstaat*, Buch III, Cap. iii.

[3] Foreign travel must be prohibited except to highly qualified persons (*der Gelehrte und der höhere Künstler*), duly authorized by the government. — *Handelsstaat*, Buch iii, Cap. vii.

End world-commerce, with the ambitions and rivalries engendered by it in the nations, and the most prolific source of war will disappear.[1] Freed from the tale of distractions and woes from this source, the closed commercial state will give full scope to the capacity that it has for comfort and culture, and will surely guarantee to every individual citizen that which in the profoundest sense is his own.

In his later years Fichte carried his socialistic doctrines equally far in another direction. He still insisted on the duty of the state to guarantee the citizen's material existence, and he declared categorically that the government must insure to each the opportunity to work for a living, while insuring at the same time that each do his share of the work provided: there must be neither pauper nor idler in the rational state.[2] But a different aspect of life from the physical engaged the philosopher's interest. After Prussia was crushed and dismembered by Napoleon in 1806–1807 Fichte joined eagerly in the search for the explanation of so astounding a calamity. He found it in the lack of a clear political consciousness in the conquered. His famous "Addresses to the German People,"[3] set forth an exalted conception of the character and mission of the Germans, with eloquent appeals for political and educational institutions suited to the realization of this mission. Under the influence of his interest in Prussia's revival his scientific conception

[1] *Handelsstaat*, Buch iii, Cap. iii.

[2] *Cf. Werke*, III, 214.

[3] *Reden an die deutsche Nation*, in *Werke*, Bd. VII. See *infra*, chap. viii.

of the state was transformed to correspond. Not the mere man, but the trained man — the man of complete moral and intellectual culture — must be, Fichte now held, the center of political theory, and the development and protection of such individuals must be the real function of the state. Fichte's elaboration of this idea, with the conception of the government as primarily an educational institution, runs parallel in many places with the lines of Plato's Republic. From such places the individualism of Fichte's early philosophy seems remote indeed.

In respect to government and constitution, as distinct from state (*Staatsrecht* as distinct from *Staatslehre*), Fichte's doctrines were more consistent and coherent than Kant's. Legislation (*Gesetzgebung*) was to Fichte as to Rousseau a term denoting exclusively the will of the sovereign people. The executive function included the judicial, and must necessarily be exercised by representatives, constituting the government (*Regierung*). The government might be either monarchic or aristocratic, hereditary or elective; it could never be democratic, that is, the people as a whole could not act as administration. To insure that the sovereign will of the people, as embodied in the laws (*Gesetze*) forming the constitution, should not be overridden by the government, Fichte conceived an institution named the ephorate that he regarded as indispensable to a rational constitution (*vernunft- und rechtmässige Staatsverfassung*).[1] The right of final judgment upon the conduct of the government must

[1] *Werke*, III, 160, 171.

inhere necessarily in the people as a whole. To assign to any organ of the government the function of deciding whether the laws were being properly administered, would be to make that organ supreme; to assign to any organ even the function of deciding when the people should be called upon to express their opinion upon the situation, would have the same tendency to exalt the government over the sovereign. Hence the need for a body of ephors, wholly distinct from the government, and having no other duty than that of setting in motion, at the time they judged proper, the machinery through which the will of the sovereign people as to the constitution and laws can be expressed.

Such was Fichte's contribution to the solution of the much debated problem, how to keep the government in accord with the constitution without permitting any branch of the government to shape the constitution at its will. That his ephors would not solve the problem is suggested by what we know of Sparta, whence the very name was derived. The Spartan ephors became practically the supreme power in the state.[1] Fichte himself in his later years lost confidence in his ephorate as a practical means of preserving the constitution, and found nothing to suggest in its place but the purely ideal conception that the functions of government should be entrusted only to all-wise philosophers, whose pure and unerring intelligence would never deviate from the straight line.

[1] *Political Theories, Ancient and Medieval*, p. 10. Ephors had figured in the theory of Althusius, but with a function only slightly resembling that assigned to them by Fichte. *Pol. The. from Luther to Montesquieu*, p. 64.

One source of Fichte's difficulties at this point was the same that made trouble for Kant — the independent position of the hereditary monarch. Where such an institution existed, if part in the constituent function were permitted to the government, the supreme law would tend to be at the mercy of the prince. How real the logical need was for such an organ as Fichte's ephors were intended to be, may be estimated by reflection upon the constitution-making influence actually exerted by two famous governmental bodies much less powerful *a priori* than a princely executive — the British Parliament and the Supreme Court of the United States.

3. *Wilhelm von Humboldt*

Before Fichte worked out his system of extensive state activity, a noteworthy theory in the diametrically opposite sense was formulated by the elder of the famous Humboldt brothers. His *Ideas for an Attempt to determine the Limits of the Activity of the State* [1] was written and parts of it were published in 1792, when the author was but twenty-five years old. In his later career, as a power in the Prussian government, he lost confidence and interest in the product of his irresponsible youthful enthusiasm, and the complete essay did not see the light till 1851, long after his death.[2] Though thus repudiated in a way by its author, the little book has a real significance in the

[1] *Ideen zu einem Versuch die Gränzen der Wirksamkeit des Staats zu bestimmen.*

[2] See Cauer's *Einleitung* to the *Ideen* (Breslau, 1851).

history of political theory. It embodies a very full and systematic expression of ideas that were closely involved in the philosophy of the time when the essay was written, and that were on the verge of widespread acceptance when it was finally published.[1]

Humboldt assumes without discussion the Kantian view as to the origin of the state in a contract between men for their respective benefit. What he emphasizes and reiterates is, that the political union thus created is merely a means — one among many — for the promotion and realization of human welfare. The state is not an end in itself. It must subserve the end of man; and the end of man is, the highest and best-proportioned development of his powers to a whole.[2] What, then, can the state contribute to this development? Shall it take the individual in hand and guide him along carefully prescribed paths to his goal? Or shall it leave him to find his own path and make his own way? This latter, Humboldt answers, is the true principle; and his essay aims to establish it on the firmest rational grounds.

The full development of humanity depends, so his argument runs, on the fullest possible development of the individual man. This in turn depends upon the unrestricted play of the powers and faculties peculiar to each (*Eigenthümlichkeiten*). Liberty, in this sense, is the condition of progress. No obstacle due to the forces of physical nature will fail to yield in time to

[1] It is an interesting coincidence that Herbert Spencer's earliest exposition of *laissez-faire*, the *Social Statics*, appeared in 1850.

[2] *Ideen*, p. 9.

the art and energy of men acting freely either singly or in voluntary coöperation. Only those obstacles to progress that arise out of the domineering propensities of men require for their removal a power that can and will constrain the action of the individual. Such a power is the state. It is necessary, inasmuch as the collisions of individuals seeking unlimited self-expression would be fatal to the ends of all of them. At the same time it is an evil, because it interferes with that freedom which is the condition of full development in each. The problem then is, to determine how this necessary evil, the state, is to be made most contributory, or more exactly, least detrimental to human advancement.

Humboldt's solution is that the action of the state shall never extend to the positive promotion of the welfare of its citizens, but shall be confined to a negative role, namely, that of providing for their security (*Sicherheit*). His demonstration of this doctrine, both in the abstract and the concrete aspects, covers substantially all that has ever been urged in support of it. Against intervention by the state for the positive promotion of individual welfare, he urges that it tends to produce a depressing uniformity among the citizens, to weaken their powers, to obstruct the proper reaction of the material environment upon their spirit and character, to divert their energy from self-development and waste it on the prescription of rules for others, and in other ways to hinder that exercise of idiosyncrasy which is the key to progress. On one or another of these grounds Humboldt insists that the state must refrain from concern in education, in religion, in the improvement of morals (*Sittenverbesserung*) — in short from all activity designed to influence the character of the people (*Nation*). Effects upon the popular spirit will flow indirectly from the legitimate operation of government; these should be all.

The legitimate sphere of the state is solely the care for the security of the citizens. By security he means "certainty of lawful liberty" (*Gesetzmässige Freiheit*), that is, certainty that the use of one's powers and the enjoyment of one's property will not be wrongfully (*Widerrechtlich*) obstructed.[1] The criterion of state intervention must be necessity, not expediency. Danger to security may come from without or from within a society, and the field of state action is accordingly twofold. War in defence of the community is one of its appropriate activities; and war, with all its objectionable incidents, Humboldt regards as a very salutary influence in the development of human character.[2] On the side of internal security the functions of the state are limited to those that fall into the four categories, police law (*Polizeigesetze*), private law (*Civilgesetze*), the regulation of judicial procedure (*Prozessordnung*), and criminal law (*Kriminalgesetze*), together with the guardianship of helpless minors and the insane. The rule throughout all these classes

[1] *Ideen*, p. 103.

[2] ". . . ist mir der Krieg eine der heilsamsten Erscheinungen zur Bildung des Menschengeschlechts und ungern seh' ich ihn nach und nach immer mehr vom Schauplatz zurücktreten." *Ideen*, p. 48. But the state must not actively either encourage war or hinder it. — P. 52.

must be that the scope of governmental intervention is determined solely by what is necessary for the protection of individuals in person and property.

This conception of the state Humboldt presents frankly as an ideal — a product of pure reason, not known to experience and not likely to be realized.[1] It is an ideal of liberty; and men in general tend to feel more interest in dominion (*Herrschaft*). The strong man builds up a far-reaching government out of the sheer exuberance of his powers; the weak man is proud to be part of the mighty machine.[2] Until a society is ripe for liberty — until men show that their fetters chafe them, it is futile to press a free constitution upon them. A taste for liberty may be stimulated by the gradual extension of opportunities to enjoy it; but the abrupt transformation of institutions does not appeal to Humboldt. Reform, not revolution, is his way of introducing higher ideas; and reform is to be not compulsory, but voluntary — is to express primarily the feelings and ideas of the people, not the will of the government. The essay is pervaded with the author's conviction that political authority not only ought to be, but in fact actually has been, of minor importance in the development of mankind. The constitution of the state, he declares, is subsidiary to the social union (*Nationalverein*),[3] from whose manifold activities spring the greatest advantages of life. In the unobtrusive working of

[1] *Ideen*, pp. 175–177. [2] *Ibid.*, p. 182.

[3] "Die Staatsverfassung und der Nationalverein sollten . . . nie mit einander verwechselt werden." *Ideen*, p. 176.

social forces the spirit and power of a people are expressed, and history shows that all great political revolutions spring from antecedent changes in this spirit and this power.[1] Experience teaches the same lesson as pure reason, that the progress of mankind is not dependent upon far-reaching governmental activity.

Humboldt's theory, taken as a whole, is a synthesis of many elements that preceding thinkers had wrought out separately. On grounds of theory similar to his Milton had excluded government from interference with the citizen's expression of opinion, Locke had excluded it from interference with the citizen's material property, Voltaire and a host of others had excluded it from interference with his religious worship, the Physiocrats and economists had excluded it from interference with his industrial and commercial life. All these were combined in Humboldt's theory, and were based logically upon the dogma of the dignity and worth of man as man — a dogma that had played a part in most of the early individualistic philosophy.

It is to be noticed, however, that Humboldt, like his predecessors, while preaching individualism, did not preach democracy. He thought of government as something outside of the socially organized people, not conceivably part and parcel of it. Even while formally accepting the dogma of the social contract, he shows no consciousness that the dogma entails the possibility that state activity may mean self-activity, and restriction upon government may be

[1] *Ideen*, pp. 178–9.

self-imposed restrictions upon the individual. Humboldt's individualism was in part that of the intellectual aristocrat, resenting, like Milton, Voltaire and *les philosophes,* the authority of lesser men who happened to possess political power, and in part that of the Prussian subject, unconsciously determined in his philosophy, like Kant and Fichte, by the actualities of the régime of the Hohenzollerns.[1]

4. *Georg Wilhelm Friedrich Hegel*

The climax of the German idealism in political philosophy was reached in the speculation of Hegel. The extraordinary genius of this thinker produced a system that surpassed in breadth and profundity those of even Kant and Fichte. Like those two predecessors, Hegel developed his political principles as part of a comprehensive system of philosophy. There was that in his system, however, which gave it a strongly marked individuality and caused it to wield an influence in political science that long outlasted others. The great distinguishing mark of the Hegelian system was the evolutionary and historical spirit that pervaded it. This element made it more acceptable to the nineteenth century, during which the confidence of the preceding century in fixedness and rigidity passed steadily away. The philosophy of history, in which

[1] Humboldt was made Prussian Minister of Culture and Education in 1809, and in this capacity conducted governmental activities that his theories condemned as deleterious. It is one of the oddities of history that the philosopher who so skilfully exposed the evils of state interference in education (*Ideen*, pp. 56–60) should have been chiefly instrumental in the founding of that remarkable monument of state interference, the University of Berlin.

Hegel developed with great fulness his evolutionary doctrine, was but an appendix, however, to a vast body of abstract speculation that was often repulsive in form and obscure in substance.[1]

Hegel's political theory proper was systematically set forth in his *Outlines of the Philosophy of Right.*[2] His announced purpose in this work was, like that of Kant and Fichte, to exhibit the state as thinkable — to develop the purely intellectual modes and processes through which the idea of the state must take shape. His problem was avowedly that of Plato. For his starting point he took the will, as his German predecessors, following Rousseau, had done. But the will, as Hegel conceived it, was not an attribute or faculty of an individual person. That will in this sense had been the basis of earlier systems, was in his opinion their fatal weakness. In this Rousseau, Kant and Fichte all had gone astray. For valid philosophy, Hegel held, will must be conceived as one aspect of pure abstract intelligence — or in the term that almost defies rendering into English — of *Geist.* Thus conceived, will is eternal, universal, self-con-

[1] Doubtless these qualities are inevitable in a literature that deals with the uttermost concepts of pure thought; the Hegelian exposition at any rate betrays no attempt to make concessions to the average intelligence, and bristles throughout with a serried array of *heits* and *keits* and *täts* that too often effectively bar access to the thought that lies behind them. Thus, for example, begins his explanation of the relation between family and civil society: "Die Allgemeinheit hat hier zum Ausgangspunkt die Selbstständigkeit der Besonderheit, und die Sittlichkeit scheint somit auf diesem Standpunkt verloren, denn für das Bewusstsein ist eigentlich die Identität der Familie das Erste, Göttliche und Pflichtgebietende."

[2] *Grundlinien der Philosophie des Rechts, oder Naturrecht und Staatswissenschaft im Grundrisse.* In *Werke*, Band VIII.

scious, self-determining. Freedom, therefore, is of the essence of will. As Hegel lucidly phrased it: The idea of the will, as a last abstraction, is the free will that wills the free will.[1]

Having posited free will thus as the absolute, Hegel develops his philosophy by presenting various stages of the process in which this absolute idea is realized. "Realization," however, does not mean to Hegel primarily presence to the senses or to experience. The reiterated postulate of his system is: What is rational is real; what is real is rational.[2] Hence the idea of the free will is realized when it is manifested in some form of thought that is produced by right reason. Thus the "realization of freedom" is but the completion of an exercise in formal logic. Such at all events is the theoretical character of Hegel's *Rechtsphilosophie*. Starting from the conception of will as active, the philosopher deduces, by the methods and formulas of his peculiar logic, a series of concepts in which he discovers a progressive approximation to that of perfect freedom. These concepts form the chapter and section heads of his system. Let us take them in his order.[3]

First comes law (*Recht*). This is the field in which the ideas of personality, property and contract are developed. All these are shown to be manifestations of the free will. A living creature is a person only

[1] *Philosophie des Rechts*, Einleitung, sec. 27.

[2] "Was vernunftig ist, das ist wirklich; und was wirklich ist, das ist vernunftig." — *Werke*, VIII, Vorrede, p. 17. *Cf.* sec. 141, Zusatz: "Nur das Unendliche, die Idee, ist Wirklich."

[3] *Philosophie des Rechts*, sec. 33.

so far as it freely wills to be so. An object is property because it is determined by the free will of a person. A human being or a people is property — slave — only because of lacking the free will to be free.[1] In this doctrine as to slavery, as wherever else Hegel's practical views come into sight through the haze of his technical vocabulary and method, law and rights are judged not by a fixed standard, but with reference to the various stages of culture and self-consciousness that history reveals.

The second phase in the realization of the free will is subjective morality (*Moralität*). Here belong those aspects of self-determination in which the individual is affected by a consciousness of other like individuals. The conceptions of purpose (*Vorsatz*), responsibility, motive, conscience are formulated and come to the front; but the full relation of the individual to the universal will is not displayed here. That is revealed in still another and final field, that of conventional or customary morality (*Sittlichkeit*), or in other words, social ethics.[2] The customs or habits (*die Sitten*) of mankind express the working of a universal cause. At the same time they bear the impress of individual choice. These considerations underlie Hegel's rather rapturous proclamations that the socially ethical (*das Sittlich*) satisfies the idea of realized free will.

[1] *Philosophie des Rechts*, sec. 57.

[2] Hegel's distinction between *Moralität* and *Sittlichkeit* can hardly be indicated by any concise expressions in English. Bosanquet, whose skill in formulating what Hegel may have or ought to have meant is so vastly superior to Hegel's own ability to make clear what he really did mean, translates *Sittlichkeit* by "Social Ethics." *Philosophical Theory of the State*, p. 264 *et seq.*

As he expresses it in his own technical terms, "what law (*Recht*) and abstract morality (*Moralität*) are *not*, custom (*Sitte*) *is*, namely, spirit (*Geist*)"; and spirit is "unity of the individual and the universal."[1] Hence, since the reduction of all concepts to terms of spirit is the end of philosophy, according to Hegel, his goal is reached in social ethics.

It is in the detailed exposition of this subject that the theory of the state is to be found. The institutions in which the socially-ethical is revealed are, according to Hegel, three, the family, civil society, and the state. His doctrine as to the family, when stripped of its Hegelian husks, is the conventional doctrine of his day. Civil society,[2] however, appears in a new light. It is made to include those relations of individual to individual that turn upon the satisfaction of economic needs, the protection of property through the administration of justice (*Rechtspflege*) and the care of the general welfare through agencies of police and corporation (*Polizei und Korporation*). Admitting that this classification attributes to civil society much that has commonly been attributed to the state, Hegel stoutly defends his own idea. What appears to be the real basis of his procedure is the zeal for artistic symmetry in the structure of his system. The adjustment of these introductory concepts is cleverly made

[1] *Phil. des Rechts*, secs. 151, 156.

[2] Hegel's term is *bürgerliche Gesellschaft*, and this Bosanquet renders "bourgeois society." To me this rendering seems misleading, because it suggests a connection that does not exist between Hegel's doctrine and certain phases of nineteenth-century revolutionary politics.

to furnish a neat and attractive setting for the capstone — the idea of the state (*der Staat*).[1]

This final goal of his system evokes the utmost exuberance of Hegel's peculiar diction. The state, he explains, is the reality of the socio-ethical idea — the socio-ethical spirit as the revealed, self-perceived, substantial will that thinks and knows itself and fulfils what it knows so far as it knows it. The state, further, is "perfected rationality," "absolute, fixed end-in-itself"; for it is the unity of the universal will and the individual will—or what is the same thing—of objective and subjective freedom; and the unity of universality and particularity is perfected rationality (*das an und für sich Vernunftige*). As such the state is of the eternal and necessary essence of spirit (*Sein des Geistes*).[2]

This exposition hardly requires the warning given by Hegel, that he is dealing with the state not as a historical phenomenon, but as an intellectual concept (*gedachter Begriff*). His phrases should have in fact no meaning to one not an adept in the Hegelian logic. But the philosopher was an artist in abstractions, and contrived to involve his dialectic in an atmosphere of mystical exaltation that suggested the proximity of undiscovered truth. Many an ardent soul was

[1] Thus, after a rather perfunctory and arid treatment of the corporation, he continues: "Der Zweck der Korporation als beschränkter und endlicher hat seine Wahrheit . . . in dem an und für sich allgemeinen Zwecke und dessen absoluter Wirklichkeit: die Sphäre der bürgerlichen Gesellschaft geht daher in den Staat über." — *Phil. des Rechts*, sec. 256. Thus the corporation fulfils the useful function of furnishing the philosopher with a smooth transition.

[2] For these and many more bits of Hegelian eloquence, see *Philosophie des Rechts*, 257, 258.

satisfied to repeat the rhapsodical Hegelian dicta about the state in the conviction that they solved anew and finally the ultimate problems of politics. The ineffable majesty predicated by the master of the state as idea, was inevitably transferred by the followers to the state as a concrete fact. In the heyday of Hegel's popularity at Berlin (1818–1831) there was no lack of philosophasters to whom the Prussian monarchy was "perfected rationality," or who saw the "eternal and necessary essence of spirit" in the stodgy Hohenzollern then on the throne.

The idea of the state manifests itself, according to Hegel, in three ways, namely, as constitution or internal public law (*Verfassung oder inneres Staatsrecht*) as external public law, and as world history. In each of these three channels he traces the progressive unfolding of freedom — the synthesis of universal and individual will. Without following the devious path by which the philosopher reaches his conclusions, we will notice some of the more concrete ideas on which he expresses himself coherently.

The fundamental fact in a particular state is the political consciousness (*Gesinnung*) of a people (*Volk*). This consciousness determines the constitution. To think of a constitution as a created thing (*ein Gemachtes*) — as having an absolute beginning, is all wrong: there may be changes made from time to time, but the constitution in some form is a fixed fact, inseparable from the idea of a state.[1] Only a crowd of individuals

[1] Hegel's expression is rather strong: "Die Verfassung ist das schlechthin an und für sich Seyende, das darum als das Göttliche

can be thought of if a constitution is not presumed; and an atomistic crowd is no concept of political science. Who should "make" the constitution, is therefore a senseless question. Not less futile is debate as to what form of constitution and government is best. A people inevitably has the constitution that expresses its spirit and culture at the given time. No other could be better for that people at that time. Another system in another community, or in the same community at another time, may more fully realize liberty; but this is true not because the system is better *per se*, but because a higher stage of culture has been reached by the people.

In what, now, according to Hegel, is the constitution manifest? In the differentiation and action of the various powers. "The state," he says, "is organism, that is, development of the idea to its distinctions."[1] The organism is the constitution, consisting of distinct powers so correlated as to sustain and strengthen the unity of the whole. Hegel's logic, like Montesquieu's, discovers three of these powers, but the German's three are not the Frenchman's. The three powers indispensable to the idea of state are, in Hegel's analysis, the legislative, the administrative (*Regierungsgewalt*), under which falls the judicial, and the monarchic (*fürstliche Gewalt*). Of these, the first two do not differ substantially from the legislative and executive of earlier philosophers. The monarchic

und beharrende, und als über der Sphäre dessen, was gemacht wird, zu betrachten ist." — *Phil. des Rechts*, sec. 273.

[1] "Der Staat ist Organismus, das heisst, Entwickelung der Idee zu ihren Unterschieden." — *Ibid.*, sec. 269, Zusatz.

power, however, is endowed by Hegel with the highest importance. It is the unifying force through which the other two powers are restrained from disrupting the state. It is the element through which the idea of a constitution is fully realized. The differentiation of legislative and executive expresses the principle of diversity that is essential to the idea constitution; the monarchic power contributes the principle of unity that makes the idea complete. Constitutional monarchy, thus conceived, fulfils for Hegel all the conditions of perfect rationality, and the development of the state into this form, he declares, is the typical achievement of the modern world.[1] In this form are comprehended and blended the three forms, monarchy, aristocracy and democracy, that satisfied the analysis of earlier and more primitive ages; for the prince represents the one, the administration the few, and the legislature the many.

The monarchic power (*fürstliche Gewalt*) is demonstrated at length by Hegel to furnish the only really philosophical principle of sovereignty. Granting that sovereignty in conception may properly be said to be an attribute of the state as a whole, he contends that sovereignty in reality and in action consists in the final decisive indication of an individual will. If the state be sovereign, yet an expression of the sovereign will must necessarily involve in last analysis a determination by some person. If sovereignty be sacredly

[1] "Die Ausbildung des Staats zur constitutionellen Monarchie ist das Werk der neuern Welt, in welcher die substantielle Idee die unendliche Form gewonnen hat." — *Phil. des Rechts*, sec. 273.

in the people (*das Volk*), nevertheless the will of the people is in every concrete instance the decision of some leader or some nominal servant. The monarchic principle is thus present and active in every state, and the fully developed political people will recognize this principle and give full expression to it in their constitutional system — will provide for its regulated and open, rather than irregular and secret, action.[1] Sovereignty, thus, is to be ascribed scientifically to the monarch.

This demonstration that the prince is an essential feature in the philosophical conception of the state is followed by an equally elaborate demonstration that the legislative power (*gesetzgebende Gewalt*) must be vested in an organ wherein prince, administration (*Regierung*) and people (*Volk*) all shall have part. Hegel's idea of a legislature is that of the diet (*Landtag*) long familiar in Germany, with modifications drawn from the British Parliament. He supports this idea with all the apparatus of his peculiar logic. Participation of prince and administration in lawmaking is essential to the unity of the state and its will — which unity the vaunted separation of powers must certainly destroy. The popular element in the legislature must appear in an assembly that shall represent the people as organic, not as atomistic. Classes (*Stände*), expressing the economic and social interests of the community, not the people as a group of individuals, furnish the basis of representation. Hegel has no sympathy with the current notion that the

[1] *Phil. des Rechts*, sec. 279.

source and end of political science is the will of the people; for in many or most cases those who sustain this dogma really mean by "people" that part of the people which does not and cannot know its own will.[1] Self-conscious, intellectual volition is all that can enter into the constitution of a rational state.

In external public law Hegel finds the state manifested in the relation of independent self-determined existence among distinct communities. International relations must be expressed in a system that recognizes the complete individuality of every politically self-conscious people. No "law" governs these relations, save the will of the particular states. The standards of conduct for the states are not the standards of private persons.[2] War, despite the amiable ideals of perpetual peace such as Kant and others have expounded, must remain, Hegel believes, an inevitable and not wholly maleficent incident in the establishment and preservation of national individuality.[3]

The final channel through which the state is revealed as perfected free will is, according to Hegel, world history (*Weltgeschichte*). To him the process of events is an unfolding of universal spirit (*Geist*). The culture of every people — its art, religion, political institutions

[1] ". . . ist vielmehr der Fall dass das Volk, insofern mit diesem Worte ein besonderer Theil der Mitglieder eines Staats bezeichnet ist, den Theil ausdrückt der nicht weiss was er will." — *Phil. des Rechts*, sec. 301.

[2] *Ibid.*, secs. 330, 337.

[3] Adepts in the Hegelian terminology probably see some such thought as this in the cryptic phrase: "Der Krieg . . . ist . . . das Moment worin die Idealität des Besonderen ihr Recht erhält und Wirklichkeit wird." — *Op. cit.*, sec. 324.

— expresses a particular stage in the activity and revelation of the absolute idea. Each successive age in world history since civilization began offers to view some people in whose spirit (*Volksgeist*) is reflected the world-spirit (*Weltgeist*) so far as that has been revealed. The process of revelation and realization of the idea, according to the principles of the Hegelian dialectic, is a fourfold process. It is not surprising, therefore, that Hegel's survey of general history detects four great world-historic political systems (*Reiche*) in whose successive careers the idea of freedom has progressed to perfect realization. These four systems are the Oriental, the Greek, the Roman and the German. With benumbing legerdemain the philosopher makes the commonplace facts of familiar history fit themselves nicely at the word into the categories and relations of his logic, and shows us mankind through all the ages marching steadily but unconsciously along Hegelian lines toward the Germanic perfection of the nineteenth century. In the modern world freedom is revealed to be the universal principle of state life. "The Orient knew and to the present day knows only that *One* [*i.e.* the despot] is free; the Greek and Roman World, that *Some* are free; the German World knows that *All* are free." [1]

Such is Hegel's generalization of the world-historical process. It displays the usual tendency of a philosophy of history — to represent the thinker's own time and place as the climax and summation of progress. But with whatever qualifications we judge the specu-

[1] *Philosophy of History*, p. 104.

lation and conclusions of Hegel, it is impossible to deny that the scope and coherency of his system of political science and the boldness and vast sweep of his historical inductions[1] reveal a mind of titanic power.

5. *Influence of the German Idealists*

Of the historical and evolutionary spirit that pervaded Hegel's politics there was little or no sign in the thought of Kant and Fichte. They represented the dogmatism of the French Revolution, while Hegel reflected a phase of the reaction that followed the downfall of Napoleon. There was thus great diversity among those whom I have classed together in this chapter. But there was also an essential likeness that justifies the classification — the conviction common to all that the vital truths of political science were to be reached rather through the processes of pure thought than through investigation of experience. Absolute verity, comprehensible to supreme intelligence, but transcending the sphere of the practical, was the goal common to these thinkers.

Like all other idealists the German philosophers achieved in fact little more than to clothe certain institutions and aspirations of contemporary politics with the sanctifying garb of a mystic form and nomenclature. To the substance of political doctrine their contributions were very slight. The strength and earnestness of their expositions and the confidence and

[1] His *Philosophy of History* contains a full and extraordinarily eloquent and inspiring expansion of the idea of world-history that is outlined in *The Philosophy of Law*, secs. 341–360.

zeal inspired in their disciples produced, however, very clear results in the form and method of political philosophy, especially in Germany. Through the refined psychological analysis that characterized the work of Kant, Fichte and Hegel the scope and classification of political ideas assumed great scientific precision. As to the further influence of these thinkers, it may be summed up as follows.

1. The idea of will, as the ultimate element in politics and law, was developed to its utmost limits. While Rousseau had exploited this idea with the clever manipulation of the amateur, Kant and Fichte, with professional exactness, set it in place as the corner-stone of a massive and symmetrical philosophy. Hegel also held to the will as the initial idea; but in his philosophical structure it was the capstone rather than the corner-stone, he building from the apex down, as was done, according to an ingenious hypothesis, by the constructors of the Egyptian pyramids.

2. Contract, as the formula through which the individual will created social and political authority, received at the hands of Kant and Fichte the highest degree of philosophical finish. No more was possible than Fichte actually did to give full scope and logical precision to the theory of the social contract. Even in his own life-time, however, as the spirit of the Revolution waned, the validity of this formula as a basis of political life began to appear less clear. Hegel dropped it entirely in his explanation of the state; and in all later political theory, the social contract, while sometimes deferred to with formal respect, has never re-

ceived the serious recognition of any philosopher ranking intellectually with Fichte.

3. The decline of the contract theory was promoted by another influence emanating from the German idealists. Whatever the degree of respect manifested by them for the dignity and rights of man as an individual, all of them save Humboldt ascribed unmeasured majesty and excellence to the state. With Kant and Fichte this ascription originated in their sense of the importance of political organization to the individual, but took eventually a shape that lost connection with its origin and suggested a cult of state and even of monarch *per se*. With Hegel the glorification of the state became a sort of Bacchic frenzy over intellectual parturition. Having brought forth the idea of the state, he set no limit to the adulation of his offspring: It is the absolute spirit, consciously realizing itself in the world; its existence has no other explanation than that God so wills; it is God.[1] Where such doctrine held sway there was inevitably a tendency for the individual to wither and for attention to center about the institutions in which this divine existence was manifest. The attributes of political authority rather than the rights of man became the core of discussion.

Finally, the doctrine of nationality as a fundamental principle of political organization received considerable

[1] "Der Staat ist der Geist, der in der Welt steht und sich in derselben mit Bewusstsein realisirt . . . es ist der Gang Gottes in der Welt, dass der Staat ist; . . . Bei der Idee des Staats muss man nicht besondere Staaten vor Augen haben . . . man muss vielmehr die Idee, diesen wirklichen Gott, für sich betrachten." — *Phil. des Rechts*, sec. 258, Zusatz.

stimulus from both Fichte and Hegel. The partition of Poland, the sweeping obliteration of ancient jurisdictions by the Napoleonic conquests and the no less arbitrary readjustments by the Congress of Vienna, all aroused fierce controversy as to the theoretical basis of the claim to independent political existence. Fichte set up, as we have seen, the ideal of a geographically isolated and economically self-sufficing community as objectively a nation. Hegel was less precise and stressed political self-consciousness as the criterion of a people (*Volk*). At the same time he attributed great significance to geographic and other physical conditions, quite in the spirit of Bodin and Montesquieu, and included the whole world in a splendid, if not wholly convincing, generalization as to the past, present and future abodes of the truly world-historic nations.[1]

It was of course an essential element in the doctrines of the philosophers that the criteria of nationality should be such as to assure to the Germans of central Europe the qualities of a political people. The conceptions worked out in accordance with this requirement played a great role in the demand for German national unity that figured so largely in the stirring history of the mid-nineteenth century.

[1] *Philosophy of History*, Introduction. America, he says, is "the land of the future, where, in the ages that lie before us, the burden of the World's History shall reveal itself. . . ." — Page 86.

SELECT REFERENCES

Bosanquet, Philosophical Theory of the State, chaps. ix, x. Bluntschli, *Geschichte*, Kap. xii (Kant); Kap. xiv (Fichte and Humboldt); Kap. xviii (Hegel). Caird, Essays on Literature and Philosophy, II, pp. 392–442. Fichte, *Werke*, Bände III, IV. Hegel, Philosophy of History, translated by Sibree, Introduction; Philosophy of Right, translated by Dyde. Humboldt, Sphere and Duties of Government. Janet, *Histoire*, II, pp. 574-627 (Kant). Kant, Philosophy of Law, translated by Hastie; Project for a Perpetual Peace. Leon, *La Philosophie de Fichie*, pp. 211–248, 465–508. Levkovits, *Die Staatslehre auf Kantischer Grundlage*. Wallace, Hegel's Philosophy of Mind, Essay V. Zeller, "*Fichte als Politiker*," in Sybel's *Historische Zeitschrift*, IX, 23.

CHAPTER V

THEORIES OF CONSERVATISM AND REACTION

1. *General Character and Influence*

BETWEEN 1789 and 1812 the wave of revolutionary doctrine generated at the French capital swept destructively over continental Europe, with little effective resistance till the boundaries of the Czar and the Sultan were reached. Adversaries of the subversive creed were mercilessly thrust aside by both the republican and the imperial realizations of the triumphant ideas. In the early years of the revolution the protests of conservatism were multitudinous and full-throated; but before the amazing transformations wrought by Jacobin and Napoleonic France they dwindled to a few faint and feeble voices from the obscure nooks and corners where the enemies and victims of the revolution found uncertain safety. In Great Britain alone anti-revolutionary doctrine was full in volume and unrestrained in expression. Edmund Burke's vehement eloquence set the pace that the lesser thinkers strove to maintain. Inevitably, however, in the true manner of the British, their philosophy centered mainly on the practical problems of their own internal and international politics. Their concern was deeper in the effect of a powerful French state on world commerce and the balance of political influence, than in the theoretical question as to the true basis and the proper organ of the power. The gigantic effort that destroyed Napoleon was directed, not against the representative of the French people, but against the disturber of the peace and equilibrium of Europe.

When, however, the great task had been accomplished and the question of readjustment was before the conquerors, speculation about what had happened became active, and the principles of the new order were warmly debated. Voices that had been silent or unnoticed during the past twenty years rang out clamorously in behalf of the institutions and the doctrines that had been overwhelmed by the revolution. The practical settlement of the questions at issue in the great wars was effected in the two treaties of Paris, of 1814 and 1815 respectively, and in the agreements reached at the Congress of Vienna (September, 1814, to June, 1815). Under these compacts the principles of popular sovereignty, constitutional government and nationality received short shrift; but nevertheless it was impossible to avoid altogether the admission that something had happened. A restoration of territory and government to the precise conditions that prevailed twenty years earlier was, humanly speaking, impossible; in determining how far the process could and should go in concrete cases the debates sometimes turned, even in the innermost shrines of reaction, on considerations of popular desire and economic or other national interest. Most significant of the evidence that some sense of progress was present at Vienna was the well-known provision in reference to the newly established German Confederation, that there should be in every state belonging to it a constitution based upon the Estates (*landstaendische Verfassung*). This species of constitution was not one that appealed to the liberals; indeed it was precisely what had been overthrown in France in 1789; but that any qualification at all of the monarchic principle should be approved at Vienna, was very suggestive.

The concession involved in this German provision had already been exceeded in fact by the act of the Bourbon Louis XVIII, whom the allied powers restored to the French throne. He so far recognized the trend of things as to proclaim a constitution (*Charte constitutionelle*),[1] guaranteeing civil and religious liberty, equality before the law and parliamentary government. Here was indeed a written constitution — the goal of the revolutionists' doctrine. But it was a constitution with a difference. While in practice it might secure the substance of free government, in its theoretical basis it repudiated the whole dogma of the revolution. The *Charte* was the supreme law; its source, however, was the will of the king, not of the people or the nation; and the authority of the king was derived, not from the people or the nation, but from God. "All authority in France," the document said, "resides in the person of the king"; out of consideration for the wish and welfare of his subjects, he has voluntarily granted the rights and governmental order established by it. As it embodied nothing of popular sovereignty, so it embod-

[1] Hélie, *Constitutions de la France*, 3me fasc., p. 884 *et seq.*

ied nothing of natural rights. The liberties accorded by it had no special sanctity as inalienable or imprescriptible; they were granted by the king and had no guarantee other than his formal oath to maintain the *Charte*.

This species of constitution, either the absolute concession by a monarch, or a compact between a monarch and the ancient estates of his realm, was put in operation in many of the lesser states of Europe in the years following the overthrow of Napoleon.[1] Both in content and in manner of establishment it expressed the moderate and conservative idea of political progress that was especially represented in the history of England. To those in whom the ends and methods of the French in 1789–93 were still ideals of eternal right, the granted charters lacked all validity and must as speedily as possible be made to give way to the will of the people. At the other extreme the reactionary element of the restored aristocracy and clergy saw only an amiable weakness in the monarch's willingness to grant privileges to his subjects, and strove with might and main to thwart every policy that led further away from the sacred system of the *ancien régime*. The particular concrete embodiment of this reactionary ideal was the Holy Alliance, created by the treaty of September, 1815, between the monarchs of Russia, Austria and Prussia. This unique convention announced, among others, the following intentions of its signatories: to take as their sole guide in both internal

[1] Borgeaud, *Adoption and Amendment of Constitutions*, p. 28, *et seq.*

and external relations of their governments, the precepts of justice, Christian charity and peace; to treat one another as brothers, and to act toward their respective subjects as fathers of families; to regard themselves as delegated by Providence to govern three branches of one family, whose sole sovereign should thus confessedly be God.

There was not much comfort for the revolutionists or even for moderate conservatives derivable from such a platform, though the treaty taken as a whole was redolent of virtue, benevolence and piety. To the extreme reactionaries, however, the religious and mystical tenor of the Holy Alliance made a strong appeal. The breaking up of society by the rationalistic revolution had confirmed in many minds of the harried and impoverished nobility and clergy the conviction that faith and the ancient church afforded the only security for mankind. Accordingly the political philosophy that came forth in large bulk after 1815 tended very strongly to theological and mystical lines. This quality was distinctive of Bonald, Maistre and lesser lights of their school. Their whole tendency was obscurantist, and their practical influence was to win some measure of intellectual support for the measures of Metternich, who himself, while skilfully plying every means to repress liberalism, was at heart no devotee, but a contemptuous cynic.

Of quite different a general tone, though at one on many particular points, was that species of anti-revolutionary doctrine whose unapproachable chief was Edmund Burke. The ramifications of Burke's influence were very extensive. His diatribes against the revolution were freely reproduced by translation and imitation all over the continent. His eloquence and fervor won attention where his reasoning fell short of the demands. But he was, as a whole, not in the class of reactionaries and obscurantists. He would never have advocated absolute monarchy; his ideal was the sort of constitutional rule that the conservatives after 1815 actually established.

2. *Edmund Burke*

At the age of fifty-nine, after a long and arduous public career as a Whig in British politics, Burke was confronted in 1789 with the necessity of judging the revolutionary proceedings in France. Many of the Frenchmen, with many approving Englishmen, believed the principles and purposes of the National Assembly at Paris to be identical with those of the Parliament at London that just one hundred years earlier effected the English revolution. The Whigs, therefore, who boasted themselves the particular bearers of the doctrines and traditions of the "glorious revolution" of 1688, were naturally expected and disposed to sympathize with the new order in France. Burke, however, took alarm at both the principles and the procedure of the Frenchmen. Their dogmas, he saw, recalled rather the Levelers of 1649 than the Whigs of 1688; and their sweeping demolition of ancient institutions, political, religious and economic, filled his conservative and aristocratic soul with horrid forebodings of democracy. England became full of unrest and agitation in sympathy with French principles. Societies for the propagation of these ideas manifested much activity. The scorn and loathing with which Burke regarded such presumptuous intermeddling of the common people with the high things of politics spurred him to energetic action against them. In Parliament he pronounced an initial invective against the French proceedings,[1] and then he put forth the famous essays in which he dealt at large with the whole history and philosophy of the revolution as he saw it. The leading work was the *Reflections on the Revolution in France*,[2] published in 1790, and the second in importance — perhaps the first from the standpoint of political philosophy — was *An Appeal from the New to the Old Whigs*,[3] published in 1791. Neither of these works presents a body of systematic political theory. Both consist in large part of violent assaults upon what Burke assumed — often quite without accuracy — to be the policy and achievements of the French revolutionary party. The splendid glow of his eloquence tends to dim the sequence of his reasoning, yet it is not so serious a task to reconstruct, from the fragments scattered through his essays, the philosophy that underlies his emotion.

Burke's hostility to the dominant principles of the revolution is directed against both their general character and their specific content. As to their general character, he detests and spurns the method of precise mathematical formulation of human rights and social

[1] In the debate on the army estimates, Feb. 9, 1790. *Works* (Boston, 1884), III, 213.

[2] *Works*, III, 231.

[3] *Ibid.*, IV, 57.

arrangements. The rigor of exact logic has, he holds, no controlling place in the ultimate explanation of political life. That proudest achievement of French philosophy, the reduction of governmental science to the brief formulas of a written constitution, is to Burke supreme foolishness. The Declaration of the Rights of Man is "a sort of institute and digest of anarchy," — "such a pedantic abuse of elementary principles as would have disgraced boys at school."[1] Just in proportion as the dogmas of this code are metaphysically or logically true they are morally and politically false. For government, Burke argues, is a contrivance to provide for the *wants* of men, after the institution of society has superseded their abstract *rights*. The provision for their wants is a matter that requires a careful consideration of means, and the organization of such means is the constitution of a state; but the matter of rights derivable from abstract reasoning about pre-social conditions no longer has importance.[2] Why discuss, he asks, a sick man's abstract right to medicine? Call in a physician, not a professor of metaphysics.

This impatience with a philosophy that is too precise and definite is abundantly illustrated by Burke's handling of the contract theory. In this he is most successful in avoiding the precision and self-consistency that offend him. Both concepts that we have seen designated by the name contract theory figure in Burke's works. He discourses on the agreement that constitutes civil society and also on that which expresses the relation between monarch and subjects. But in

[1] *Works*, III, 221. [2] *Ibid.*, III, 310 *et seq.*

neither case will Burke give such definiteness to the contract as to justify the conclusions drawn from it by the revolutionists. The dangerous clarity with which Hobbes and Rousseau and their followers set forth the terms, the parties and the content of the social pact, has no charm for Burke. He takes up the habit of Bolingbroke and the other English essayists, and around the vague outline of the contract as they present it he throws the multiplied incoherence of his dazzling rhetoric:

> Society is indeed a contract . . . but the state ought not to be considered as nothing better than a partnership agreement in a trade of pepper and coffee . . . to be taken up for a little temporary interest and to be dissolved by the fancy of the parties. . . . It is a partnership in all science, a partnership in all art, a partnership in every virtue and in all perfection. As the ends of such a partnership cannot be obtained in many generations, it becomes a partnership not only between those who are living, but between those who are living, those who are dead and those who are to be born. Each contract of each particular state is a clause in the great primæval contract of eternal society, linking the lower with the higher natures, connecting the visible and invisible world, according to a fixed compact sanctioned by the inviolable oath which holds all physical and all moral natures each in their appointed place. . . .[1]

Burke could feel perfectly confident, after penning this famous rhapsody, that no logic-chopper would ever use it to sustain a revolution.

In his *Appeal from the New to the Old Whigs* Burke was obliged to grapple at close quarters with the doctrines of the revolutionary party. A host of keen critics[2]

[1] *Reflections*, in *Works*, III, 359.
[2] Thomas Paine, in his *Rights of Man*, was one of the keenest.

replied to the *Reflections* and extorted from the author something more definite in both attack and defence. Burke took up the fundamental dogmas of the revolutionary school and opposed to them the bases of his own belief. That sovereignty resides constantly and inalienably in the people; that the people may lawfully change their government at will; that a majority counted by the head is the final and unquestionable organ of the people's will; that the assignment of precisely equal weight to every individual's judgment is a requirement of political justice; that no people has a constitution until some formal written document shall have been adopted by popular vote: — all these dogmas, which according to Burke are the substance of his adversaries' philosophy, he rejects with the most positive energy. In their place he maintains a view that is substantially as follows:

Political society and government may have their origin in the consent and agreement of individual men. To that extent the will of the people is the source of authority and may be called sovereign. But beyond that beginning, in the life and action of a state duly constituted, it is utterly wrong to regard the individual will as a predominant factor, or any number of such wills as the abode of paramount authority. The man born in an established society is under obligation from his birth to respect the institutions of that society. To assert that he is free to disregard them at the behest of his own will, is to assert the principle of anarchy. Duty must be recognized as above will. Duties rest upon men irrespective of their formal consent. They arise from conditions and relations in which volition and choice have no part. Without conceding this, society is impossible. The relation of parent and child is not a voluntary one — certainly not on the part of the child, possibly not on that of the parent; but the moral duties that arise out of the relation are essential to social development. So the political and social circumstances amid which a man is born are not his choice; yet they impose duties upon him.

> [No] man or number of men have a right (except what necessity, which is out of and above all rule, rather imposes than bestows) to free themselves from that primary engagement into which every man born into a community as much contracts by being born into it as he contracts an obligation to certain parents by his having been derived from their bodies. The place of every man determines his duty.[1]

This keen and powerful attack upon the dogmas of popular sovereignty and the right of revolution Burke supplements by a not less vigorous handling of the claim that a numerical majority wields the authority that the people possesses. His argument, concisely put, is, that in establishing a state unanimity is indispensable, on the showing of the advocates of popular sovereignty themselves, and after the state is established the people as a mass of independent units no longer exists, having been replaced by the organization and relationships created by the social union; neither before nor after the formation of government, therefore, is there any place for mere majority rule.

To the suggestion that the conduct of government by

[1] *Works*, IV, 167.

majority votes of the people may be prescribed by the very terms of the agreement by which a society is instituted, Burke's reply is his doctrine that the state that follows nature is necessarily aristocratic. That a number of men, of various endowments, should be able to act as one body, presumes, Burke holds, some kind of leadership by the wiser and more expert. Only thus can there be hope of attaining the ends of the association. This appears in the state of nature that precedes the organization of government. A natural aristocracy is to be seen in every "large body rightly constituted." In a nation it is seen in the class of those who by birth, wealth or intellect have a particular fitness for public functions [1] — the men of light and leading. To submerge these in the great mass of lesser men and give them only the weight of their numbers, would be violence to the natural order of things and the enthronement of anarchy.

As to the theory of a constitution, Burke has nothing positive to offer beyond the exposition and eulogy of the constitution of England. In this he sees social and political forces operating with the regularity, ease and effectiveness of nature herself. The organs of government — King, Parliament and courts — have their authority from the law and custom of the land, which express the compact on which the constitution rests. The rights of the people have their definition, and the interests of all classes their protection, in this law and custom. Life, liberty and property are secure, not

[1] Burke's description of this class is probably the most comprehensive and effective ever penned. *Works*, IV, 174–5.

because any abstract philosophy requires it, but because it is embodied in the law. Political convenience, not logical formulas of right and justice, is the foundation of policy. Liberty and authority are both duly regulated. "The whole scheme of our mixed constitution is to prevent any one of its principles from being carried as far as, taken by itself and theoretically, it would go." Check and balance are of the essence of the system. Each part, while serving its own particular end, limits and controls the other parts. Hence, "in the British constitution there is a perpetual treaty and compromise going on, sometimes openly, sometimes with less observation."[1] In this, as contrasted with the insistence that any principle shall be applied in its abstract perfection, Burke finds the special merit and philosophical justification of a constitution.

It is clear from the foregoing that Burke's spirit is the spirit of the statesman rather than the closet philosopher. His thought centers about the state as a going concern rather than as a concept of pure thought. To reason from the ultimate thinkable in politics is to him unreason. The experience of mankind and the institutions in which human nature has expressed itself are the final source from which political principles are to be derived. In holding to this idea Burke places himself among those notable thinkers who make up the historical school of political science. His eulogy of Montesquieu illustrates the type of his philosophy, while confirmation is found in the indignant and reiterated attacks on Rousseau.[2] Yet Burke, while rejecting

[1] *Works*, IV, 207–8. [2] *Ibid.*, III, 459; IV, 25 *et seq.*, 211.

metaphysical and *a priori* politics, did not escape certain presumptions not different from theirs. He was no mere empiricist. When he bade political philosophy cease to go further in its research than where actual institutions were revealed, and when he denounced the innovating spirit as fraught with peril, he spoke in the name of a divine and a natural order that determined human affairs. God and Nature were both adduced as sponsors for his dictates of political wisdom. Behind the working of actual systems Burke believed there was a moral purpose, fixed by a superior intelligence, and claiming, therefore, the reverent support of men. This mystic strain of thought is discernible in various places, but is not so conspicuous as to give a distinct character to his doctrines. In other representatives of anti-revolutionary theory this particular strain assumed great prominence and shaded off into utter obscurantism.

3. *The Marquis de Bonald*

The Marquis de Bonald, a French nobleman whose life (1754–1840) spanned the revolutionary age in its utmost vicissitudes, philosophized in the form and method that to Burke were most abhorrent. Metaphysical and religious dogmas at the foundation and mathematical precision in deduction from them produced a system of political science as harmonious and symmetrical as that of Siéyès or Condorcet, but of a content contradicting theirs at every point, and surpassing even Burke in justification of the *ancien régime.* Bonald's theory is set forth in his *Essay on the Natural*

Laws of the Social Order,[1] and in his *Primitive Legislation*. The *Essay* and the "Preliminary Discourse" of the *Primitive Legislation* exhibit in forceful and informal style his antipathy to the dogmas of the revolution — an antipathy less emotional and more purely intellectual than Burke's. The *Primitive Legislation* presents Bonald's positive system in a series of formal and closely articulated propositions, beginning with "Beings and their Relations," and running through "Harmony of State and Religion" into the details of administration and education.

Bonald's point of view is that of Catholic Christian philosophy. His reiterated indictment of the revolutionary theories is that they are not only unsocial, but atheistic — that they ignore the essential oneness of political and religious society. In last analysis human knowledge, Bonald holds, is concerned with phenomena under three categories — cause, means and effect. This triad of categories, which inevitably recalls the generalizations of Campanella and Vico,[2] is exemplified, according to Bonald, in the individual man by the will, the organs through which it acts, and the objects to which its action is directed; in the family by father, mother, children; in society, whether political or religious, by a sovereign power, the agents through which it acts, and the subjects under it (*pouvoir, ministre, sujets*). This trilogistic *motif* runs all through Bonald's

[1] *Essai analytique sur les lois naturelles de l'ordre social*, in *Œuvres*, Tom. I; *Législation primitive considérée . . . par les seules lumières de la raison*, in *Œuvres*, Tom. II, III, IV. See also his *Théorie du pouvoir politique et religieux* in Tom. V.

[2] *Political Theories from Luther to Montesquieu*, pp. 150, 385, 388.

thinking and is exploited with much ingenuity. The Christian Trinity obviously enough illustrates it; and it is made the basis of a striking interpretation of world-history, wherein the Hebrew culture is said to have revealed the great cause, pagan philosophy to have revealed and analyzed the effects, Christianity to have revealed the universal means — the mediation of Jesus Christ.

Social philosophy proper Bonald begins with a definition of society. It is the association of like beings for the purpose of their reproduction and preservation.[1] The essence of such union is the inter-relationship of the three elements, *i.e.*, of power and ministry for the welfare of the subjects.[2] Here is the brief formula that sums up the nature of family, of church and of state — a sovereign power to will, a ministry to execute, and subjects to obey and profit by the combination. Such an arrangement expresses the universal and eternal rule of nature. Such was the beneficent system that prevailed throughout Christendom till the sixteenth century. Since that fatal Lutheran and Calvinistic epoch the natural order has been overthrown — in the state by popular sovereignty, in the church by Presbyterianism and in the family by divorce.[3]

To sustain his anti-revolutionary thesis it is necessary for Bonald to prove the rationality and utility of hereditary absolute monarchy and of privileged nobility;

[1] "La réunion des êtres semblables pour la fin de leur reproduction et de leur conservation." *Œuvres*, II, 133.

[2] ". . . Le rapport du pouvoir et du ministre pour le bien et l'avantage des sujets." *Ibid.*

[3] *Œuvres*, II, 141.

for these represent respectively the "power" and the "ministry" of his natural state. Monarchy he argues is in a sense inevitable. That is to say, the definite impulse of some one human will is what in fact produces every action. In popular government this is no less true than in monarchic. *Many* may think and talk, but some *one* in last analysis gives the determining volition. The difference between a monarchic and a popular sovereign is merely this, that in one it is always certain, and in the other it is never certain, whose will is to prevail. Hence the greater stability of the monarchic state; and as stability is of the essence of order, and order is indispensable to the preservation of men in society, monarchy is the natural system. Bonald's complete argument goes far beyond what is here outlined, and results in this comprehensive dogma:

> The public power must be *one*, masculine, property-owner (*propriétaire*), perpetual; for without unity, masculinity, property, permanence, there is no real independence.[1]

The agent or servant (*ministre*) of the supreme power is the nobility (*la noblesse*). This institution Bonald upholds with reasoning equal to Burke's, if not with equal eloquence. The nobility has its end not in adorning the society or in honoring individuals, but in serving the state. It is a function, a duty. It affords an opportunity by which a man who has proved his ability by success in serving his family may be exalted into the service of the state. Under popular governments the only goal of success in private life is wealth. The man who enters the public service merely uses his

[1] *Œuvres*, III, p. 84.

temporary authority as a means to increase his fortune. A permanent service in the hands of those whose ability is assured by inheritance or personal achievement, is the only guarantee of an administration of public affairs that can conform to nature.

For the dogma that nature's rule is equality, Bonald's scorn is extreme. The Declaration of Rights, he says, is merely a series of indefinite maxims "put at the head of a constitution as in Virgil the false shades and deceitful dreams are placed at the entrance to Hades."[1] Equality is incompatible with the first principle of order; for "order among men is nothing but the art of causing some to go ahead of others so that all may reach the goal in time (*à temps*)."[2] And Bonald points out with grim satire that the Declaration of Rights contains an assertion of the right of property, to satisfy those who by luck or diligence have reached their goal, and a contradictory assertion of equality, to satisfy those who are yet to arrive.

The purely theological basis of Bonald's politics is to be seen in his doctrines as to sovereignty and law. The power of the monarch is not sovereign. The fundamental axiom of the social order is: "Sovereignty is in God; . . . power is from God." The law (*la loi*), therefore, is "the will of God and the rule of man for maintaining society."[3] Natural law and natural right have for Bonald no importance except so far as they express the will and purpose of God. Nature signifies only the *ensemble*, in a created thing, of end and means for its realization. At different stages in the develop-

[1] *Œuvres*, II, 186. [2] *Ibid.*, II, 189. [3] *Ibid.*, II, 205.

ment of man, for example, different institutions are natural to him. In the domestic condition celibacy is not natural; in the political condition it is natural.[1] There is thus no invariable criterion of natural law and right save in the will of the Creator. This will, and hence the substance and foundation of all real legislation through human power, Bonald thinks is to be found clearly revealed in the Bible, and may be discovered also in the immemorial traditions of society when they have not been corrupted or obscured by written codes. The unconsciously developed customs and morals (*mœurs*) of a people are its true fundamental law; and nothing is more futile than the effort to put this law into writing. To stereotype the constitution is to destroy it. On the title-page of his *Primitive Legislation* Bonald places the sentence: "A people that has destroyed its customs in seeking to give itself written laws, has obliged itself to write everything, including its customs." This he considers a perfect *reductio ad absurdum.* In the order of God and of nature law, like custom, has no precise time and place of origin. "Bad laws have a beginning, but the good, emanating from God, are eternal as he. At whatever moment men put them in writing, they come from an earlier time, and like man himself, they existed before they were born."

The point of view here exemplified was not peculiar to Bonald, but belonged to the whole reactionary school. It is found in Burke, who vents his scorn for "blurred shreds of parchment" where man has scribbled what

[1] *Œuvres*, II, 243.

nature derides. Most perfect of all, however, was the clear and profound argument directed against the theory of the written constitution by the most brilliant of the continental reactionaries, Joseph de Maistre.

4. *Joseph de Maistre*

This distinguished representative of French literature and philosophy became a Frenchman only by virtue of the revolution which he so detested. A Savoyard nobleman, he shared in the disaster which overwhelmed the court of Turin when the armies of the French Republic swept over Italy, and the exile that began thus in 1797 was prolonged to 1817 by his appointment as ambassador to the Czar. The sojourn at the Russian court was responsible for his most famous work, the *Soirées de St. Pétersbourg,* wherein all the varied phases of his intellectual interest are fully illustrated. Before he went to Russia, however, he set forth the basic features of his political philosophy in his *Considérations sur la France,* published in 1797. The doctrines of this work that bore specifically on the nature of constitutions were elaborated in a separate monograph, the *Essay on the Source of Political Constitutions* [1] (1814). A very full and systematic exposition of his ecclesiastical philosophy was embodied in the volume of *The Pope* (*Du Pape*), written when Napoleon held the pontiff in captivity, but published only in 1817.

It has been truly said that Maistre's political theory is inseparable from his theology. He was thoroughly

[1] *Essai sur le principe générateur des constitutions politiques.*

mediæval in this respect. As familiar with the secular and rationalistic thought and learning of the eighteenth century as Aquinas was with that of the thirteenth, Maistre, like St. Thomas, found an absolute limit to the dominion of that thought and learning in the dogmas of the Christian faith, and the authority of the Roman Church. His conception of the papacy is not far from that of Hildebrand. The monarchy is indispensable to the existence of the church as it is to the existence of the state, and infallibility is the attribute of the Pope precisely as sovereignty is the attribute of the secular prince.[1] The two terms designate, indeed, but a single concept, regarded, however, from different points of view. It has been by no mere chance, Maistre insists, that the history of the Christian era shows the monarchic principle dominant in both state and church. This is God's way, and it is the only way in which man's destiny on earth can be fulfilled.

From such premises the conclusion, so far as concerns the theories of the revolutionary propaganda, can easily be drawn. The fundamental fault of these theories is, Maistre feels, an overweening confidence in the power of the human reason. There is a mystery in the state that mortal intelligence cannot penetrate; and the pretence of politicians that they can create governments and constitutions is the emptiest of dreams. The power of man is exhausted in naming and modifying that which already exists. To hold that a state can be called into being by an act of the human will is like holding that a tree is "made" by

[1] *Du Pape*, liv. i, *passim*.

the man who plants and cultivates the seed. To hold that a body of written formulas is the actual constitution, or that a mass of written statutes are the real laws of a people, is to ignore the eternal verities of political science. The indisputable truth of the matter, Maistre declares, is summed up in these dogmas:

The roots of political constitutions exist prior to all written law.

A constitutional law is and can be only the development or sanction of a preexisting and unwritten right.

What is most essential, most intrinsically constitutional and truly fundamental, is never written, and indeed never could be without destroying the state (*sans exposer l'Etat*).

The weakness and frailty of a constitution are in exact proportion to the number of constitutional provisions that are written.[1]

What Maistre has chiefly in mind in the development of these dogmas is the futility of the human will and purpose in the supreme matters of politics. It is the vanity of vanities to expect liberty and rights to flow from the drafting of a constitution. No constitution results, he says, from deliberation. Men labor upon the circumstances with which they find themselves surrounded and produce what they call, and seriously believe to be, constitutions and laws; but the practical operation of their system is likely to bring results quite different from what was expected. No nation can give itself liberty by the simple process of promulgating a Declaration of Rights. That which is sought must exist in the soul of the people by the act of the Creator in order that it may be actually manifest in

[1] "Essai sur le principe générateur," in *Œuvres*, p. 116.

the institutions of government. A free nation may write a free constitution, but a free constitution can never make a nation free. Self-consciousness in a people, as in an individual, obstructs rather than promotes the expression of the true character. "When a nation begins to reflect upon itself, its laws are already made."

Maistre does not depend wholly upon his abstract principles for support in this attack upon the theory of the written constitution. His wide knowledge of history and of contemporary politics enables him to sustain his thesis by some clever interpretations and comments. From antiquity he adopts the well-worn idea of the lawgiver, like Solon and Lycurgus, whose fortune in establishing successful institutions was due, Maistre holds, to the inspiration through which the superman was able to divine the true spirit of the people.[1] It was always distinctive of such a lawgiver that he was of royal or aristocratic blood, that he refrained from putting his system in written form, that he acted rather from impulse and instinct than from reason, and that his chief dependence in enforcing his authority was a certain moral force that constrained the wills of men. These characteristics, Maistre maintains, all go to support his doctrine that no laws, in the scientific sense of the word, are the product of deliberate human volition; for those great sages to whom

[1] "Lorsque la Providence a décrété la formation plus rapide d'une constitution politique, il paraît un homme revêtu d'une puissance indéfinissable : il parle et il se fait obéir ; mais ces hommes merveilleux n'appartiennent peut-être qu'au monde antique et à la jeunesse des nations." *Considérations*, chap. vi, sec. 8.

the legislative function has been particularly ascribed for ages were really oracles of God, not to be judged by merely human standards.

In modern conditions Maistre depends largely, of course, on the English constitution as the type of what goes on in fact in every nation. As to America, which he knows will be cited against him, he will only say that it is not yet time to cite it.[1] It has indeed a written constitution, it has abjured monarchy, it has adopted many advanced democratic institutions; but much of this he finds to be merely the expression of ideas and practices that have been familiar in the history and institutions of the people, and thus to be part of their true, but in no sense of a new, constitution. As to what is really novel in their system — what is the outcome of their deliberation and discussion, all that is the frailest of frailties, and foredooms the system to weakness and decay.[2]

Of all constitution-making, that is the most hopelessly inane, Maistre of course believes, which pretends to formulate a fundamental law that will meet the requirements of every nation — that will express the

[1] This was written probably in 1796.

[2] As an example of the over-confidence of the Americans in their ability to determine their affairs by reflection and choice, Maistre refers to the project of a new city to be founded for the capital of the United States. The plans for this city, he says, are circulating through Europe, but he is sceptical as to their realization. Very likely a city will be built, he admits, but "nevertheless, there is too much of deliberation, too much of the human, about the business; and it would be safe to wager a thousand to one that the city will not be built, or that it will not be called Washington, or that Congress will not have its seat there." *Considérations*, chap. vii, end.

universal principles of governmental organization and action. The jaunty assurance of Siéyès, Condorcet and the other revolutionary leaders on this point excites only contempt in Maistre. To him a constitution presumes a nation, and is in fact nothing but the solution of the following problem:

> Given the population, the customs (*mœurs*), the religion, the geographical situation, the political relations, the wealth, the good and bad qualities, of a certain nation, — to find the laws that are suited to it.[1]

A more sane and rational statement of the problem than this could hardly be made. Yet, taken in connection with the other doctrines of Maistre's philosophy, it puts in a high light the dreary and hopeless character of his system from any but the obscurantist point of view. For he insists, as we have seen, that every effort of the human intelligence to find the laws suited to the nation's needs must be futile — that to formulate, or even to become conscious of, the most essential of these laws is to destroy the state.

5. *Ludwig von Haller*

The principles and dogmas of the anti-revolutionary philosophy received a highly systematic formulation at the hands of a German-Swiss thinker, Ludwig von Haller, of Berne. Haller was driven into exile by the sweep of the revolution over his native city, but returned in 1806 to become professor of public law in the university. His experiences had caused him to ponder very carefully the political problems of the day, and

[1] *Considérations*, chap. vi, end.

he returned from his exile satisfied that he had discovered the cause that was at bottom responsible for all the existing turmoil.[1] This was the almost universal acceptance among civilized peoples of the idea that authority of man over man originated in voluntary bestowal by the subject individual. The deadly error of this doctrine was manifest, he held, particularly in the various forms of the social-contract theory, and he set himself to the task of making that theory forevermore untenable by rational beings. The outcome of this pious purpose was his work, in six substantial volumes, entitled: *Restoration of Political Science, or Theory of the Naturally Social State opposed to the Chimaera of the Artificially Civil State.*[2] Eighteen years elapsed between the completion of the first volume (1816) and the appearance of the last (1834), and the trend of events during this interval was manifestly away from the conditions that he held to be ideal; yet he never wavered in his conviction that his political theory embodied ultimate truth and must in the long run be realized in practice. Indeed, it was the essence of his thought that however divergent in appearance institutions were from the principles of his system, the proper analysis must always reveal those principles determining the life and action of the institutions.

As indicated by the title of his work, Haller believed that for two centuries political philosophy had been

[1] His intellectual processes in connection with this matter are set forth with garrulous naïveté in the preface of his work.

[2] "Restauration der Staats-Wissenschaft, oder Theorie des natürlich-geselligen Zustands der Chimäre des künstlich-bürgerlichen entgegengesetzt."

wholly perverted by the doctrines, for which he held the Roman jurists largely responsible, that men were by nature equal and that authority was an artificial concept or quality, originating in delegation by the subject. After a vigorous polemic against these doctrines and the philosophers who had upheld them,[1] he unfolds in a rigidly logical manner the principles of his own system, tests them at every step by pure reason and history and often also by uniformities of usage in different languages (to which Haller, like Maistre and Bonald, attributes great importance), and expounds at great length the organization and action of the governments that illustrate his ideas.

His initial grievance against the contract school of thinking is its assumption that it particularly expresses the system of nature. He is as eager to speak the voice of nature as are his adversaries, but her voice to him is far different. Not equality but inequality among men is her rule as he sees it. All men have indeed the same rights, which are fixed by the divine and natural law of justice and love. The ancient formula — Live rightly, injure no one, give to each his own — is nature's rule of conduct to every man, and insures to every man alike the justice that inheres in the operation of these injunctions. But in respect to the power to satisfy the

[1] His attack on the social-contract idea is very comprehensive: whether considered as an historical fact, or as a mere hypothesis, or as a purely philosophical idea, it is false, impossible and self-contradictory. This broad platform of condemnation enables Haller to mete out a goodly measure of contempt to the prevailing idealism of the Germans. Kant he frequently refers to as the "sophist of Königsberg." For an opinion of Haller by Hegel, see the latter's *Werke*, VIII, p. 309 *et seq.*

needs of mundane life, and in respect to the kind and intensity of these needs, nature's rule is endless diversity and inequality. This fact, Haller holds, is the key to the whole system of social relations. Here is the open but hitherto unnoticed secret of human authority. He who has the power and resources, of whatever kind, that enable him to be independent of every other in satisfying his own needs, and to contribute to the satisfaction of the needs of others, — he is the natural ruler, and those who depend on him are natural subjects.

This principle explains not only the authority of government, but also every other species of authority exercised by man over his kind. It appears in the relation of the child to the adult, of the weakling to the strong man, of the stupid to the intelligent, of the poor man to the rich man, of pupils to their teacher, of the invalid to his physician, of the client to his lawyer, of the mass of men in any collective enterprise to the leader. Human society in general is but an infinite multitude of such relationships, in which the salient fact is control on the one side and subjection on the other. Because these conditions are due immediately to the diverse and unequal circumstances inherent in earthly existence, they must be regarded as natural in the strictest sense of the term. Thus Haller establishes his thesis that authority needs no exercise of human volition as its basis, and that no distinction can be made between the natural and the civil or political state, so far as mastery and subjection are concerned.

As to that species of authority which is called political,

it differs from other species, according to Haller, in degree only, and not at all in kind. He is very impatient with that doctrine by which a grand, dim, mysterious entity called the state is set apart from and above all other human institutions. Governmental authority is in truth, he holds, merely the name for an *ensemble* of superiorities that insures to its possessor a far-reaching independence and an abundance of means for aiding the less favored. An individual who, by reason of wealth, energy, sagacity, or other qualities, inherent or acquired, is able, without dependence on his fellows, to satisfy his own needs and theirs, will inevitably gather about him a group of less happily situated persons, and the association thus naturally formed is a political society. Or a group of equally powerful and equally independent men, who have deliberately united for the promotion of their common interests, will attract a group of less powerful and dependent individuals, and will exercise over them the sway of a government. Here is the whole story of the origin and nature of the state. And here is the whole basis of a classification of states. In the first of the two cases described there appears the monarchy (*Fürstenthum*), in the second, the republic (*Republik*). No other forms are possible.

Political authority, as thus explained, is at the farthest remove from the character ascribed to it by the revolutionary school of thought. It originates not in any conferences or discussions involving masses of men, but partly by the operation of natural forces directly, partly by individual agreements (*Dienstver-*

träge); it comes not from below, but from above; it arises not all at one time, but at various times by successive aggregation; and thus the holder of the authority has it not at all from the ruled, but from nature, and therefore through the grace of God. From the point of view of the subject, on the other side, it is clear that he gives up no liberty and no right whatever, but serves the superior either because naturally dependent on him, or voluntarily for the sake of food, protection, education, or other things that make life agreeable. Subject, like ruler, enjoys his just and lawful (*Rechtmässige*) liberty after, as well as before, the establishment of the political bond. There is nothing of unrighteous coercion in either the entrance into the bond, the continuance in it or the termination of it. All merely illustrate the great principle of nature, that where power and need meet, a relation of mastery and subjection is inevitable,[1] and inures to the advantage of all concerned. No deliberate volition of man is necessary to this result. The more powerful rules even if he does not will it or seek it;[2] the needy is subject even if no one desires service from him and every one wishes him to be free.

The state, thus, is not different in character from the countless other relationships that make up the sub-

[1] ". . . dass da wo Macht und Bedürfniss zusammentreffen ein Verhältniss entsteht, kraft welchem der ersteren die Herrschaft, dem letzteren die Abhängigkeit oder Dienstbarkeit zu Theil wird, dass aber desswegen nicht minder der Gerechtigkeit ganz gemäss und zu beiderseitige Vortheil abgeschlossen ist." *Restauration*, I, 359.

[2] Thus the man of genius in art, literature or science will have followers, Haller observes, and his authority will be respected, even though he knows nothing of it.

stance of human society. It differs from them only in the degree of power and independence concerned. The ancient distinction between natural and civil or political society is baseless. For what is called civil society is but the highest grade of natural society. Nor is any distinction possible between the state and other associations on the basis of the end or purpose (*Zweck*) involved. Justice, human rights, general welfare, culture, *etc.*, that are ascribed by various thinkers to the state as its peculiar end, are in fact, Haller holds, the ends of many other forms of association as well. The truth is, he says, that states as such have no common end, but differ from one another as do other kinds of association. The individuals who constitute the state have certain aims that are common to all of them — subsistence, protection, *etc.*, — but these are not the aims of the state. It is a state by virtue of the power that makes its sovereign above such aims. Concisely defined, the state is a complete and perfected social union, existing for itself and through itself alone.[1]

As to the independence that makes a man or group of men the nucleus of such an association and the sovereign, it is nothing of an innate or indefeasible right. It is merely a gift of fortune (*Glücksgut*), and the highest of such gifts. It may be acquired by one's own strength and exertion, by contract or gift from other possessors, by happy chance (*zufälliges Glück*), or, as is most usual, by a combination of all three of these methods. It may be lost by any of the chances that history makes so familiar; for what, Haller asks, is

[1] *Cf. Restauration*, I, 463.

political history but the narrative of the acts and conditions through which individuals and corporations have acquired, maintained and lost again their complete independence? The important consideration is that the possession of political sovereignty by any particular person at any particular time is a matter of fact, and not of right in any moral sense.

As to the manner of using this supreme power, there is plenty of room for the discussion of right. Since the sovereign is such merely by reason of his power and independence, his conduct of the administration is merely the management of his own affairs, and cannot be legally (*Rechtlich*) called in question by any one. But like every individual the sovereign is morally bound so to manage his affairs as not to injure, but positively to promote, the rights of others. More specifically, his function is to satisfy the needs of his subjects, and not to increase those needs in number or intensity. Where such increase appears, there is tyranny. The sum of the whole matter is that the sovereign is bound only by the moral law, which Haller identifies with the law of nature and of God. Under this law political society exists for the amicable exchange of reciprocal benefits, and this end limits, in a moral sense, the authority of the ruler.[1] Haller's exposition of this doctrine offers nothing essentially different from what was commonplace in political philosophy for two thousand years before him.

Between the two possible kinds of state, monarchy and republic, there is no basis, in Haller's theory, for

[1] *Restauration*, I, 514.

a preference *a priori*. Each is a natural product of particular circumstances. History assures him that monarchy has been more common, more efficient and more durable, but he bases no absolute judgment as to abstract merit on this. Three species of monarchy are discoverable, he holds, in both experience and logic: the patrimonial (*Erb- und Grundherrliche*), the military, and the spiritual (*Geistliche*). The first is based on the possession of a great landed domain, the second on successful military leadership and conquest, the third on the promulgation and establishment of an intellectual, a moral, or particularly a religious dogma or creed. Usually a monarchy founded on the second or third principle drifts sooner or later into the first class.

Haller's long and systematic analysis of the organization, action, and principles of perpetuation (*Makrobiotic*, he terms the discussion of these principles) characteristic of each of these species, is a mass of corollaries derived very logically from the theory already described. All the acts and policies of the prince are to be judged like the acts and policies of any other individual in carrying on his private affairs. Thus, making war is but the exercise of the natural right of self-defense, and the troops of the prince are merely his hired or voluntary assistants. Compulsory service in the prince's army is wholly without warrant, according to Haller, and the practice of conscription is denounced as one of the most deplorable results of the revolutionary philosophy.[1] Again, the prince is the supreme law-maker, but by no means the sole law-maker.

[1] *Restauration*, II, 84 *et seq.*

He is a law-maker only as every man is a law-maker. For law, Haller argues, is but a binding expression of will, and whatever is just is binding; therefore, since every man may express his will, every such expression that is just is law.[1] The prince's law differs from the private man's only in the extent of the power that insures the enforcement. Likewise the judicial power (*Gerichtsbarkeit*) belongs to the prince only as it belongs to every man. It is but a phase of the natural duty to help another in the maintenance of his right. Finally, the revenue of a prince must on principle and as a rule be derived from his own property. Taxes may be imposed on serfs or on those vanquished in a just war; but the prince has no right *a priori* to take the property of his free subjects, and if circumstances make it imperative, for the good of both prince and subjects, that they should help him financially, it must be done through free grant by the subjects.[2]

A republic, in Haller's theory, differs from a monarchy only in that the power and independence constituting sovereignty are possessed by a corporate group rather than by an individual.[3] The republic is not preeminently or distinctively a product of nature. Men have no innate tendency to this species of corporation. In flat rejection of Burke's scornful dogma[4] that the state is not to be likened to a commercial or other utili-

[1] For the theory of law and legislation see *Restauration*, II, cap. 32.

[2] *Ibid.*, II, 317 *et seq.*

[3] "Von den Republiken oder den freien Communitäten," is the title of Haller's Zweiter Theil, constituting the sixth volume of the *Restauration*.

[4] *Supra*, p. 179.

tarian association, Haller holds that there is no essential difference between them. When a number of men, substantially equal in power and therefore naturally independent of one another, unite for the promotion of some common interest, and by virtue of their union and strength become independent of every other society or individual, there is a republic. The specific end for which the society is formed may be of any description, and is by no means, as some pseudo-philosophy pretends, necessarily the maintenance of justice. As a matter of experience the ends most usually sought by the members of a commonwealth are security against external foes, better food supplies, extension of commerce, increase of property, and the promotion of religion, science or art. These ends are of course the basis of numberless corporations that have not the character of a commonwealth. All that distinguishes the latter is the possession of power and resources enough to make it wholly independent.

We need not follow into details Haller's discussion of the republic. It is everywhere saturated with the mediaevalism that characterizes his treatment of the monarchy. But despite the backward look of his system, that makes it so much more a justification of the past than a forecast of the future, some of the most characteristic features of his thought have been very conspicuous in later political and social science. Thus the emphasis laid by him on the mechanical, as contrasted with the volitional, influences underlying political institutions suggests the later fashion of interpreting all state life in terms of economic analysis. His refusal to see any distinction in kind between the state and other forms of association places him in line with certain phases of sociological theory. His uncompromising hostility to the idealism that enveloped the concepts of politics in a metaphysical mist illustrates a type of thought that was to find noteworthy expression in the doctrines of Comte and of the English Utilitarians.

In leaving Haller it is not uninteresting to reflect that while he doubtless established his chief scientific thesis, namely, that political authority is natural rather than artificial, he at the same time furnished the revolutionists with a justification of their proceedings on his own principles. For it is very easy now to see — what was less obvious in Haller's day — that the net result of the transformations in Europe was the assumption by certain social classes of the authority that was naturally theirs by virtue of their superiority in moral, intellectual and economic power.

SELECT REFERENCES

Bluntschli, *Geschichte*, Kap. 16. Bonald, *Essai analytic*; *Législation primitive, Discours préliminaire*. Burke, Works, Vols. III, IV. Faguet, *Politiques et Moralistes*, pp. 1–121 (Bonald and Maistre). Haller, *Restauration*, Band I, Vorrede. Laski, Authority in the Modern State, chap. ii (Bonald). Maistre, *Considérations sur la France*, chap. vi; *Essai sur le principe générateur*. Morley, Miscellanies, II, pp. 257–335 (Maistre). Sybel, *Historische Zeitschrift*, Vol. I, Essay on Maistre.

CHAPTER VI

THE ENGLISH UTILITARIANS

1. *Progress of Social and Political Reform*

THE ideas that underlay the American and French revolutions at no time lacked sympathy and support in England. Opposition to every tendency toward increase of power in the monarch was the traditional policy of the aristocratic leaders who dominated Parliament, especially in the Whig party. Outside of the aristocratic circle, however, an insistent opinion developed in the last quarter of the eighteenth century that was adverse not only to royal power but also to the power of Parliament itself. A succession of agitators — John Wilkes, Horne Tooke and others — and a group of pamphleteers who were less conspicuous but not less thoughtful — Cartwright, Priestley, Price — voiced a feeling in the English middle class that the House of Commons was neither in its source nor in its action a representative of popular liberty. Before the outbreak of the French revolution this sentiment gained sufficient influence in the parties themselves to lead to a formal project for parliamentary reform. The project failed, and when the proceedings in France took on their extreme form it became impossible to make further progress in England in the desired direction.

Under the influence of the republican movement in France, however, an advanced radicalism gained many adherents across the channel in Great Britain. Thomas Paine and William Godwin were perhaps the most significant exponents of the radical dogmas. Of Paine's ideas we have already taken notice.[1] Godwin's attack on the whole doctrine of private property and political organization made less impression on his contemporaries than on the succeeding generations in which socialism and anarchism took form.[2] Yet his views, as well as Paine's, found many supporters in the non-political classes of England; and the demands among these classes for natural rights and a working popular sovereignty had to be repressed with such severity as to leave the radical movement practically paralyzed until the wars of the Napoleonic era were ended.

During this interval, however, the social transformations that were effected by the revolution in industrial method and organization brought a powerful support to the doctrines that had been in abeyance. The trades-union movement and a variety of demands for a wider realm of free activity among the lower classes of society became, after 1820, a manifest source of serious danger to the existing government. The industrial classes began to insist with dangerous vigor on the reform of Parliament that would give them some share of the power exercised by it. Demands for a readjustment of the electoral districts were accompanied by demands of a farther-reaching kind for great extension of the suffrage, for the secret ballot and for an immediate responsibility of members of Parliament to their

[1] *Supra*, p. 110. [2] *Infra*, chap. ix.

constituents. Some measure of concession to these demands was involved in the great reform bill of 1832. This bill was, however, a distinctively Whig measure and, therefore, lacked the quality of thoroughness and logical principle that was so antipathetic to Whig policy in general.

In the turmoil of agitation during the decade preceding the achievement of the reform but a single group of the agitators displayed a coherent and systematic body of principle. This was the group that clustered about Jeremy Bentham and recognized in his dogmas the core of a sound political system. Almost all the radicals who made the reform movement famous acknowledged some degree of relationship to Bentham's philosophy. Romilly and Brougham and John Cam Hobhouse and Sir Francis Burdett and William Cobbett all drew inspiration from that source. Their activity, however, was chiefly by way of partisan political propaganda and not through appeal to the reflective sense. Their support came from the unthinking classes very largely. The smaller group of men devoted themselves to a concerted effort for a coherent philosophical system that should supply the unassailable foundation for the practical measures proposed. This little group gave to political science the only distinctive contribution that was furnished by British thought until after the middle of the nineteenth century. Benthamite utilitarianism and individualism made for itself a place in English thought and in world philosophy of an importance that was out of all relation to the small number of thinkers who sustained it.

Bentham lived to see the substantial triumph of the movement for parliamentary reform. He died in the year of the success of the measure. Long before this he had seen the realization of many reforms that had been near to his heart in legal procedure and administration. After his death the radical doctrine that he had contributed so much to promote continued to disturb the serenity of the British political mind. The Chartist movement, with its far-reaching demands for democracy, was based on principles to which the Benthamite philosophy had given a firm foundation. The remodelling of municipal administration, the sweeping reform of the poor law, the abandonment of protectionism, and finally the great advance toward universal suffrage insured by the reform bill of 1867—all these were impregnated with the spirit of the utilitarian philosophy.

While these prodigious transformations in the social and political system of Great Britain were going on, the philosophical system that was associated with them lived its life and passed into a decline. It had taken its form through Bentham and James Mill; it practically lost form and all cohesion with the maturity of John Stuart Mill. Its influence can readily enough be traced in many leading aspects of political philosophy at the end of the nineteenth century, but here its principles are dissociated from one another and animate independently various systems of thought that would have been repellent to Bentham and the elder Mill. While it lasted, however, English utilitarianism was one of the most potent forces in the intellectual life of all Western Europe and of America as well.

2. *Jeremy Bentham*

When, upon the cessation of the long wars in 1815, the dormant program of political and social reform was vigorously revived, Bentham had been active in the field for forty years. Since 1776 he had maintained, through the widest extremes of favoring and of adverse conditions, a pressure for the adoption of new principles and new practices in government and law. The normal English suspicion of innovation had been, by the course of events in France, hardened into an impassable barrier, and Bentham's endless and ingenious propositions for change had been bootless. The post-bellum problems that enlisted British attention, however, brought his spirit and his philosophy into prominence and influence. A number of strong and eager minds received from him the impulse that shaped their contributions to various branches of social science. Among the notable names of this group are those of David Ricardo, James Mill, George Grote, John Austin and John Stuart Mill, who in ethics, economics, history and jurisprudence made a deep impression on the intellectual life of their time. Because the systems of all these men and many others were clearly rooted in that of Bentham, he became the symbol of a powerful current in the general movement of political philosophy.[1]

The starting-point of Bentham's political theory was his conviction that there was need of extensive

[1] All aspects of the Benthamite group and its thought receive full, just and sympathetic treatment in Sir Leslie Stephen's admirable work, *The English Utilitarians*. These volumes can never be superseded as an exposition of a remarkable episode in the history of the human intellect.

reforms in English law and judicial procedure. His father wished him to become an ornament of the legal profession and guided his education with that end in view. At the very entrance to the career of a practitioner, however, the young man balked. He found himself confronted with a mass of obscurities, fictions and formalities that were altogether revolting to him. The critical faculty was most conspicuous in his intellectual equipment, while respect for the antique and the historical *per se* was entirely lacking. Among the venerable principles and practices of conservative England's law and politics he became, therefore, a veritable bull in a china shop. His demands for the removal of obvious abuses in the substance and administration of the law were met by the usual conservative eulogies of the system. The Common Law, he was told, was sanctified by its ancient origin and centuries of growth and by the quality impressed upon it by the fine intellects of the jurists who loomed so large in the glories of the national tradition. To meddle with the structure that they had reared was to court disaster to the state.

For such views Bentham had no respect whatever. Neither the antiquity of an institution, nor the reputation of any man past or present who was responsible for it, carried any weight with him in its justification. The law of today must be shaped, he held, by the legislator of today in accordance with the needs of today; and the sole criterion of those needs must be the greatest good of the greatest number of men. Contribution to this good will justify the summary abrogation of a practice or a principle that originated a thousand years ago and has been approved by the best minds of thirty generations. Contribution to this good will justify the introduction by law of a practice or a principle that never till the present day entered the thought of man.

Thus Bentham banished from debate the whole apparatus of historical research and all the implications of sanctity that were involved in mere age and mystery. He did not deny that the long prevalence of a law or an institution might suggest that it was useful. There was nothing conclusive, however, about the suggestion.

The test of utility — of contribution to the greatest good of the greatest number — really proved to be, in last analysis, conformity to a body of principles worked out by Bentham himself as a complete and final guide for all who might be interested in morals and legislation. The philosopher's conviction that he had deduced from human nature itself the universal motives of men's actions and therefore the certain rules for regulating their social relations, was deep and unwavering. Legislation became in his mind merely the process of shaping these fundamental rules so as to fit with nicety the superficial peculiarities of a particular community; the substantial requirements for all communities were the same. On the basis of this comfortable conviction Bentham not only contributed, sometimes as a volunteer and sometimes on invitation, to the codification and revision of private law in a number of countries, but he even offered to furnish on demand to any people a code that he could guarantee as sound in every particular and certain to promote the true end of every government, the greatest good of the greatest number.[1]

It is not necessary here to enlarge upon the validity or otherwise of Bentham's ethical system, or upon the influence, undoubtedly very great, of his principles of lawmaking, especially codification, in the rising science of jurisprudence. For the substance of his distinctively political theory we have to go to one of the first of his multitudinous writings that was published, the *Fragment on Government*.[2] This work was written in 1776, when Bentham was but twenty-seven years old; yet, though he lived to be eighty-four and wrote to the very end, it was never superseded as a presentation of his fundamental principles of political science. The work was evoked by Blackstone's famous *Commentaries on the Laws of England*, wherein was embodied a complacent optimism that singularly excited Bentham. The commentator went deeply into the history of the law, and in the preoccupation of his antiquarian interest he from time to time gave eulogy and justification to customs and principles that had long lost the

[1] He was especially hopeful of securing the adoption of his ideas by the temporarily triumphant revolutionists in Spain and Portugal in the twenties of the nineteenth century, and his influence was not without importance both in these lands and in the newly independent republics of Spanish America. For the United States his admiration was great, and he conceived a project for assuring to the republic the advantages of a truly scientific body of law. In 1811 he made a formal proposal to President Madison that authority to frame a code should in some way be conferred upon the philosopher. For a full account of this queer incident, see Reeves, "Jeremy Bentham and American Jurisprudence," an address before the Indiana State Bar Association, 1906.

[2] In the *Works*, Vol. I. An excellent reprint of the first edition is that of F. C. Montague, whose Introduction is most valuable.

original ground for their existence and continued in use only, as Bentham believed, to enhance the dignity and emoluments of the bench and the bar. Blackstone's opening chapters, moreover, on law in general and the basis of legislation, embodied a feeble and incoherent collection of current ideas about the nature and origin of government [1] — ideas that ran counter to Bentham's whole conception of the subject. Accordingly the *Fragment* was produced primarily as an annihilating criticism of Blackstone. Incidentally to this feature the positive doctrines of Bentham were set forth in pretty complete and more or less systematic form.

As to the origin of political society, he practically disclaimed all interest in the subject. The distant past could furnish no light, he believed, to guide our reasoning on the rights and duties of the present. Even if it could be shown that deep in the bygone ages a formal contract bound all then living Englishmen in a social and political union, it would have no special bearing on the laws and constitution of today. Nor would such a contract, if regarded not as an historical fact but merely as a logical concept, explain any assertion of authority by government or any obligation of obedience on the part of any subject. Every form of a contract theory of the state is rejected by Bentham.[2] Contract, consent, agreement, furnish no basis for political rights and duties. The ultimate reason why men submit to the requirements of law and of government is,

[1] See above, p. 73.

[2] *Fragment*, chap. i, secs. xxxvi, *et seq.* Bentham expands, without modifying, the argument of Hume. *Cf. Political Theories from Luther to Montesquieu*, pp. 383–4.

not that they or their ancestors have promised to do so, but that it is for their interest to do so. In Bentham's own well-known phrase, men obey the laws because "the probable mischiefs of obedience are less than the probable mischiefs of disobedience." Governments exist because they are believed to promote the happiness of those who live under them.

The recognition of this simple and all-pervading motive of human action, a calculated self-interest, renders superfluous the historical guesses and the dialectical fictions by which philosophers of the contract school explain the difference between the natural and the political or civil state of man. Discard all such rubbish, Bentham says, and look at the simple facts of the case. Consider any group of men living in more or less intercourse with one another. If in this group there is on the part of some of the members a habit of paying obedience to other members, whether one or more in number, the group altogether constitutes a political society. If there is in the group no such habit of obedience, the group is a natural society. That is all there is of it.[1]

The libraries of disquisition on the state of nature, with its iniquities or its blessedness according to the

[1] *Fragment*, chap. i, sec. x: "When a number of persons (whom we may style *subjects*) are supposed to be in the *habit* of paying *obedience* to a person, or an assemblage of persons, of a known and certain description (whom we may call *governor* or *governors*), such persons altogether (*subjects* and *governors*) are said to be in a state of *political society*." Sec. xi: ". . . When a number of persons are supposed to be in the habit of *conversing* with each other, at the same time that they are not in any such habit as mentioned above, they are said to be in a state of *natural society*." Italics are Bentham's.

fancy of the writers; on the devious and complex process through which men emerged from the natural into the political state; and on the survival of rights and duties from the earlier in the later condition: — all these were banned to peremptory worthlessness by the Benthamite formula. The essence of a state was merely a habit of obedience. Such a dogma surely left no room for the history or the mystery which played so large a part in the political theory of the conservatives and the reactionaries.

Nor was Bentham's criticism less sweepingly destructive when directed toward the conceptions of law and rights that had been the stronghold of much of the revolutionary contention. Subjects who sought to throw off the habit of obedience so far as concerned a particular sovereign, could never cover their procedure with a legal warrant. To allege in justification of revolt the prescriptions of a law of nature and a body of rights and duties under that law, seemed to Bentham but quibbling with words. So vague and elusive an entity as "nature" he could never tolerate as a guide. Accordingly he set forth a conception and definition of law and rights and duties that effectually eliminated that confusing element. His ideas were fundamentally those that had been formulated by a no less acute English intelligence, Thomas Hobbes, two centuries before; but Bentham carried the common conceptions to a fruitful development and derived from them a distinction between politics and ethics that Hobbes would not admit, and further the substructure of a science of jurisprudence in which Hobbes had little or no interest.

A law, in Bentham's thought, is the expression of a will in the form of a command.[1] In a political society, that is law which is enjoined by the authority which the members of the society habitually obey. The making of laws is the characteristic function of this authority, which is the sovereign. Because law is the expression of a will, sovereignty can be predicated only of a being of which will can be predicated. Nature or reason or justice cannot be the supreme power in a state, because they cannot make law; God and man are the only forms of existence possessing will; therefore law in any precise sense must emanate from one of them. Thus divine law and human law are intelligible concepts; natural law and the law of reason are meaningless and wholly misleading. But divine law — the will of God — is not ascertainable with certainty; some human will, therefore, must in every instance be the abode of the supreme power in a political society.

How far the supreme power extends, and what are the rights and duties of the individual members of the society in respect to it, are questions that Bentham answers by the application of his utilitarian philosophy. The existence and the location of sovereignty are a matter of fact, and give no occasion for questions of right and duty. But given the existence of a sovereign, is the scope of his power without bounds? Can he legislate on every subject and to every effect whatever? Is there no line beyond which his prescripts are *ipso facto* void?

[1] *Fragment*, chap. iv, sec. xi, note. *Principles of Morals and Legislation*, at end, in *Works*, I, p. 151.

Bentham can see none. "The supreme governor's authority," he says, "though not infinite, must unavoidably, I think, unless where limited by express convention, be allowed to be indefinite."[1] The only conceivable restraint on the sovereign is his own judgment as to the probability of effective resistance by the subjects. And their attitude will always be determined in last instance by the calculation of their interests — by their comparison of the evils that will follow resistance with those that will follow obedience to the ruler's commands.

With this doctrine and its exposition and corollaries Bentham set himself in direct antagonism to the predominant philosophy of the revolutionary and reforming parties of his day, with whom he was in many respects wholly sympathetic. Their confidence in written constitutions as guarantees of rational government, and in the simplification of legislation in every respect, he shared and applauded. But bills of rights, limitations upon the power to amend the constitution, and all other devices for restricting the supreme authority, he regarded as unsound in theory and worthless in practice. They rested largely for justification, he said, upon the idea that the distinction between free and despotic governments depended on the greater or less degree of power possessed by the supreme authority of the state. In fact, the ultimate sovereigns in all states possess precisely the same unlimited and undefined power. Whether any particular government is considered free or despotic depends on a variety of cir-

[1] *Fragment*, chap. iv, sec. xxiii.

cumstances connected with the distribution and application of this power in its exercise.[1]

For the common declaration in constitutions that men have by nature rights that the sovereign authority must respect, Bentham felt great contempt. That it expresses any political truth or imposes any real barrier to the sweep of the supreme power, he demonstrates to be logically and actually inconceivable. His analysis of the conception of rights is clear and conclusive in this connection. A right, he explains, is a term without meaning, except when taken in connection with a duty. The two concepts are inseparable correlatives. A has a right only in so far as B and C and the rest of the alphabet have the duty of leaving him free to act in a certain way. But duty, in Bentham's philosophy, has no basis but interest. The duty of B and C to let A alone — to respect his right — has reality only when letting him alone will have consequences more agreeable to them than the consequences of molesting him; or, conversely stated, when violation of his right will bring greater evil upon them than recognition of it. The right can, therefore, be said to have actual existence only when the evil to follow its violation is definite and certain. This evil is the sanction of the right, and where the right is established by a law, the penalty

[1] For example, the manner in which the supreme power is distributed among the persons who collectively enjoy it; the degree of ease with which governors and governed may change roles; the extent to which the governors are bound to give reasons for their actions to the governed; the opportunities for complaint and opposition on the part of the governed, that is, the liberty of the press and of association. — *Fragment*, chap. iv, sec. xxiv.

which the law provides is the guarantee that the right is real.[1]

Bentham's assumptions and definitions may not always be approved; his doctrine that duty has no basis but self-interest has been as stoutly assailed in the nineteenth century A.D. as the same doctrine was assailed in Athens in the fourth century B.C. Nevertheless, the precision of his thinking confirmed in political theory conceptions and distinctions that have been of the utmost value in the clarification of the subject. Blackstone was not the only one of his generation to make a logical mess of it when discussing rights and duties. The whole philosophy of the revolution time is pervaded with unclearness and confusion about them. Bentham let into the situation a penetrating light.

Duties, he said, fall into three categories, according to the character of the sanction for the correlative rights. A political duty is determined by the penalty which a definitely known person, namely, a political superior, will inflict for the violation of certain rights. A religious duty is determined by the punishment to be inflicted by a definitely known being, namely, the Creator. The third species, a moral duty, depends upon circumstances hardly certain and definite enough to be called punishment, yet such as to create an unpleasant state of mind in the person concerned, by putting him

[1] *Fragment*, chap. v, sec. vi, note. For an elaborate attack upon the French Declaration of Rights, see Bentham's *Anarchical Fallacies*, in *Works*, Vol. II, p. 487. Sir Leslie Stephen's analysis of Bentham's doctrine is particularly just and illuminating. — *The English Utilitarians*, I, 289, *et seq.*

in disagreeable relations with that indefinite body of individuals known as the community in general.[1]

Taking rights in the same classification, Bentham contends that political discussion requires the nicest discrimination in the uses of the word. A legal right is a clear and intelligible expression. It means a faculty of action sanctioned by the will of a supreme lawmaker in a political society. A moral right is a clear and intelligible expression, though less free from ambiguity than the other. Its sanction is the opinion or feeling of a group of persons who cannot be precisely identified, but who nevertheless are able to make their collective or average will unmistakably manifest. A natural right, on the contrary, is an expression that has neither definite meaning nor any form of usefulness. Nature is a vague and undefinable entity. It may indeed be used as synonymous with God, in which sense it may serve a good purpose. In any other sense, however, it denotes something that cannot be thought of as endowed with will, and is therefore incapable of making law: or something that is clothed with human attributes only by most obvious metaphor, and is, therefore, to be ignored in all serious discussion of rights and duties. Like "law of nature," "natural rights" is a phrase that can contribute only confusion in a rational system of political science.

These definitions and distinctions, applied to the ultimate problems of political theory, give these conclusions. As against the supreme power in a political society the subjects cannot have a *legal* right of resist-

[1] *Fragment*, chap. v, esp. sec. vii, note.

ance or revolt. Their *legal* (or as Bentham generally calls it, their *political*) duty is unconditional obedience. A *moral* right and a moral duty to disobey and resist the supreme power is, on the other hand, the conditional attribute of every subject.

Looked at from the point of view of the sovereign there is neither legal right nor legal duty in respect to the subject. Moral rights and duties, however, are ascribable to the sovereign, first, in so far as the collective opinion of the sovereigns of the world — the so-called law of nations — is operative as a norm of conduct for governments; and second, in so far as the danger of resistance and revolt by the subjects sets a real, if indeterminate, control upon governmental procedure. Within the hazy limits imposed by these restrictions the hand of the sovereign is free. Its policies are determined and justified in last instance, not by their conformity to the prescriptions of a vague and conjectural law of nature, nor by the obscure terms of an imaginary contract, but by their utility, that is, by their fitness to promote the greatest happiness of the greatest number of the human beings affected by them.

Bentham's chief interest was in devising systems and methods of legislation that would surely conform to and serve this great end. His services to ethical and juristic science in connection with this work were of the utmost value. With sublime confidence in the infallibility of his judgment he formulated codes of international law, of constitutional law, of civil law, of criminal law, which, though failing of adoption by the denser-witted practical statesmen of the day, embodied, nevertheless, principles and suggestions that have not failed of fruitfulness in later generations. His distinctive field was, however, that of ethics and jurisprudence — what may be called the realm of the supra-political. His distinctions in the various species of law contributed decisively to the elimination of ethical and juristic conceptions from the domain of the science of the state. The complete separation of jurisprudence from political science he did not work out. He was too keenly concerned in various phases of practical reform to make a perfect job of his theory. The necessary advance in this direction was made by a disciple of Bentham — a less original and less picturesque, but hardly a less acute intelligence, John Austin.

3. *John Austin*

The distinctive work of Austin was that of more exact definition and more scientific arrangement of Bentham's principles in the field of jurisprudence. So far as this task touched upon political science the contribution of Austin is to be found in his well-known, if little read, lectures on "The Province of Jurisprudence Defined."[1] In these he seeks to mark out with the utmost possible precision the respective domains of law and ethics. Only by way of incident does he present noteworthy conceptions in the field that belongs properly to politics. His method is wholly *a priori* and he proceeds, like Bentham, entirely

[1] Under this title are included the first six lectures of the general course on *Jurisprudence* that makes up the great part of the two volumes of his published work. The six lectures are in Vol. 1, pp. 81–351.

by definition and deduction. Part at least of the improvement that is made on the master is due to the system and methods of the German jurists, whom Austin studied with care when preparing his work. Bentham somewhat ostentatiously despised the Germans.

The thesis to which Austin devotes his first interest is that jurisprudence as a science must be limited to the field of what he calls "positive law." His definition of law is substantially Bentham's: an expression of will by a determinate being that a certain course of conduct come to pass, failing which, an evil will come upon one who deviates from that course. Of law as thus conceived there can be but two species, divine and human; natural law is an ambiguous and misleading term, having definite connotation only when regarded as a kind of divine law. Human law falls into two classes: first, rules that are imposed by political superiors in independent societies, to use the phraseology of Austin, or in other terms, rules that are laid down by the sovereign in a state; second, rules set by men who are not political superiors, as, for example, by one sovereign to another or by parent to child. In this second class fall also those rules which are set merely by the opinion of an indeterminate body of men, such as the laws of fashion, the laws of honor, and very much of the mass of customs, understandings and conventions that are commonly referred to as constitutional and international law. This whole class receives from Austin the designation "positive morality," while "positive law" is restricted to the rules that emanate from the will of the sovereign. It is this latter species alone that in Austin's view should constitute, as I have said, the subject matter of the science of jurisprudence.

While we are not concerned with the fate of Austin's juristic doctrines, we may observe in passing that they failed to evoke enthusiastic approval from the class of thinkers for whom they were particularly devised. That was due, not to any lack of force and cogency in their presentation, but largely to the shock and repulsion which they produced in the circles of the old-fashioned and respectable jurisprudence. The adepts of the ancient system stood aghast to see Austin take the most venerated principles of the constitution and the law of nations, bundle them up with such low-bred imperatives as the laws of fashion and honor, deny them even the name of law, and mark them with the new-fangled and unintelligible label, "positive morality." Even at the present day staid and world-famed members of the Hague Tribunal will fidget at the bare mention of Austin, because by his classification their personal judgments about international relations are morality but not law.

Having developed his conception of positive law as the subject of jurisprudence, Austin sought to be equally explicit as to the source of this law. This brought him to his doctrine of sovereignty, which is his most influential contribution to political theory proper. Like Bentham, and in terms obviously suggested by the Benthamese formula, Austin defines sovereign and state (or, as he calls it, "independent political society") in a single sentence. The classic and familiar definition is this:

> If a *determinate* human superior, *not* in a habit of obedience to a like superior, receive *habitual* obedience from the *bulk* of a given society, that determinate superior is sovereign in that society, and the society (including the superior) is a society political and independent.[1]

There is *prima facie* an air of the utmost scientific precision and finality in this sentence. Austin himself made no claim of exaggerated efficacy for it in solving all the problems of politics. He was confident only that it was well adapted to the promotion of exactness in the field of jurisprudence. He pointed out that the words "habitual" and "bulk" are not terms of mathematical precision, but leave room for a large margin of uncertainty, so that his formula will not surely give an answer to the question as to whether a given society is to be classed as an independent political society.[2] But where the answer is clearly affirmative, the sovereign as defined must be regarded as the source of all the legal rules to which obedience is habitually given. So far as these rules are in the form of statutes, they are obviously the expression of the sovereign will. So far as they are contained in the judgments of the courts, they must be regarded as emanating from the sovereign through his judicial agent. So far as they are mere custom, they are willed by the sovereign in that he permits them to prevail, because what he per-

[1] *Jurisprudence*, Vol. I, p. 226. The development and defense of this definition constitute the subject matter of the whole of lecture vi, pp. 224–348.

[2] See the careful explanations on this point in *Jurisprudence*, Vol. I, pp. 233 *et seq.*

mits he commands, and they are *ipso facto* superseded the instant the sovereign will to that effect — that is, a positive law — is promulgated.

Austin's sovereign, thus, is absolute — above every restriction by law, free from all connection with legal rights and duties. Yet the Austinian conception gives no such effect of the overwhelming as the characterization of sovereignty which Blackstone, improving on Bolingbroke, put into his commentaries: "However they [the various forms of government] began, or by what right soever they subsist, there is and must be in all of them a supreme, irresistible, absolute, uncontrolled authority, in which the *jura summi imperii*, or the rights of sovereignty, reside."[1] This impressive aggregate of English adjectives, "topped off," as Bentham says, with "a piece of formidable Latinity," gives the idea that unlimited power is the necessary attribute of every state — that the conception of restriction in any respect, by any force or influence whatever, is incompatible with the conception of sovereignty. Such an interpretation of Blackstone's has been often carried over into the interpretation of Austin's definition, and the blending of the two has been responsible for much of the criticism of the Austinian doctrine.[2] That the sovereign must be in every state determinate, was unquestionably of the essence of Austin's definition. Adding to this the requirement that the sovereign must have power without limit in scope and vigor, the problem was presented of discovering in every state,

[1] *Commentaries*, I, 46. *Cf. supra*, p. 74.

[2] *Cf.* Henry Sumner Maine, *Early History of Institutions*, lect. xii.

as an indispensable condition of its being a state, a definite, countable or otherwise identifiable man or group of men, whose effective will was in last analysis the cause of all political phenomena. The effort to detect a sovereign of this awe-inspiring sort in such a political society as the United States, for instance, was naturally exhausting and unfruitful, and Austin has been made to bear the reproach of authorship of a worthless doctrine and theory of the state.

In reality Austin's sovereign, by the terms of the definition, was supreme only in respect to positive law. Austin never denied that other forces than positive law were operative in social life. He was not blind to the influence of custom, of habit, of what is called constitutional law and international law; but he denied to them the character of law and held merely that so far as social life was considered as determined by the will of a definite superior, there must be an end to the gradation of such superiors — a discoverable being whose will there was none above to overrule. To one who seeks the source of law and finds one will after another, in the hierarchy of governmental organs, superseded by a superior, the one which is not and cannot be superseded is the sovereign. Only in the legal, not at all in the moral or physical, sense could Blackstone's quartette of stirring adjectives be properly applied; only as maker of positive law is the sovereign supreme, irresistible, absolute, uncontrolled.[1]

[1] See Austin's explanation of his two classes of states, monarchy and aristocracy, I, 244, note: "The habitual independence which is one of the essentials of sovereignty, is merely habitual independence of laws imperative and proper. By laws which opinion

Austin, like Bentham, is at some pains to explain the application of their theory to the case of federal governments. In the *Fragment* Bentham, as we have seen, lays it down that the authority of the sovereign is without definite bounds "unless where limited by express convention."[1] This qualification he considers necessary in order to include the German, Swiss and Dutch systems of his day in the category of political societies. In such systems, he points out, the habit and disposition of obedience, which is the basis of sovereign power, may be present as to one kind of acts and absent as to another. Hence the governing person or persons may be supreme as to one kind of acts and not as to another, provided that the latter sort "be in its description distinguishable from every other." If an act in the field exempted by the convention is a clear and definite indication that the moment for resistance to the government has arrived, the limitation on the sovereign is manifest. Bentham's whole treatment of this point turns on the assumption that the partition set up against the intrusion of the government can be made perfectly distinct. He allows nothing for the possibilities of interpretation and construction. He thinks in the line of divided sovereignty, or sovereignty in spheres, that brought such bitter experience to the United States.

Austin, on the other hand, stands rigidly on the dogma that sovereignty is indivisible.[2] A group of political

imposes, every member of every society is habitually determined." See also the discussion of "the limits of sovereign power," I, 270.

[1] *Cf. supra*, p. 219.

[2] *Op. cit.*, I, 264, *et seq.*

societies associated under some form of governmental union will always prove on close inspection to fall into one of the two classes, a composite state, or a confederacy of states. The distinction is that in the composite state there may be detected a body possessing in respect to the whole group the attributes of sovereignty in the strictest sense; while in the confederacy sovereignty in the strict sense inheres in each member of the union. The United States is the only example given of the composite state, and Austin's solution of the problem of the location of sovereignty in the American system perfectly illustrates his theory. The solution is this:

> . . . the sovereignty of each of the states, and also of the larger state arising from the federal union, resides in the states' governments as forming one aggregate body: meaning by a state's government, not its ordinary legislature, but the body of its citizens which appoints its ordinary legislature, and which, the union apart, is properly sovereign therein.[1]

This solution well illustrates at once the acuteness of Austin's perception and the precision of his intellectual processes. He penetrates to the innermost recesses of the American constitutional system, with all its complexity, and brings to view the supreme legislator that his philosophy requires. Whether his analysis gives adequate weight to all the facts of the situation, is a question that has excited violent debate. Certainly those critics of Austin have ground for complaint who ask whether it is useful to hold that so incoherent a body as he refers to can properly be called "determi-

[1] *Op. cit.*, I, 268.

nate," or that "habitual obedience" scientifically characterizes the relation of a people to a supreme governor that formally enunciates its will only twice in a century. For the sovereign enacts positive law only by way of constitutional amendment, and no amendment was in fact made in the Constitution of the United States between 1803 and 1865, or again between 1870 and 1913. The far-reaching development of political institutions during those intervals can be ascribed to the will of the Austinian sovereign only by recourse to the convenient, if often overloaded principle, that what is permitted is commanded.

The character of Austin's philosophy in this respect is well revealed by his views on liberty.[1] Political or civil liberty he defines to be the freedom of action left or granted by a sovereign government to its own subjects. So far as concerns law in the proper sense, the sovereign is under no restriction as to widening or narrowing the bounds of liberty. Yet restrictions of an extra-legal kind may be, and in fact always are, operative in determining these bounds. The customs, habits and traditions of a people, the understandings and agreements that make up their domestic constitution and their foreign relations, and the principle of utility itself, demanding the ascertainment and enforcement of that which is for the maximum happiness — all play a part in defining the limits within which liberty is prescribed by law.

Austin has no patience with the enthusiasm that exaggerates the role of liberty in the scheme of politics.

[1] *Jurisprudence*, I, 281.

He is very severe in his comment on "the ignorant and bawling fanatics," as he sweetly calls them, "who stun you with their pother about liberty," and consider it the principal end for which government ought to exist. In his opinion "political or civil liberty is not more worthy of eulogy than political or legal restraint." Whether the one or the other is the more serviceable in promoting the end for which all government exists, is the criterion of preference.

This end is, in Austin's as in Bentham's opinion, the greatest possible advancement of human happiness. The quantitative measurement of happiness is based in the approved Benthamite manner upon elementary arithmetic. The aggregate happiness of mankind is the mere sum of the aggregates of happiness found in the various societies into which mankind is divided; and the happiness of each of these groups is the arithmetical sum of the quantities of happiness attaching to the individuals constituting the group. The difficulties in the way of any mathematical reckoning of human satisfactions were fully appreciated by the utilitarians, but they were ready with the claim that their method of calculus was no more vulnerable than any other and was decidedly simpler.

On one point of ever-growing importance Austin was emphatic with more than his usual ponderosity: the criterion of utility must be the maximum welfare, not of a particular community at the expense of the rest, but of all mankind. The patriotism that would disregard the interests and welfare of all but a single nation he stigmatizes as stupid and atrocious. Equally repugnant to sound philosophy, he maintains, is any theory that a single element of happiness, as for example property, is the paramount object of the sovereign's interest. On this ground he runs atilt with the economists of his day, who tended to regard the state as primarily, if not exclusively, an institution for promoting the accumulation of wealth.

Finally, we may note that Austin, in the manner of his sect, took especial pains to repudiate the most cherished dogmas of the continental and advanced English radicals as to natural rights and the social contract. He paid his compliments also to the popular doctrine that government depends for existence and for action on the consent of the governed. This is true, he said, only as a statement that the governed, for some reason or another, habitually obey the sovereign; it is not true in the sense that the bulk of the community prefer the existing form to every other form of government, and that if they did not, they could, without inconvenience, overthrow the existing. So far as men are controlled by reason the fundamental ground for the existence of a given government is that of its utility; that is, the subjects either are satisfied that it is promoting their welfare as well as possible, or are convinced that a change would on the whole produce more evils than it would remedy. Only highly developed and enlightened men, however, are controlled by reason in a thorough way. In undeveloped and unenlightened communities the grounds for the existence of a particular government are to be found in unreflecting custom or in irrational but immovable sentiment or prejudice.

4. *John Stuart Mill*

James Mill was born in 1773; John Stuart Mill, his son, died in 1873. The century covered by these two lives fixes very fairly the chronological bounds within which the Benthamite utilitarianism rose, flourished and passed away by absorption into later philosophic growths. James Mill was the disciple and intimate friend of Bentham in the post-Napoleonic days when the dogmas of the aged philosopher were at the height of their fame and influence. The younger Mill received during those days the abiding impressions of a precocious youth, from not only his conscientious father, but also his not less positive tutor, John Austin.

The practical politics of Great Britain during the twenties, thirties and forties of the nineteenth century involved on the domestic side the fiercely fought battles for Parliamentary, administrative and economic reforms, and on the foreign side the problems of effective sympathy with the movements for constitutional government on the Continent. It was a stirring epoch, and a philosopher who could present a rational theory of politics never lacked an audience or a subject. The elder Mill formulated in 1820 the utilitarian theory of government[1] in rigid conformity to Bentham's dogma. Forty years later the more talented son set forth a theory which, while faithful in most fundamentals to the dogma of the father, disclosed nevertheless in many features of the development a pliability that tells of the passing of the original Benthamism.

[1] See his *Essays on Government, etc.*, esp. the first essay.

The systematic expression of John Stuart Mill's political theory is to be found in his work *On Liberty* and that on *Representative Government.* When these were published, in 1859 and 1861 respectively, Mill had achieved great distinction as a philosopher and was, through his famous *Political Economy,* one of the most influential thinkers of the time. On all the chief questions of public interest and debate his vigorous pen had been busy, and his general political doctrine had thus been pretty fully revealed. The function of the two essays referred to was to throw into coherent and properly correlated form conceptions that had as yet lacked this manner of presentation.

Mill's political theory knew nothing of "the state" under that name. "Society" was the term by which men in their ultimate collective aspect were habitually designated, and "government" named indiscriminately the genus and the chief species of political institutions. This use of terms meant something. It pointed backward to the philosophical systems of the eighteenth-century physiocrats and economists, and to the just completed work of Auguste Comte wherein the foundations of sociology were well laid. At the same time it looked forward to the long debate in which the state, as a distinct concept of political science, was to be pushed by German theory to a position of preëminence over society, government and the individual as well.

Mill, true to his utilitarian training, holds that government is made by men for their social well-being. Human will and purpose always are operative in the life of political institutions. Though other factors enter into the problem, a government functions at any particular time only so far as the people whom it controls are willing to accept it, and are able, as well as willing, to do what is necessary to keep it going and fulfilling its end. "Social well-being," the end of government, Mill thinks of as meaning the possession of desirable qualities by a number of concrete human beings, not the perfect adjustment of the abstract relationships which make these men a society. Hence the fostering of such qualities — summed up as virtue and intelligence — is the first criterion of good government. Only second in importance is the character of the machinery itself, — the degree in which it is adapted to make the best use of such qualities as the individuals possess.[1]

Mill is not uniformly successful in avoiding recognition of anything in a social group beyond what is in the individuals composing it. His nominalism is less rigid than that of his father. More or less, perhaps, under the influence of Comte's spirit, he often ascribes to a community attributes that cannot be readily predicated of a mere sum of human beings. But Comte's famous criteria of the happy society, "order and progress," Mill flatly rejects. He objects to the terms on various acutely distinguished metaphysical grounds, but seems most influenced in rejecting them by their failure to involve adequate stress on the qualities of the concrete human beings who make up a society. These qualities must, as stated above, be the first consideration in any estimate of the social well-being. What must be the fundamental condition in the relation between the gov-

[1] *Representative Government*, chap. ii.

ernment and the individuals over whom it exercises authority, is set forth by Mill in his celebrated essay *On Liberty.*

The thesis of this essay is:

> . . . that the sole end for which mankind are warranted, individually or collectively, in interfering with the freedom of action of any of their number, is self-protection — that the only purpose for which power can be rightfully exercised over any member of a civilized community, against his will, is to prevent harm to others. His own good, either physical or moral, is not a sufficient warrant. [Chap. i.]

So far as his actions concern the interests of no person but himself, "advice, instruction, persuasion, and avoidance by other people if thought necessary by them for their own good, are the only measures by which society can justifiably express its dislike or disapprobation of his conduct."

Mill's development of this doctrine, on the basis of utility, broadly conceived, as the standard of right, embodies a complete and symmetrical philosophy of individualism and *laissez faire.* Freedom of thought and expression he defends with Miltonian fervor and more than Milton's acumen.[1] Individuality as an element of well-being he sustains with the reasoning that William von Humboldt had developed from different premises,[2] and he proclaims with the German that the repression of originality in thought and conduct, whether by law or by public opinion, is the essence of despotism and is fatal to the progress of the race. Mill manifests the intellectual man's apprehension of the

[1] *Political Theories from Luther to Montesquieu,* p. 244.

[2] *Supra,* p. 149.

tendency of the growing democracy. When individuality is repressed by the law of a monarch or an aristocracy, the evil of it may be counteracted by the custom of the masses; but when the masses make the law of repression, custom unites with legislation to confirm the evil. Mill sums up effectively all the claims to exemption from governmental interference that were to be found in the social and economic conditions of the middle of the nineteenth century. These conditions, especially as exemplified in Great Britain, were evidently the chief inspiration of his philosophy. When he proceeded to discuss the form of government that would best apply the basic principles of liberty as he conceived them, it was likewise to his own land that he went for his chief inspiration.

Ideally the best form of government Mill held to be that in which "the sovereignty, or supreme controlling power in the last resort, is vested in the entire aggregate of the community," every citizen not only having a voice in the expression of the sovereign will, but also, at least occasionally, an actual part in the discharge of some public function. The excellence of such a form of government was deduced from two principles: first, that any task is done best by those whose rights and interests are immediately involved; and second, that the faculties of men — moral, intellectual and practical — are most developed and improved when they are in active exercise.[1]

This form of government is no novelty in the speculations of political theory. It is the ideal of a host of

[1] *Representative Government*, chap. iii.

thinkers since, and including, Aristotle. It is indeed a form of state rather than of government, though Mill ignores such a distinction. He names it "representative government," and makes it conform strictly to its name by ascribing to it as its essential characteristic this:

> . . . that the whole people, or some numerous portion of them, exercise, through deputies periodically elected by themselves, the ultimate controlling power, which, in every constitution, must reside somewhere. This ultimate power they must possess in all its completeness. They must be masters, whenever they please, of all the operations of government.[1]

Mill thus commits himself to the dogma of a determinate and absolute human sovereign combining the peculiarly ill-assorted thoughts of Austin and Blackstone. There will always be, he says, a single depositary of ultimate power, whether by constitutional prescription or by unwritten custom.[2] In this position Mill separates himself from the French liberals like Guizot, who insisted that absolute power in any human depositary, even "society" or the "people," was incompatible with rational liberty, and that "the principle of the representative system is the destruction of all sovereignty of permanent right, that is to say, of all absolute power upon earth."[3]

Mill's obvious interest, however, is not at all the abstract foundations of political life, but the concrete

[1] *Representative Government*, chap. v.

[2] Note his phrase "the positive political morality of the country" — one of the rare instances in which Austin's terminology is adopted by a later writer.

[3] Guizot, *Representative Government*, Course II, lecture 18.

institutions in which it is manifested. Hence it is his discussion of various questions relating to the constitution and action of the representative body that gives chief significance to his work. The British Parliament is always in his mind as the typical instance of such bodies, and the current propositions for reform of that Parliament may be detected at every turn in his thought.

The proper functions of the representative body as he describes them are very much like those assigned by Aristotle to the *ecclesia* in the city state, that is, not administration or even legislation, but a general scrutiny and censorship over the officers on whom the responsibility for these functions immediately falls. The parliament should watch and control the government, insure the publicity of its acts, compel their justification, and, when the men constituting the government contravene "the deliberate sense of the nation," expel them from office and "either expressly or virtually appoint their successors."[1]

That this system of government has its weaknesses, Mill freely admits. The most dangerous of them he thinks is the exposure to the unjust domination of the numerical majority. An inevitable tendency of popular government toward "collective mediocrity" enhances the peril from this source, so that power gravitates surely toward the less intelligent classes of the people. To counteract this Mill believes that recourse must be had to a system of proportional representation through which a minority of the electors may secure a number of members corresponding to their numerical

[1] *Representative Government*, chap. v.

strength. Thus the evils of extending the suffrage would be minimized, and the instructed minority would have a share in the government that would make always for progress. Under such a system the able man would be sure of coming to the position where his ability would tell for the common good, instead of remaining submerged beneath the surge of the mediocre and worse.[1]

Other doctrines of Mill touching the suffrage confirm the very qualified character of his radicalism. The right to vote should be extended to women, but should always be limited, regardless of sex, to those whose attainments in culture should have reached through reading and writing and the rule of three. Plural voting should assure a proportionate weight to the superior intelligence. Finally, voting should be public, not secret, save when some peculiar circumstance dictates the contrary. The secret vote, he argues, creates and strengthens the idea that the suffrage is a personal right rather than a public trust — that it may be used for the voter's own interest rather than with a primary view to the public interest. "If it is a right," Mill asks, "if it belongs to the voter for his own sake, on what ground can we blame him for selling it, or using it to recommend himself to anyone whom it is his interest to please?"[2]

Such questions and discussions illustrate the practical bearing of Mill's theory in this later stage. The Reform Act of 1867 was already in debate and it furnished the basis of his argument. On the practical issues of the times he was a liberal rather than a radical.

[1] *Representative Government*, chap. vii. [2] *Ibid.*, chap. x.

His speculative doctrine remained immovably, however, that of his early training. Truth and righteousness in society and government were discoverable only through the process of logical deduction from the utilitarian dogmas as to the nature and end of man. That the history and conscious experience of the race might embody some aspects of political truth that escaped the sweep of the Benthamite system, was a proposition that made no appeal to Mill. Before his death, however, Darwin's epoch-making treatise was producing a great transformation in the manner of men's thinking; Herbert Spencer and Henry Sumner Maine had announced their first discoveries of profound social and legal truth in the lives of the most primitive peoples; Freeman and Stubbs were inspiring the search for the origins of English liberty among the institutions of the Anglo-Saxons; the historical method began to dominate the whole intellectual attitude of both British and Continental thinkers; and with these developments the whole utilitarian system went into eclipse. For a generation after Mill's death the primary interest of political philosophy was to explain political institutions not in their being but in their becoming.

5. *Conclusion*

Whether we do or do not approve of utilitarianism as an ethical system, we get a sense of refreshment on turning from the political theory of the American and French revolutionary school to that of Bentham and Austin. There is an impression, initially at least, of contact with concrete realities instead of remote or intangible abstractions. Thus the state of nature, the law of nature, the social contract — all seem, when presented to view by the revolutionary theorists, historically far-distant and dim, or logically beyond the ready reach of the average mind. But when Bentham says that the social contract is a myth, that the law of nature is merely a state of mind on the part of the person who speaks of it, and that the state of nature is nothing more occult or remote than the condition of a group of persons in the habit of conversing with one another, the entrance to political science seems open to all.

The purpose to give simplicity and precision to political terms was always strongly present in Bentham and Austin, and their success was notable — perhaps too great. Compare their definitions with the pale, elusive, unsubstantial concepts which the German idealists evoked from the metaphysical deeps and clothed with the names and attributes of state and society and sovereignty and government. Hegel, for example, defined, or described, the state as "the realization of the social-ethical idea — the social-ethical spirit as the revealed self-perceived substantial will that thinks and knows itself." Such a collection of words, if it meant anything to anybody, certainly meant nothing to the average man, and served only to involve political ideas in confusion and mystery. Any such result it was the particular function of the utilitarians always to resist. To Fichte, following Rousseau, the essence of the state was will; to others it was personality; to others it was organism; to others it was a sacred, inscrutable effluence of God. What hardihood was required of him who sought an intimate knowledge of things political, the mere enumeration of these conceptions makes comprehensible.

Then come Bentham and his utilitarians with the frank assurance that the essence of the state is merely a habit — the habit of obedience. A political society, they say, is nothing more or less than a group of living human beings, actuated by motives that are familiar in the experience of everybody. Its actions are determined, not by agreements or compacts made by past generations or conceived to have been made unconsciously by the present, but, like all other human actions, by the consideration of the pleasure and pain, the happiness and woe, of living individuals. All institutions, traditions, customs and ceremonies, of whatever antiquity, dignity or good repute, are worse than useless unless they promote directly and immediately the greatest happiness of the greatest number of men. When in the place of the abstractions, fancies and mysteries of the idealists and the obscurantists, these simple and winning propositions are presented, the inevitable reaction from the hearer is that of approval and acceptance.

Historically the Benthamite and Austinian theory fills a large place in political philosophy. It has passed, however, the high tide of its influence. Its ethical formula has proved practically no more fruitful than others, and distinctly less available as against the cynical; for there has become inseparably connected with the lofty phrase, the greatest good of the greatest number, the scoffer's supplement: "and the greatest number is number one." Its dogmas as to law and sovereignty have contributed very much to the clarification of a complex situation. Yet it is impossible for any but the strongest intellects today to stem the current of usage that deliberately includes under the name law many social imperatives other than the will of a political superior. The Austinian sovereignty has lost the plenitude of its power. As announced by its discoverer, it was the determinate human superior to which habitual obedience was given in every community worthy of the name of independent political society. For half a century the most acute speculators in things political sought with meticulous diligence to isolate and put on view such a sovereign in each of the leading states of the world. Outside of Great Britain, with its omnipotent Parliament, the search was generally in vain. So the Austinian sovereignty was ignominiously decorated with a commonplace adjective, and as "legal" sovereignty became the partner, if not the inferior, of a newly discovered entity, the "political" sovereign.[1]

Finally, the utilitarian theory of the state failed of a sure grip on the thinking world through the intensity of what the medievals would have called its nominalism. This was a defect of its most significant quality. In the hatred of vagueness and abstractions Bentham and Austin rejected everything that failed of the most literal participation in the life of a human individual. The happiness which was the goal of their philosophy must be reckoned not in any terms of generality; it must be the mathematical sum of the emotions ex-

[1] Dicey, *Law of the Constitution*, pp. 66 *et seq.* Ritchie, *Darwin and Hegel*, p. 238.

perienced by a definite number of actual men. Sovereignty must inhere in a determinate man or group of men, that is, in case of a group, a number of individuals every one of whom could be separately identified and every one of whom exercised a will in such a way that the algebraic sum of their wills would be the will of the sovereign, or law. Political society itself, or the state, must be thought of only as an aggregate of individuals. And the attributes of this aggregate could be nothing but the totality of the attributes of the individuals.

It is easy to understand how useful such ideas were in correcting the vagueness and mysticism of Burke and Hegel and Maistre; but it is no less easy to understand how incomplete the system was which refused to recognize that a social group of men possesses attributes distinct from those of its component members and lives a life that is other than theirs. Though group psychology is full of pitfalls for the unwary, a theory of the state that ignores it is an inadequate thing. Bentham and Austin and Mill in fact never reached a theory of the state. The limit of their political science was, in terms of a distinction that also was ignored or unnoticed by them, a theory not of the state, but of government.

SELECT REFERENCES

Austin, Jurisprudence, lect. vi. Bentham, Fragment on Government, especially chaps. i, iv, v; "Anarchical Fallacies," in Works, Vol. II. Dicey, Law of the Constitution, pp. 64–79. Lewis, Use and Abuse of Political Terms, secs. iv, v, xii. Maine, Early History of Institutions, lects. xii, xiii. Mill, James, Essays on Government, *etc.*, pp. 3–32. Mill, John Stuart, On Liberty, chaps. iii, iv; Representative Government, chaps. iii, v. Ritchie, Darwin and Hegel, pp. 227–264. Stephen, The English Utilitarians, Vol. I, pp. 130–136, 307 *et seq.;* Vol. II, pp. 74–97; Vol. III, chap. iv.

CHAPTER VII

THEORIES OF CONSTITUTIONAL GOVERNMENT

1. *The Struggle for Constitutions on the Continent*

WHILE Great Britain worked out in comparative calm the adaptation of her political system to the needs of the nineteenth century, progress in the same direction in the rest of Europe was attended with a long series of convulsions. From the fall of Napoleon's empire for full two-thirds of a century agitation was continuous and wars were not infrequent for the realization on the Continent of political ideas that had been made prominent by the French Revolution. Until the middle of the century the history of the period is punctuated with insurrections; after 1850, the type of disturbance changes to international war.

Insurrection made its first imposing appearance in the early twenties, when the Carbonari and the Free Masons rose in Italy and Spain respectively, and temporarily converted Bourbon despotisms into a semblance of constitutional governments. At the same time Portugal went through a similar experience, and the Greeks won the interest and sympathy of Christendom by throwing off the yoke of the Sultan.

Before the widespread ferment attending these movements had subsided a more terrifying shock was given to conservatism by the reappearance of revolution in France. In July, 1830, the Bourbon Charles X was driven from the throne and the Orleanist Louis Philippe was put in his place. All Europe was filled with unrest and alarm lest these events should be the prelude to such developments as had followed the uprising against the brother of Charles in 1789. Only at two widely separated centers, however, were there serious consequences. Poland rose against the Czar and was ruthlessly crushed back into subjection; the Belgians broke away from the connection with the Dutch that had been arranged by the great powers at Vienna, and were assisted by these same powers to set up an independent neutralized monarchy.

After the turmoil of these affairs there was a fretful interval of peace. Then came the most violent of all the insurrectionary convulsions, that of 1848. France was again the first to set up the standard of revolt, and she was easily first in the unexpectedness of the outcome. None would have predicted when the insurrection began that the French government was about to pass from constitutional monarchy to republic and from that, within four years, to a second Napoleonic empire. Central Europe on this occasion furnished tumults that in fervor and complexity fairly rivalled those in France. All the German and all the Italian peoples were aflame with political passion. Berlin and Vienna and Rome were the scenes of bloody conflicts. At Frankfort a famous assembly of Germans labored long but futilely on the project of uniting Germany under a constitutional government. At Buda-Pesth a short-lived independence of the Hapsburger cheered the hopes and stimulated the florid eloquence of the Magyars. On every side it seemed as if the old order was finally destroyed. But when after two tempestuous years the tumult ceased, the Hapsburger and the Hohenzollern ruled their dominions and their neighbors as before, and on the face of things Central and Southern Europe showed little change.

Beneath the surface, however, a transformation had been effected that was readily perceived when trouble again appeared among the nations. Not internal but international conflicts assumed the chief place in European politics, and the projects of the warring powers were in an ever-increasing measure determined by considerations of national growth and consciousness. The operation of this influence is not hard to discern in the Crimean War and in the Italian War of 1859; in the great Bismarckian conflicts of 1866 and 1870 the consolidation of German national unity was the avowed end and the most efficient instrument of the triumphant Prussian policy. Nor was the notion of nationality lacking to the Russo-Turkish War of 1877–78; for Serb and Bulgar received through this war the birthright of substantial independence.

Looked at from the point of view of political philosophy, the sixty-five years (1815–1880) of strenuous statecraft just surveyed shows three bodies of doctrine occupying successively the chief place in the current speculation. The first was constitutionalism, which dominated thought till the middle of the century. The second was nationalism, which reached the climax of its sway over men's minds in the sixties. The third was socialism, which was on the high road to universal absorption of philosophy when the period closed. It is the purpose of the present chapter to set forth the salient features of the doctrines that accompanied the spread of constitutional government throughout Western and Central Europe.

Despite the strong reactionary and obscurantist influence manifested in the Holy Alliance, the governments actually organized in the states whose monarchs were restored by the Congress of Vienna, furnished abundant evidence that the ideas of the revolution had not lost all their force. Especially conspicuous was the idea that some kind of constitution — of fundamental law, written or unwritten — was of the essence of a rational and workable system. Various practical conditions[1] confirmed the old tendency to regard a formal written document as in the only full and precise sense a constitution. Hence the demand for some such well-defined legal basis for the government, whether monarchic, aristocratic or democratic, became the central feature in the program of the Liberal party in every state. Concession to this demand went steadily on among the princes of the Continent, strongly resisted only by Austria, Russia and Prussia. After the crisis of 1848 the Hohenzollern and later the Hapsburger gave way, and by 1880 practically every Christian state of the Continent save Russia was governed under a written constitution.

[1] Among them the fact that where French dominion, after long sway, was destroyed and a sweeping reorganization was necessary, the restored princes were almost compelled to formulate the principles that were to characterize their government, in order to save their subjects from hopeless confusion and anarchy.

During the agitations and conflicts that attended the progress to this end, theoretical debate developed new and striking doctrines only as to the content, not as to the desirability of the written code. There was the greatest diversity among the actual constitutions as to the organization and action of the governments. In every state there was continuous strife between parties devoted to the application of liberal and conservative interpretations respectively to the fundamental law, or to the expansion of it in the sense of their interests. As to the essential requirements of constitutional government, theory was practically unanimous in holding that there must be some guarantee of rights to the individual and some reciprocal check and balance among the legislative, executive and judicial powers. It was further held by all but the ultra-conservatives that rational government required the participation of some form of deliberative assembly, representing in some way the body of the population. All these requirements had been understood and met in France in 1789 and the following years, but the swift progress of those years into anarchy remained a potent warning to the Liberals of the next generation and interposed a barrier for decades against every suggestion of republicanism. Hence the chief problem of those who speculated on the theory of constitutional government was to find a safe and useful niche in the system for the monarch.

Thus until after 1848 the theories of the constitutional state, *Rechtsstaat*, as the Germans called it, were largely concerned with the effort to reconcile the functions of a representative assembly with those of a hereditary monarch, to insure the liberty of the subject individual against the historical and traditional omnipotence of the reigning individual, and to partition sovereignty neatly between the prince and the people or banish the troublesome concept from the ken of philosophy.

2. *Types of the Realized Constitutions*

The concrete provisions of the constitutions on certain fundamental points furnish a clear revelation of the theory that was prevalent. What is contained in the codes themselves as to the origin of their prescriptions and the power to modify them, as to the relation of the constitution to ordinary legislation, as to the part of the prince in the making and the execution of laws — constitutes the most useful path of approach to the speculative doctrines of the time.

France led off, as we have seen, in the promulgation of a *Charte Constitutionelle* by Louis XVIII at his restoration in 1814. So far as this document itself furnished evidence, the authority on which it was based was the will of the monarch. To withdraw it or to make changes in it of any kind whatever, seemed equally in his discretion. He was, finally, the definitive interpreter of its provisions in any doubt as to their meaning or operation. Under this last principle the clause giving the king the ordinance power was construed by Charles X, in 1830, as a warrant for royal decrees setting aside certain statutes and contravening the Charter itself. The result was the revolution that put Louis Philippe on the throne. A revision of the

Charter was effected in connection with this event, and the phraseology of the instrument, like the proceedings by which the revolution was effected, disposed finally of the idea that the will of the monarch was the basis of the constitution, and gave most support to the doctrine that the fundamental law rested upon a compact between the king and the elected representatives of the people. To this system pertain those famous specimens of Gallic phrase-making — "A throne surrounded by republican institutions" and "The king reigns but he does not govern." The constitution was no more successful than these ingenious party formulas in giving precision to the royal function. The politics of the July monarchy turned always on the critical question whether the superior power in the state should gravitate to the king or to the elected representatives of the people.

In many of the lesser states of Europe the course of events was much like that in France. Few princes, however, had as much success as Louis XVIII in imposing on their subjects constitutions of exclusively royal origin. In most cases the fundamental law took shape as the result of a formal agreement between monarch and estates-general, and was treated by all parties as beyond amendment save by consent of all who were concerned in its establishment. As the old estates-general was superseded in the new constitution by the bicameral legislature, this organ became the coördinate factor with the monarch in the guardianship of the supreme law. Formal modifications of the constitution required the joint action of parliament and crown; but a strong and resolute prince rarely failed to impress upon the established system, by interpretation and administrative practice, the principles that favored his own particular policies. The written constitutions of the nineteenth century proved little more effective than the unwritten law and custom of England in the seventeenth for the speedy and final elimination of the royal prerogative from the high places of authority.

A particularly good illustration of this is to be found in the early history of Prussia under the constitution of 1850.[1] This instrument, formulated by royal authority in agreement with representative bodies, was promulgated by Frederick William IV as fundamental law for the state. It embodied guarantees of individual rights on a generous scale, and it assigned an important part in legislation to a chamber that was in some measure representative of the people. Both the terms of the constitution, however, and the interpretation that was at once adopted in practice maintained for the monarch a scope of authority that left no room for the intrusion of democracy, or for the transformation of the government from the royal to the parliamentary type. The principle of separation of powers, with check and balance in the interest of popular liberty, received no recognition. To the king was ascribed the whole executive power, the controlling influence in the legislative power, and, moreover, the broad authority to issue ordinances for the execution of the laws.

In general the government in Prussia under the

[1] English translation by Professor J. H. Robinson in *Annals of the American Academy of Political and Social Science*, Vol. V, Supplement.

constitution continued to be, as before, a government by the king, subject only to the new condition that in matters of lawmaking he would act in conjunction with the chambers. How little this restriction meant when a critical issue arose was revealed in 1862 when Bismarck became the king's chief minister. It was explicitly laid down in the constitution that the revenues and expenditures of the state should be determined annually by the budget, which must be voted as law.[1] For four years, however, during which the chambers would not agree on any budget, the government administered the finances according to its unrestricted will. Certain grounds for this action were found in the constitution, though Bismarck afterwards admitted that they were without serious value. What really enabled him to carry through his policy against the violent opposition of the Liberal party was the steadfast assertion of the doctrine that the responsibility for the conduct of the government in Prussia was in last analysis in the king, and that he must do his duty, in conformity with the constitution if possible, otherwise without reference to it.[2]

[1] Article 100 of the constitution ran as follows: "Taxes and contributions to the public treasury shall be collected only insofar as they shall have been included in the budget, or authorized by special laws."

[2] The technical question was, what should be done when the two houses could not agree on a measure indispensable to the existence of the government. The upper house of the legislature was controlled by the ministry, and could thus readily be made the means for effecting a disagreement with the more popular chamber. Bismarck, having created this situation, took the high ground that the king must save the state from the anarchy threatened by the failure of the chambers to perform their duty.

In addition to this dogma of the general residuary power in the king the monarchic principle was sustained in Prussia and elsewhere by a special theory of the nature of law and legislation that was developed by the jurists of the public law. The common assumption that the participation of the chambers in legislation implied that their function in the matter was equal or superior in importance to that of the prince was declared to be erroneous. A dual process is involved, so the argument ran, in what is commonly spoken of as law-making. First the content of an act of will is determined; second, the will is expressed in the form of a command. In only the first process do the chambers take part. They aid by their deliberations in fixing the content of the future law. But when their proceedings are entirely completed, the result is by no means law. It still lacks the essential element — the command that subjects conform to the indicated rule or be punished. This final and decisive element it is the function of the king exclusively to supply, through the performance of his duty to promulgate the laws. Only through this royal act is law technically "made." So long as this ultimate act remains the function of the monarch, it is idle to speak of sovereignty as resting anywhere but in him.[1]

Closely associated with this support of the monarchical principle was the distinction carefully worked out between statute and ordinance. So far as the prince was

[1] For a clear exposition of this doctrine, which was long conspicuous in continental public law, see Jellinek, *Gesetz und Verordnung*, p. 312 *et seq.*

formally vested with the executive power, his right to issue commands that were incidental to the execution of the laws was conceded in all constitutions. But in practice the administration of public business in every governmental system required frequent acts of authority that could not be thought of as related to any specific expression of legislative will. Where constitution or statute set definite bounds to such acts, the ordinance power ceased; but within this limit there was room for the assertion of a degree of power that gave great support to the theory of monarchy. Charles X of France lost his throne, as has been stated, through an attempt so to extend the ordinance power reserved to him by the constitution as to justify the contravention of constitution and law. In the amended constitution under which Louis Philippe assumed the crown it was specifically provided that the power to issue ordinances should not extend to suspending the laws or dispensing with their execution. This principle was incorporated in the widely influential Belgian constitution of 1830, through which it was ultimately passed on into the public law of many German states.[1]

All the forms of doctrine devised for the support of the monarchic principle were animated by a purpose to assail at one point or another the dogma of the separation of powers. This dogma was the stronghold of popular sovereignty. Not by logical necessity, but by revolutionary history and tradition, Montesquieu's famous classification and distribution of the functions of government had become the distinctive attribute of

[1] Jellinek, *Gesetz und Verordnung*, p. 99.

liberal constitutionalism. A king thus was held to be, like the legislative chambers and the courts, one of the three agencies for carrying into effect the will of the sovereign people. Against this idea the conservative lawyers invoked, as we have just seen, the testimony of both history and the working of the constitutions themselves. Speculative philosophy came also to the front in the same cause with criticism that played havoc with the very foundations of the whole doctrine. It was declared to be incomplete and otherwise defective in its analysis of the functions of government, and confused in its distribution of functions among the various organs. The upshot of all the criticism, however, tended to be the demonstration that the chief practical weakness of the doctrine was the failure to make perfectly clear the necessity of the monarchic element. An ingenious effort to reformulate the familiar theory and make it serviceable alike for liberals and for monarchists was the leading feature of a philosophy that had some vogue in France at the time of the Bourbon restoration.

3. *Benjamin Constant: His Theory of the Royal Power*

Benjamin Constant, 1767–1830, was one of the most influential writers of the French Liberal school in the last two decades of his life. The basis of his doctrines was the sovereignty of the people. This he developed, however, rather in the general spirit of Montesquieu than in the spirit of Rousseau. He contraverted forcefully the dogma of an absolute sovereignty anywhere. Neither in any individual nor in any class nor in society as a whole, he held, could there be a right to the unqualified exercise of its will. Like Locke and Montesquieu, he would recognize no authority on earth as without limits — "neither that of the people nor that of the men who claim to be its representatives nor that of kings, by whatever title they reign, nor that of law. . . ."[1]

Constant's sympathy with the spirit of the English system led him to the formulation of a somewhat novel and striking doctrine as to the royal power. His idea was obviously derived from the working of the British constitution in his own day as distinguished from the operation of it which had been responsible for Montesquieu's view. According to Constant, the three powers enumerated by Montesquieu and recognized in most written constitutions were not exhaustive of the functions of normal government. From the experience of France, in particular, he concluded that even in republican government the old analysis was inadequate, while for constitutional monarchy there were discernible five species of power, each of which should be properly vested in a special organ. The five that he enumerates are these: the royal power, the executive power, the power that represents permanence, the power that represents opinion, and the judicial power. Of these, the executive power belongs to the ministers, the judicial power to the courts, the power representing permanence to a hereditary assembly, and the power representing opinion to an elective assembly. Above them all stands the royal power, whose characteristic function

[1] Constant, *Politique Constitutionelle*, Vol. I, p. 13.

it is to regulate and harmonize the movements of the four, to the end that coöperation rather than reciprocal obstruction may prevail among them.

It had been a common and a troublesome criticism of Montesquieu's doctrine that in operation it tended inevitably either on the one hand to deadlock or on the other hand to the clear predominance of one of the powers over the others. Constant's doctrine aimed to meet both these tendencies by ascribing to the royal power the single function of maintaining each of the others in its proper place and thus preserving the governmental machine in equilibrium.[1]

Constant is interesting and ingenious in illustrating from history the serious consequences that resulted from a failure to develop the balancing influence. The constitutional monarchy as found actually in the England of his day seems to him to solve the great problem for which before no solution was attainable. The English king embodies a neutral and intermediary power which is distinct from the executive power. This distinction between the royal and the executive, that is, between the king and the ministry, is the most conspicuous feature of Constant's doctrine. While the old defenders of monarchy saw in this distinction merely a purpose of reducing the monarch to a nullity, Constant made it the means of elevating the monarch to a position of the most serious significance in the government. The trend of his argument was to put the control of the ministry wholly in the king. The greatly mooted point as to whether the monarch should be obliged to dismiss

[1] *Op. cit.*, Vol. I, chap. ii.

ministers that were not acceptable to the representative body, was left more or less in the background. Constant pointed out with special zeal the importance of an unfettered discretion in the monarch in respect to his ministers.

> The executive power [that is, the ministry] is deposed without being prosecuted. The king has no occasion to convict his ministers of an error, of a crime or of any guilty undertaking in order to dismiss them. He dismisses them without punishing them. Thus all that is necessary happens without anything that is unjust; and, as always results, this method, because it is just, is also useful from another point of view. It is a great vice in any constitution to leave to powerful men only the alternative of keeping their power or going to the scaffold.[1]

The effort of Constant to find a logical justification for the monarch by considering him an organ of government rather than the sovereign of the state, was quite characteristic of the desires of thinking men in those days of transition from monarchic to popular sovereignty. His spirit was the spirit that dominated both France and England in the days of the July monarchy. It fell short, however, of successful opposition to the growing force of democratic sentiment. The hereditary principle was always a stumbling block to those who sought to give to the monarch a serious function in government, while at the other extreme the demand for universal suffrage was the element of weakness in the cause of undiluted popular government. The trend of things, however, was steadily toward democracy.

[1] *Op. cit.*, Vol. I, p. 23.

4. *Guizot, the Doctrinaire*

This admirable representative of French culture in the first half of the nineteenth century was more distinguished in historical than in political science, and in the practical than the theoretical aspects of government. During the decade of the twenties his lectures at Paris on the origin of representative institutions in Europe gave him a prominent place in the rising group of national historians. Devoted with all his soul to the July monarchy, he became the mainstay of Louis Philippe's government, and as prime minister bore the responsibility for its downfall in 1848. Exile in England brought about a renewal of his researches in history, enriched by the teachings of a highly instructive career in statesmanship. His lectures on the origin of representative government were, after careful revision, given to the public. These, with his famous course on the general history of civilization in Europe, fixed his reputation for scholarship and literary power. At several points in his historical narrative he turned aside for philosophical reflection, and it is from these digressions,[1] colored as they are by the teachings of his dramatic public career, that we are able to derive the fundamentals of his doctrine as to representative government.

Like Benjamin Constant, Guizot rejected the concept sovereignty as an element in rational political theory. To him the term meant, if it meant anything, an absolute right of making law for a social group of human beings — an absolute dominion of a human will over

[1] These are to be found chiefly in *Representative Government*, Pt. I, lects. vi–viii; Pt. II, lects. x, xv–xviii.

other human wills. Such dominion was to him merely the essence of tyranny, against which history showed that society in all its grades and forms had always protested. This universal protest sufficed to satisfy him that the ascription of absolute power to human beings, whether one or many or all, "is an iniquitous lie." Not will, but the instinctive sense of justice and reason that dwells in every human spirit, must be the ultimate basis of political obligation.

Guizot energetically assailed the long potent dogma that stressed the part of the will in the theory of the state. Liberty he held to be as little dependent on will as was authority. That the individual can be bound only by his own will, as Rousseau assumed, was to Guizot absurdity. The individual is bound, as his will itself is determined, by the conscious or unconscious operation of the ideas of reason, truth and justice that inhere in his being as man.

> . . . man has not an absolute power over himself in virtue of his will: as a moral and reasonable being he is a subject, — subject to laws which he did not himself make, but which have a rightful authority over him, although, as a free agent, he has the power to refuse them, not his consent, but his obedience.[1]

From this rather optimistic assumption as to the psychology of the individual, Guizot's nominalism made easy for him the conclusion that political authority rested elsewhere than in human volition. For society was to him but a collection of individual men, and was subject, therefore, to no other principle than that which controlled in the life of each.[2]

[1] *Rep. Govt.*, Pt. II, lect. 10. [2] *Ibid.*, Pt. I, lect. 6.

According to this reasoning sovereignty, as an absolute norm of authority in a state, could be attributed neither to any individual nor to any number of individuals, but only to reason, truth and justice — the abstract ideals to which men inevitably tend to conform. In other words, there was no place in political philosophy for that concept which Hobbes and Rousseau, Blackstone, Bentham and Austin had made the corner-stone of all sound doctrine, even of all possible doctrine. The monarch of the *Leviathan*, the community of the *Contrat Social*, the "supreme, irresistible, absolute, uncontrolled" authority that was placed at the summit of the English law by Blackstone, and the determinate human superior from which Austin had set out — all were banned to the scrap-heap by Guizot. With that group of earnest and talented Frenchmen who were known as the *Doctrinaires*, he strove to solve the problems of France after 1815 by denying sovereignty to both Bourbon and people, and striving to satisfy the aspirations of the times by glorifying the rationality and justice of the *Charte*.[1]

On the basis of his idea about sovereignty Guizot developed his conception of representative government — the main subject of his speculation. Governments fell, he held, into two classes, according as they did or did not attribute absolute sovereignty to human beings, one or more. All of the first class were despotic. Representative government was of the second class,

[1] For a good account of the political doctrines of the group to which Guizot belonged see Merriam, *History of the Theory of Sovereignty since Rousseau*, chap. v, "The Sovereignty of Reason."

based on the denial of the right in any man to make law for himself or anybody else, and on the assumption that all political power is to be directed to approximating the realization of reason, truth and justice. A corollary of the last dogma was that power in the government must be assigned to those who were most capable of approaching reason, truth and justice. The whole operation of the system tended to gather up from the different parts of the community where it was to be found the talent best adapted for the realization of this high end, and to open to this talent the opportunity to promote through the conduct of government the best interests of the community. Guizot did not claim that the working of representative government would be perfect; but he believed that it would come nearer to the maintenance of true liberty and to the true end of the state than any other system thus far devised. The conditions in which the excellence of representative government would be manifest he laid down summarily to be these: That individual liberty should be understood to consist in the power of a man to conform his will to reason; that the guarantees of liberty should aim to secure the conformity of all wills, both of governors and of governed, to reason; that actual power should be in no case absolute, but in every case merely legitimate; and that power is legitimate when it is recognized and accepted by the free reason of the men over whom it is exercised.[1]

The conscious end sought by Guizot in his theorizing was to banish from political science the conception of

[1] *Rep. Govt.*, Pt. II, lect. 10, at end.

absolute power. Definitive power he recognized as permeating every governmental organization; the last word *in any one* of its various fields of action must be the right of some person or persons. But the right in any person or persons to say the last word in *every* field of action, he held incompatible with rationality. It was the formal end of representative government — the highest achievement of political speculation — to provide that every species of definitive power should meet with restraints enough to prevent it from assuming omnipotence. The widest and highest of these powers must especially be so organized as to insure that it do not usurp absolute authority, but act always within the rules of reason and justice. "The art of politics, the secret of liberty, is, then, to provide equals for every power for which it cannot provide superiors."

This was in substance the old theory of the check and balance in government — familiar for generations. Guizot's immediate practical purpose was to gain for the written constitution of France the credit of a complete and final embodiment of this theory. He demanded for the *Charte* the same exaggerated reverence that had been accorded by great-minded Englishmen like Burke to the unwritten constitution of England. At the same time he freely and regretfully conceded that the peculiar success of the English system, a product of unconscious growth and adaptation to concrete demands, was not to be expected of any government that was planned and instituted complete at a given moment of time. He was too strongly imbued with the historical spirit to feel any confidence in constitutions scientifically made to order.[1] All that he hoped from the *Charte* was that it should serve as a sea anchor, steadying France till the perils of a-priorism and self-consciousness should pass away, and she should be able to relapse peacefully into the benign influence of his particular ideas of reason, truth and justice.

The eternal verity that Guizot found in the *Charte* was its guarantee against any exaggeration of power in either monarch or people. The balance between these two equally menacing elements he believed to be there justly maintained. It was his pathetic fate to see himself and all his theories repudiated by France, and absolutism triumphant through democracy and monarchy in turn.

5. *Tocqueville and Realized Democracy*

While the cause of constitutional monarchy was upheld by the doctrines that were represented so well by Constant and Guizot, there was no lack of speculation on republican and fully democratic lines. Most of this, however, was more ardent than novel, and tended merely to reproduce and reiterate the ideas that were dominant at the end of the preceding century. A sensational diversion from the monotony of the discussion in this branch of liberalism was created by

[1] See his criticism of the analytical method in modern political science, in *op. cit.*, Pt. II, lect. xv, *ad init.* It was the fortune of the English system that it developed naturally and spontaneously out of facts, when the science and artifice that distinguished modern times were unknown. *Loc. cit.*

the priest Lamennais, who in 1834 began his twenty years of futile enthusiasm over the idea of democratizing Catholic Christianity.[1] He became eventually a full member of the socialistic group, in whose doctrines democratic philosophy found a really new and productive field of development in and after 1848. This type of speculation we shall take up for consideration later. At the present point attention must be given to a discussion of democracy that was wholly distinct in method and in spirit from those that had become traditional.

It has appeared in earlier pages of this volume that the political systems of the Americans had been of more than negligible influence in motivating the French Revolution of 1789. With the submergence of republican ideas in the Napoleonic period and that of the Bourbon restoration, the great experiment of the United States ceased to receive much attention. Liberal exiles from the disturbed regions of the Old World found a safe refuge but little comfort in the crude communities of North America. The adherents of constitutional monarchy assumed, without much investigation, that the peculiar people across the ocean could furnish no suggestions that would be of use where royalty was of the essence of rational government. Then, in 1835, the first volume of Tocqueville's *Democracy in America* appeared, and throughout the intellectual circles of Western Europe both democracy

[1] His *Paroles d'un croyant* appeared in 1834. For a full and impartial account of his life and works, see Spuller, *Lamennais*, Paris, 1892. Suggestive also is Laski, *Authority in the Modern State*, chap. iii.

and America took on a new aspect and a new significance in political speculation.

A general analysis of Tocqueville's famous work cannot be undertaken here. Its scope far exceeds the field in which we are interested, and its influence in our limited field was not of the greatest. On certain points, however, in the working of democratic government under a written constitution, Tocqueville's acute observation and brilliant literary expression established a new canon in political science. We shall confine our attention in this place to his method in general and to his exposition of two or three features of the constitutional system in action.[1]

In method Tocqueville continues the line of Aristotle, Polybius, Machiavelli, Bodin and Montesquieu. The last-named is at many points an openly imitated model. Like all these great thinkers, Tocqueville makes the observation of facts the basis of his philosophizing on politics. He differs from Aristotle and Bodin in making no effort to work out a complete science of the state; and he differs from Montesquieu in confining his comment to the laws and customs of a single people. To Machiavelli's *Discourses on Livy* the *Democracy in America* has a striking kinship: the Florentine's search among Roman institutions for lessons that shall profit the Italian republicanism of the fifteenth century is closely paralleled by the Breton's investigation of America for the benefit of French republicanism in the nineteenth. But Machiavelli

[1] The *Democracy in America* is the only work that shall concern us here. His other writings had no important bearing on the history of nineteenth-century constitutionalism.

took his facts at second hand, while Tocqueville wrote on the basis of personal observation. At this point the French philosopher comes into close connection with Polybius, whose analysis of the Roman state sprang from the note-book of the foreigner. As Polybius's conception of the Roman constitution formed the basis of all systematic speculation on the subject later among the Romans themselves, and as Montesquieu furnished the English with the first coherent theory of their constitution, so Tocqueville's exposition of the American democracy has been the source of many of the commonplaces in the conception of their institutions that has became traditional among the people of the United States.

The tenacity with which Guizot and other liberals resisted every intrusion of democratic ideas was due in large measure to the memories of the Jacobin régime. It was firmly believed that no constitutional provisions, however astutely devised, could prevent a government based on popular sovereignty from becoming sooner or later an odious despotism. Universal suffrage was sure to be the electoral law, and this would inevitably mean the tyranny of a majority, regardless of all restrictions that might be imposed by a constitution. Tocqueville's great service was to set in a clear light the agencies, both within and without the formal prescriptions of the written fundamental law, through which, in the American system, this dreaded evil was mitigated and postponed, if not escaped altogether.

He pointed out, in the first place, the qualifications permeating the principle of sovereignty. His own conception of sovereignty was wholly lacking in precision, tending on the whole to agree with that of Guizot and Constant. It was the ultimate lawmaking authority, but it was not absolute in any human will, whether individual or collective. It was in last analysis justice and reason only; and what was just and reasonable, he declared, with confusing inconsequence, was to be found in the will of the majority of all mankind.[1] Such inconsistency in thinking about sovereignty was, however, not out of place in a discussion of the American political system; for there was as yet no consensus in the United States as to the abode or even the attributes of this elusive entity, and the many constitutions, state and federal, with all their elaborate formulas, gave no conclusive demonstration that sovereignty belonged either to the states, individually or collectively, or to the people as a whole, or to the people segregated in the several state communities. Each of these views, as well as various others, was propounded from time to time by speculative minds, but the most common idea was that supreme power was divided between the United States and the individual states, each being sovereign in its sphere.

This was the dogma adopted by Tocqueville, without question as to the solution of the difficult problems of logic suggested by it. The theory served his purpose by exhibiting at the very base of the system an agency through which the perils of democracy were avoided. Since the constitution itself denied certain

[1] *Democracy in America* (Reeve-Bowen trans.), I, p. 330 *et seq.* Compare p. 154.

powers to the states and certain others to the general government, there could be no claim to absolute authority by either branch of the dual system. Moreover, there must be a natural tendency of the states to resist illegitimate extension of its powers by the general government, and *vice versa*. Thus was revealed a new item in the list of checks and balances through which liberty was insured — an item that was excluded by the nature of the case from every unitary system.

Tocqueville was quite aware that this principle had been employed in a crude form in earlier confederations of states; but he detected and set forth with clearness the features of its application in America that gave a distinctive character to the United States, whose government he thought must be designated as incompletely national rather than strictly federal. It was at all events, he believed, a new type of political organization, for which a special name had not yet been devised.[1] Its appearance had been due to the special needs of the Americans immediately after achieving their independence. Whether the new devices would be available for other peoples was far from certain; the late attempt of the Mexicans to use them had proved a dismal failure.[2] In any case,

[1] *Op. cit.*, I, p. 201. Tocqueville seems to have been unfamiliar with the German distinction between *Staatenbund* and *Bundesstaat*. Pfizer published in 1835 an influential work on German public law in which he sought to show how the German *Bund* had in it the making of a *Bundesstaat*. — See Bibliography, *infra*.

[2] "The Constitution of the United States resembles those fine creations of human industry which insure wealth and renown to their inventors, but which are profitless in other hands. This truth is exemplified by the condition of Mexico at the present time." — *Ibid.*, 211.

however, it behooved the philosophical observer to note critically and dispassionately the new phenomenon in political science.

The chief feature that made the United States unique among federal systems was the assignment to the general government of the power to enforce its authority over citizens by direct action of its own officials rather than indirectly through the officials of the states. This afforded, Tocqueville thought, a necessary corrective to the anarchic tendency that commonly manifested itself in confederacies. It strengthened the central government as against the states. On the other side the integrity of the states was guaranteed by their possession of all residual authority outside of the limited field ascribed to the United States. Against both governments the rights of the individual were secured, not only by the constitutional restrictions familiar in Europe, but especially by two devices that aroused the liveliest curiosity and interest in the philosopher. These were, first, the extreme decentralization of administration, and second, the exalted political function of the judiciary in its power to pass upon the constitutionality of legislative and executive acts.[1] These two elements in the American system were first brought into prominence among European thinkers by the descriptions and eulogies framed by Tocqueville. From his time to the present day they have been continuously in the focus of historical, constitutional and juristic discussion.

The origin and influence of these two features of

[1] *Op. cit.*, I, chaps. v and vi.

American political life are set forth with great accuracy and impartiality by Tocqueville. He finds in both of them an important part in the successful career of constitutional democracy. The exclusion of a remote and unfamiliar authority from the management of local affairs has a wholesome effect upon the interest and activity of the community in its own business, and so by suggestion upon its concern in the wider sphere. Self-government in the towns and counties is the primary manifestation of the democratic spirit that is essential to the whole system. It furnishes also a most significant item in the list of reciprocal checks upon the undue extension of governmental activity. Where it prevails there is no opportunity for the development of the oppression that is likely to accompany a wide-reaching authority in the central administration.[1]

Of somewhat similar significance is the position assumed in the American system by the judiciary. In the mere fact that the courts have a decisive voice in interpreting the constitution and in passing upon the validity of statutes, Tocqueville sees a check upon both legislature and executive that is wholly unknown in Europe. It restores to something like an equal place in Montesquieu's triad of separated powers that one which had been reduced to practical nullity,[2] and thus strengthens again the guarantees against tyranny.

[1] Tocqueville's reflections upon the nature and effects of centralization in government and in administration, the two being carefully distinguished, constitute one of the most famous and influential passages in his work. See *op. cit.*, Vol. I, p. 107 *et seq.*

[2] *Supra*, p. 115.

Nor is the manner less praiseworthy than the fact of this exaltation of the judiciary by the Americans. To set the court up in open political conflict with the legislature would be, Tocqueville sees, disastrous; but when the invalidity of a statute is determined as a mere incident of a private lawsuit, "in an obscure debate on some particular case," the danger of trouble is reduced to the minimum.[1]

The treatment of these two capital items in the American system well illustrates Tocqueville's general purpose. He aims to show that the democracy which for the first time in history appears successful in a large population and territory rests essentially, not on the prescriptions of the written constitutions (though these documents are so numerous and so skilfully framed in the United States), but on the history and character, the environment, manners and morals of the people. Neither decentralization nor the power of the courts to nullify legislation is formally embodied in the written constitutions, but both have become vital elements in American polity. It is not to be inferred, therefore, that the deliberate incorporation of these institutions in the fundamental law of another nation would at all insure the benefits that flow from them in the United States. Thus Tocqueville guards against undue stress on the volitional and conscious forces in political life, and teaches that democracy, though certain to prevail ultimately throughout the civilized world, will not come by the making of constitutions, however ingenious, but gradually, by the

[1] *Op. cit.*, I, p. 128.

unnoticed transformation of social conditions and ideals.[1]

The evil of democracy that Tocqueville finds inevitable and most dangerous is the tyranny of the majority. Universal suffrage (that is, manhood suffrage) he regards as of the essence of democracy, and universal suffrage means the ultimate control of all legislation by the mass of the people. Constitutions, as well as ordinary statutes, will be made to conform to the majority will. Nor will there be any relief in an appeal to public opinion against injustice that is confirmed by law; for the same majority that makes the law makes public opinion. With whatever mitigations American practice has imbued this hard rule, its sway is manifest on all sides. One who holds ideas outside the circle drawn by the belief of the majority can have no political career or desirable social relations. In this is a tyranny more odious and more deadly than that of any monarch.

Tocqueville's despairing insistence on this point of menace to democratic institutions is remarkable and betrays the influence of some cause that blurs his usually acute perceptions of the realities of things. For he seems to think of a majority as a definite, unchanging aggregate, whose will and purpose are beyond the influence of external conditions, instead of a casual group,

[1] An interesting light on Tocqueville's insight into practical and contemporary tendencies in France, whose special problems were always in his mind, is thrown by his relations to the revolution in 1848, whose approach he predicted. From the advertisement to the twelfth edition of the *Democracy in America*, published in 1850, it appears that he did not divine the approach of the Empire.

ceaselessly changing in physical constituents and psychological character.

As a whole, however, his estimate of the forces and tendencies inherent in the American system and in democracy in general is amazingly acute and judicious. His great work had an instantaneous and continuing effect on political theory on both sides of the Atlantic, and served in particular to counteract in a marked degree the exaggerated confidence of liberals in the efficacy of the written law.[1]

6. *German Constitutional Theory: The Bundesstaat*

Tocqueville's exposition of the American federal system did not fail to enter substantially into the speculations of contemporary German politics. The agitation throughout the German states that culminated in the affairs of 1848 was focussed chiefly at two points: first, the constitutional position of the monarch in the various states; and second, the union of these states and of the whole German people into a strong and efficient federation.

As has already been indicated, the monarchic principle generally prevailed over republicanism in constitutional practice, and received a well-developed theoretical support. The prince was conceived as a wholly self-dependent political entity, possessing far-

[1] Of all the many judgments on Tocqueville's work, that of Bryce, published just before the appearance of his own great study of the United States, has for many reasons the most interest and value for students of political theory at the present day. See his essay, "The Predictions of Hamilton and Tocqueville," in the Johns Hopkins Studies in Historical and Political Science, Series V, No. IX; also in his *Studies in History and Jurisprudence*, p. 301.

reaching powers in the government. Whence these powers were derived was variously answered. Some said, with the voice of the antiquated obscurantist, "from God"; others said, "from nature"; others, "from history"; others still, "from the nation or the state." What no defender of the monarchic principle would say was, "from the people." It was axiomatic with this school of thought that the people no more made the king than the king made the people. The kingship, historically considered, took form and developed *pari passu* with the people (*das Volk*), and the two, king and people, constituted the state. Neither without the other would suffice to maintain its existence.[1] Each must have its logical and independent place in any constitution that may be formulated for the state.

As to the powers that are indispensable to the kingship in a constitutional monarchy, there was also much difference of opinion among the philosophers. All agreed that the king must be more than a mere executive, that his headship of the state must mean real directing power, not the passivity of a symbol or figurehead. The concrete functions essential to this character ranged in theory as in practice through the whole gamut of possibilities. At one extreme the royal

[1] This is substantially the doctrine of Waitz, in his essay on "Das Königthum und die verfassungsmässige Ordnung," in his *Grundzüge der Politik*, p. 128. For other shades of doctrine in this matter in the fifties, when the excited debates of the revolution time were giving way to calmer reflection, consult Stahl, *Rechts- und Staatslehre*, II, Kap. 12, Abschnitt iii, "Das monarchische Princip." Also, Bluntschli, *Allgemeine Staatslehre*, Buch 6, Kap. xiv–xvi.

sphere was held to include the sole initiative and an absolute veto in legislation, and an ordinance power with no limit save the explicit terms of the law. At the other extreme the royal part in legislation was restricted in substance by the assignment of concurrent initiative to the chambers, and in operation by the imposition of more or less extensive responsibilities upon the ministers; while the ordinance power and the whole complex of authorities inherent in the idea of "governing" (*Regierung*) were subjected to narrow definition by the constitution itself. In this matter of the monarchic principle German theory made a little advance in scientific formulation, but practically none in substance, beyond what had been involved in the French constitutional debates from 1789 on. Where German theory brought novelty into the European discussion was at the point where the unification of Germany became the dominant practical issue.

The movement for German unity in 1848 took practical form in the famous constitutional assembly at Frankfort.[1] This body framed a constitution that failed, however to go into actual operation. The failure was due to facts that were quite apart from the theories expressed in the document. The work of the Frankfort Assembly and the whole movement that centered in this work had their chief source in the feeling of national unity among the German peoples. This sentiment of nationality was a conspicuous feature

[1] Brief notice in Hazen, *Europe since 1815*, chap. viii; fuller in Müller, *Political History of Recent Times*, sec. 17. Summary of proceedings in Mollat, *Reden und Redner des ersten deutschen Parlaments*.

of European psychology by the middle of the nineteenth century, and its philosophical aspects will engage our attention later.[1] Here we have to consider the peculiar doctrines involved in the framing of a written constitution that should satisfy the aspirations of the peoples.

From 1815 to 1848 Germany was politically a league of states (*Staatenbund*), whose sole organ of union was a diet consisting of delegates appointed and controlled by the governments of the various states. These governments were in all but a very few cases monarchic; hence the full sovereignty of every one of the princes was, in accordance with the prevailing ideas of the time, presumed without debate. To the rising liberal and nationalistic sentiment of the time the need of the situation was that Germany as a whole should in some way be made to figure as a state. There was no desire save among a few visionaries to abolish the individual states. The feeling, however, that they should be united in some such manner as to make Germany superior in power and dignity to any of its component parts, and equal to France or Great Britain, was passionate and widespread. Germany, the demand was, must be no longer a confederacy, but in the full sense of the word a state.

History furnished many instances of confederation through which groups of states effected certain common purposes by means of powers delegated more or less permanently to a common government. Not till the most recent times, however, had there appeared a form

[1] *Infra*, chap. viii.

of organization in which the elements and attributes of the common government made the union as a whole as truly a state as was each of its constituent members. Switzerland and the United States of America were known by 1848 to have assumed this character.[1] The constitutions of these two unions therefore had a great influence in shaping the projects and theories of those who were promoting German unity. Especially stimulating was the system of the American republic, after Tocqueville's penetrating analysis had brought to the attention of Europe the peculiar principles embodied in it. The constitution of the United States furnished the Frankfort constituent assembly with much that was most significant in the ill-fated project that resulted from its deliberations. Likewise after the futility of this particular written constitution was proved, German theorists about political science continued to perfect on the lines of American debate the logical concept of the *Bundesstaat*.

That republican government was the universal form in the United States while practically all the German states were monarchic, was held by many to render the theory of the American system wholly inapplicable on the other side of the Atlantic. There was indeed no room for doubt that the tenacity with which the monarchic principle was maintained had much to do

[1] In Switzerland a long series of bitter political controversies culminated in 1847 in civil war, the War of the *Sonderbund*. Certain of the cantons sought to reject the authority of the general government. After the secessionists had been suppressed by force a new constitution, in 1848, made secure for the future the permanence of the union and the authority of the general government.

with the failure of the Frankfort project. Yet those were on firm logical ground who held that the essential principle of the *Bundesstaat* was in no way affected by the special form of government in either central power or member-state, and that the Germans at Frankfort in 1848 gave the first expression in history to the monarchic type of this new form of union, as the Americans at Philadelphia in 1787 gave the first expression to the republican type.[1]

There was no disposition to deny to the Americans priority in detecting the basic feature of the *Bundesstaat.*[2] And what was this feature? Merely what Tocqueville had laid such stress on, a general government so complete in organization and so endowed with power as to be able to perform its functions and enforce its authority without recourse to the governments of the member-states. Where such a general government existed, there was implied a people seeking to realize the ends of political life, some through this organization and others through the state governments. But the organization of a people to attain the ends of political

[1] *Cf.* Waitz, *Grundzüge der Politik*, pp. 209–210. But Waitz apparently believed that the *Bundesstaat* existed among the Greeks.

[2] Treitschke, in his *Historische und Politische Aufsätze*, II, 113, declares that the fundamental principle of the *Bundesstaat* was first clearly developed by Alexander Hamilton in the *Continentalist* and the *Federalist*. The principle was, that when a political organ is endowed with a right, the power necessary to the exercise of the right must be presumed to go with it. From this it followed that in a union of states the central government must have power to enforce its laws upon the individual citizens. This *bahnbrechende* idea was discussed by the Americans solely with respect to their peculiar practical problems. Waitz was the first, Treitschke says, to treat the idea systematically and "with the profound earnestness of German science."

life is, as Waitz lays down,[1] the definition of the state. Where the organization takes the form of a single government exercising all the necessary powers in every field, there is a unitary state (*Einheitsstaat*); where the powers are divided between two governments, each independently exercising its own, there is a union-state (*Bundesstaat*).[2] Sovereignty, as designating independent and final authority, may properly, in the judgment of Waitz and others, be ascribed alike to the union-state and to the individual state, each in its proper sphere. For sovereignty is conceived as meaning authority that is supreme and unquestionable, but not authority that extends over all conceivable subject matter.

On this point of the divisibility of sovereignty, as on pretty much every other phase of the general question, there were sharp differences of opinion among the Germans. The course and substance of their controversies involved little that had not been exhibited in the legal and political arena of the United States. The dogma of sovereignty according to spheres had been propounded by all the leading American publicists. The "Union" that Daniel Webster had become immortal in defending was the obvious prototype of the Frankfort *Bundesstaat*. John C. Calhoun's trenchant attack on the doctrine of divided sovereignty, though

[1] ". . . die Organisation eines Volks zur Erfüllung seiner höheren Lebensaufgaben. . . ." — *Grundzüge der Politik*, p. 163.

[2] It has been commonly assumed that the proper English equivalent of *Bundesstaat* is "federal state." But many acute reasoners, like Professor J. W. Burgess, insist that while government may be federal, state may not, and the expression "federal state" is meaningless. "Union-state" as the rendering of *Bundesstaat* would seem to be immune to this particular objection.

apparently not yet well known across the Atlantic, was not exceeded in effect by the parallel criticism of like-thinking Germans, and his dogma of state-sovereignty was destined to furnish, when made readily accessible,[1] valuable aid and comfort to the partisans of *Particularismus* in the Empire that Bismarck brought into being.

Neither the German nor the American theorists were successful in so defining the *Bundesstaat* as to insure to it general recognition as a new species of the genus state. The Germans were embarrassed by their monarchic principle. This, taken in connection with their doctrine that sovereignty was divisible, made every reigning prince the absolute possessor of some, if not all, of the governmental powers in his dominions. To superimpose on these "sovereigns" a monarchic government whose chief must be recognized as endowed with powers and dignity as exalted and indefeasible as theirs, was possible in theory; but the resulting system would inevitably involve such diffusion of power and uncertainty of its tenure as to suggest confederacy or anarchy rather than the definiteness of a state.[2]

[1] The works in which Calhoun most systematically developed his doctrine were published only in 1851, the year after his death.

[2] The Frankfort assembly, after completing its constitution for Germany, offered to Frederick William IV of Prussia the headship of the new government, with the title "Emperor of the Germans." The dignity was declined partly because the offer came, not from the princes of the German states, but from the representatives of the people, and partly because acceptance clearly would be followed by a difficult and uncertain war to enforce the new system upon Austria and many other states. All the circumstances showed that the particular *Bundesstaat* formed at Frankfort had in it none of the elements of order and progress.

A more coherent and admissible concept of the *Bundesstaat* as a real state was developed by those who relegated the monarch to the position of a mere executive, and regarded a people as the essential and self-sufficient basis of whatever was entitled to the name of state. In the people was to be found, according to this view, the source of all the powers vested in both state and federal governments and the final authority in deciding where ran the line of partition between them. The people was the constituent entity and the constitution was the people's will as to how the functions of state life were to be divided for exercise between two organizations and distributed among the various departments of each. A *Bundesstaat*, then, was a state in which the sovereign people had a dual rather than a single governmental organization, and assigned to each branch a part, not of sovereignty, but of the powers to be exercised for the good of the state by the government.

This explanation of the *Bundesstaat* had few or no supporters in Germany. It smacked too much of democracy and dangerous radicalism. There was indeed endless iteration of the cry that the Frankfort assembly was the constitution-making organ of the German people, and that the fundamental law there formulated was the people's will. Yet conscientious philosophers, even of advanced liberal views, were slow to take this doctrine seriously; for the German princes were in theory distinctly set off from the German people, and in practice it was clearly the princes rather than the people that determined the fate of the Frankfort movement.

In America the conception of the *Bundesstaat* outlined above became after the middle of the nineteenth century predominant among reflecting men.[1] The idea that sovereignty was divisible lost its hold through the powerful logic of Calhoun, and the growing might of triumphant democracy nourished the dogma that in the people must be found sovereignty, not only in the sense of the power to say the last word in matters of governmental practice, but in that more comprehensive sense for which Blackstone furnished the formula — the power that is "supreme, irresistible, absolute, uncontrolled." With sovereignty and the making of governments and constitutions an indefeasible attribute of the people, the federal system could be neatly fitted into the theory of the state. Not that it was a new species of state. With the distinction between state and government duly regarded, there was clearly no such thing as a "federal state," as the expression went, but merely a unitary state with a federal government.

But the clearing up of theory by American facts and ideas did not serve to solve all the problems that were inherent in the conditions. To make it clear that sovereignty was in the people did not save the United States from a barbarous civil war, in which the location of sovereignty was a leading issue. The old question recurred with appalling consequences — Who constitute the people in whom sovereignty inheres? Is the partition of powers between the two govern-

[1] *Cf.* the interesting discussion in Merriam, *History of the Theory of Sovereignty since Rousseau*, chap. ix.

ments determined by the collective inhabitants of the individual state, or by the total population of all the states? There was no more decisive answer to this question in the American system than there was to the issue between princes and people in the German.

Waitz said in discussing the league of states (*Staatenbund*) that the only significance of this form of union in history was that it commonly was a step in the transition from a group of states to a single state. The *Bundesstaat* he considered to have in it more of the element of permanence — to be in fact a distinct and valuable addition to the forms of political life. There is rather more indication in the history of this species of union down to the present time that it is as unstable and transitional as the *Staatenbund*. Its role has clearly been, in America and Germany, to prepare the way for the advent of a national unitary state, with a federal government.

7. *Conclusion*

The foregoing chapter has called attention to the distinctive features of constitutional theory on the Continent till well past the middle of the nineteenth century. The written constitution became the almost universal form of fundamental law. As to the character and content of it, theory on the legalistic side dealt particularly, as we have seen, with the doctrine of sovereignty, the function of the monarch and the nature of the union-state.

On all these subjects the prevailing thought in the theories we have noticed was to ignore in a large measure the concept state and concentrate attention on government. Sovereignty, in the sense of authority that was "supreme, irresistible, absolute, uncontrolled," was excluded from consideration, or altogether from recognition as a rational idea. No determinate human superior such as the English Austin had insisted on was thought of as essential to government that was truly constitutional. The French liberals and *Doctrinaires* would hear of nothing but reason and justice, applied to the prescriptions of a nicely balanced system of checks among the departments, as the supreme directing power in political life. The supporters of the monarchic principle claimed for the prince only an indispensable, not an absolute authority; monarch, people and representative bodies each had a part in the government as determined by the constitution. The expounders of the union-state showed a dual government, each branch of which was restricted to a sphere, whose limits the constitution must be depended on to make clear.

For theoretical as well as practical completeness there was required in each of these systems of doctrine some entity on which the various elements of authority could rest. The nice balance among the various departments of the government, even when the royal power was added to the older elements as a regulator, could not be rationally explained as existing and functioning of itself and for itself in France. Prince and representative body were in almost every state of Central Europe in strife as to the scope of their respective powers; neither would concede the right of the other to partition the disputed field; an authority with competence to determine competence was inevitably suggested. In the dual government of the *Bundesstaat* the situation was very much the same: delimitation of the respective spheres of the central and the state governments became promptly a problem in both theory and practice. And finally, monarchy and union-state alike presented always the fundamental question: for whom and by whom, in last analysis, is the complex organization of authority created and maintained?

To say, as was in fact said, that a sufficient answer to these questions must be found in the constitution, was but to carry the issue one step further back and raise the controversy as to the source and end of the constitution. To evade the long familiar debate over the constituent power was more or less unconsciously always in the minds of the moderate men who led in the political discussions between 1815 and 1848. They feared to ascribe to either people or prince so unrestricted a power as that to create a constitution. They would shut their eyes to the very human motives and passions that entered into the formulation of a constitution by either prince or assembly of representatives, and would assume the concrete result to be the expression of impersonal reason and righteousness.

This attitude had been the normal one among the expositors and eulogists of the unwritten constitution. England, the example *par excellence* of this species, was assumed to have developed a nearly perfect political system through the operation of institutions and forces unrecognized and uncontrolled by the conscious intelligence of men. The English nation was the real creator of the system. In like manner, it was felt, the written constitutions that came forth so numerously in the nineteenth century expressed the spirit and will, not of the delegates or the princes who formulated them, but of the historic and ethnic aggregates of which these constitution-writers were the unconscious organs. Here, then, was to be found the real and ultimate source and interpreter of the fundamental law. Neither the constitution nor any of the organs defined and authorized by it was the last element in the political series. Behind all the definite and personal elements lay in every case that supra-human and impersonal factor that was variously called "people" (collective and abstract, not distributive and concrete), "state" and "nation."

The last of these terms became in the first half of the nineteenth century the most characteristic of the theory which we are indicating. Side by side with the development of constitutionalism in political philosophy the conception and influence of nationality received elaborate investigation and assumed much prominence. The theorizing on this subject must now be considered.

SELECT REFERENCES

Bluntschli, *Geschichte*, Kap. 17. Brie, *Der Bundesstaat*, Abth. I. Bryce, "Predictions of Hamilton and Tocqueville," in Johns Hopkins Studies, Series V, No. IX. Calhoun, Disquisition on Government. Constant, *Politique constitutionelle*, Vol. I, chap. ii. Guizot, Representative Government (translation), Part I, lects. vi–viii; Part II, lects. x, xv–xviii. Jellinek, *Gesetz und Verordnung*, Abth. I, Kap. vii; Abth. II, Abschnitt i, and Absch. ii, Kap. iv. Tocqueville, Democracy in America (translation), I, chaps. iv–viii. Treitschke, *Hist. und Pol. Aufsätze*, II, 109–191. Stahl, *Rechts- und Staatslehre*, Band II, Abschnitt iii, Kap. 12. Waitz, *Grundzüge der Politik*, pp. 129–218.

CHAPTER VIII

THE THEORY AND PRACTICE OF NATIONALISM

1. *The Struggles for National Independence and Unity*

From the American Revolution down there was continuously manifest in the larger affairs of political life the influence of the ideas which eventually blended into the definite concept of the national state. The expression of these ideas was for the most part either merely visionary and sentimental or directed to some immediate practical end. In America the fervid oratory of Patrick Henry and the clever pamphleteering of Thomas Paine stirred the imaginations with the suggestion of unity and power, while the sententious phrases of Jefferson in the Declaration of Independence and the sober warning of Hamilton in the Federalist, "a nation without a national government is an awful spectacle," revealed a pretty wide and deep understanding of the doctrine that was developing.

In France, during the period of revolutionary turmoil, the idea of nation was hardly distinguishable from that of people. Yet here, as in America, a practical problem set the consciousness of a distinction in a clear light. Under the theory of the social contract a people was merely a group of individuals united by an agreement that had no basis save in the free choice of each of the individuals concerned. This was the theory of the revolutionary leaders, but their practice showed the influence of other ideas. In America it was not by virtue of their free choice that Indians, negroes and loyalists were excluded from membership in the new-born people and even from the enjoyment of their natural rights as men. In France, after the establishment of the republic, those who preferred a monarchy logically ceased to be Frenchmen. In practice, however, they were more often treated as bad Frenchmen than as aliens. And this was a recognition of their own contention, that they remained Frenchmen without reference to the desire of any number of their fellows to exclude them from the category.

There was clearly implied in these facts a criterion of membership in a political community quite distinct from that set up by the theory of the social contract. The individual's antecedents, not his present will, became the conclusive test. His race, his color, his language, his religion, his former political convictions — all entered into the consideration. Geography, too, had its influence in the matter. In La Vendée practically the whole population refused to associate politically with the Frenchmen that surrounded them. But La Vendée was one of the old provinces of France; hence the clearly manifested will of the Vendéans received no recognition from the authorities of the republic. In America the people of Rhode Island manifested a pronounced indisposition to come into the union formed by the Constitution of 1789; whereupon there was serious talk among even the radical popular-sovereignty people of Massachusetts and Connecticut, to the effect that the Rhode-Islanders should be coerced into the desired relations with the rest of the Americans.

These instances in the procedure of the peoples who were special exponents of the revolutionary doctrine testified to the prevalence of feelings and ideas that greatly qualified the principles upon which the revolutions were supposed to be based. Something more than the caprice or even the reasoned preference of individuals was evidently operative in fixing the limits of a normal political society.

The problems here involved assumed great prominence through the transformations of the political map of Europe and the world by the wars of French expansion and the readjustments that followed the downfall of Napoleon. So far as general principle rather than immediate expediency was appealed to in the process, the French professed respect for the popular will in fixing the boundaries of states, while the Congress of Vienna stressed historical and traditionary conditions. Each side, however, resorted often to the principle of the other, and the settlement of 1815 was followed by deep and bitter dissatisfaction in both dynasties and peoples.

In the negotiations at Vienna the doctrine that nationality should be the basis of independent statehood came strongly to the front in providing for the future of Poland, Italy and Germany. It was held that the Poles, the Italians and the Germans were each so homogeneous racially as to furnish the natural material for a state. The eminent Niebuhr set the principle of race so high as gravely to argue that Saxony, in standing by Napoleon after all the other Germans had deserted him, had been guilty of treason to the German race, and must pay the penalty in loss of autonomous life.[1] These far-reaching conceptions of national rights did not show any appreciable influence in the territorial arrangements actually effected at Vienna; but Poles and Italians and Germans voiced a loud chorus of protest against the violation of their ideals, and never ceased their denunciation till it had produced the most important results in both theory and fact.

The revolt of the Greeks and their war for independence was the occasion for a great impulse to the cause of race nationalism on sentimental and pseudo-historical grounds. For a generation before the insurrection broke out a remarkable propaganda of education had been carried on through which the more intelligent of the Greeks were trained to believe that they embodied the heritage of language, spirit and general culture that had been transmitted by classic Hellas. Liberals of Europe and America eagerly seized this conception of the modern Greek, and saw in the petticoated bandits who were harrying the Turks the worthy posterity of Solon, Lycurgus and Demosthenes. Enthusiastic support was given to the insurgents by pen and purse and sword. The cause of the Greeks was

[1] Die Gemeinschaft der Nationalität ist höher als die Stats-Verhältnisse welche die verschiedenen Völker eines Stammes vereinigen oder trennen. Durch Stammart, Sprache, Sitten, Tradition und Litteratur besteht eine Verbrüderung zwischen ihnen, die sie von fremden Stämmen scheidet . . . Aus diesem Nationalitätsverhältnisse entstehen die Rechte einer Bundesversammlung, oder ihres Hauptes, zu ächten, wenn ein einzelner Stat der Nation untreu und zum Verräther an ihr, im Bündniss mit Fremden, wird. — Quoted in Bluntschli, *Geschichte*, p. 635.

won, indeed, less by the agitated activities of their idealizing friends than by the fleets and armies of those very prosaic politicians, Nicholas of Russia, Charles X of France and George IV of Great Britain. Yet more significant for the future than the work of these monarchs was the spread of the doctrine, feared and detested by all of them, that a nation was morally entitled to a national government.

In 1830 the Belgians, who had been yoked up with the Dutch by the Congress of Vienna, asserted and maintained by force their claim to national independence. The Poles at Warsaw, in the following year, fought a desperate but unsuccessful fight to escape the dominion of the Czar. Their failure, attended by tales of ruthless massacre and by the appearance of swarms of exiles throughout western Europe, probably contributed even more than their success could have done to the spread of nationalistic idealism.

By the middle of the century, when the revolutionary drama of 1848 was unfolded, nationalism was the central force in the whole great commotion, outside of France. Even Great Britain had to deal with the trouble-making principle, as it was invoked by the malcontents in Ireland. Middle Europe, from the Baltic to the Mediterranean, was a seething caldron of nationalistic aspiration. In most cases the immediate end sought was the release of a self-conscious people from the control of a government that was felt to be alien. Along with this went a wild craving for the consolidation of hitherto separate communities of kindred speech into a single political system.

The principalities and provinces of the Italian peninsula flamed with hatred of their Hapsburg and Bourbon rulers, drove them out, and groped excitedly about for union among themselves. But the time of Italian unity was not yet, and when the tumult and the shouting ceased Italy was still merely what Metternich had called it, a geographical expression.

Throughout the dominions of the Austrian Emperor almost every one of the races subject to him struck for some kind and measure of national autonomy. The Czechs at Prague demanded a revival of the ancient realm of Bohemia. The Magyars at Buda-Pesth deposed the Hapsburger from the throne of Hungary. The Serbs of Croatia set up the standard of revolt against the Hungarians. Here again, however, the end of the troubles found the authority of the House of Hapsburg practically intact, and its subjects as heterogeneous as ever.

At Frankfort, in the assembly that convened to frame a constitution for Germany, centred the most important of the nationalistic movements of this time. The popular demand that led to the meeting of the convention was irresistible both from its diffusion and its intensity. For a generation the growth of the idea of a unified and powerful Germany had been remarkable from both the sentimental and the rational point of view. History and fancy had combined to reveal or construct an inspiring past of the German nation and its heroes, Arminius, Charlemagne, the Hohenstaufen; and prophetic vision depicted a future that should see the Teuton again moulding the Gaul and Latin to his will. But the political unity of the German race, on which this vision depended, required the dismemberment of the Austrian Empire and a notable expansion of the power of Prussia. Neither of these requirements could be secured in 1849, and the work of the Frankfort assembly went to shipwreck. Germany became again a disjointed congeries of political units, but the men and the ideas that were destined to realize the national desire had been revealed.

The ebullition of 1848, in both its nationalistic and its constitutional phases, was largely controlled by sentiment and emotion. An influential and often dominant part was played by orators, poets, literary men and professors. Witness Kossuth in Hungary, Arndt and Uhland, Dahlmann and Waitz at Frankfort, Lamartine in France, and Mazzini at Rome. Within twenty years after the failures of these men the principle of nationality achieved the wonderful triumphs manifest in a unified Italy, a unified Germany, and a unified United States; but the men most responsible for these results were of a different type from the leaders of 1848. Louis Napoleon, Otto von Bismarck, Camillo di Cavour and Abraham Lincoln were hard-headed politicians, whose methods subordinated the ideal and sentimental to the practical. Hence the nationalism exhibited in the results of their work was hard to reconcile at some points with the doctrine of the earlier days. The German nation that Bismarck consolidated included many Germans who bitterly opposed his procedure, and left out the great masses of Germans who were subject to the Austrian Emperor. The United States that Lincoln left included millions of Americans who had fought a bloody war to free themselves from his government. In the earlier conception of a nation it was the expression of the popular consciousness and will. In the conception that prevailed in the German and the American development nationality became an instrument of aggression and was used to justify the overriding of popular desires. Where race, geography and history were held to have decreed that there must be a single people under a single government, no adverse choice or preference of any fraction of the people was allowed to prevail.

From this position the advance was easy to the conception of a nation's duties externally, as the supplement to its rights internally. Its spirit and culture must be projected into the uttermost parts of the earth. Whatever inferior nations refused to profit by their opportunities must be forced to do so. Thus nations in the modern world became, like mere dynasties and despots in the older time, ruthless rivals for the endless extension of their power.

2. *Theory of the State as Sovereign Person*

While soft idealism and hard practical politics were coöperating to produce the results just considered, rational theory labored conscientiously to set the nation in its proper niche in the structure of political science. The doctrines that were developed as to the nation had a close relation to the concept of the state that was most characteristic of the mid-nineteenth century. A consideration of this concept affords the best line of approach to the theory of nationalism.

It is in the scientific literature of the Germans that the most important contributions to the theory of the state are to be found. The practical problems of parliamentary government absorbed the attention of thinking men in Great Britain and France. The British were satisfied to accept the complacent optimism of the Whigs or the ethical dogmas of the Utilitarians as an adequate substitute for a real theory of the state. The French still feared to confront again the consequences of pushing the theories of 1789 to their logical limits, and the peculiar faculty of the Gallic mind for exact analysis and well-articulated synthesis was diverted to the newly opened fields of socialism and sociology.

German theory as to the nature of the state followed, through the middle of the nineteenth century, the channels into which it had been directed chiefly by the genius of Hegel. As we have seen,[1] his system combined the conclusions of a transcendental metaphysics with those of a wide ranging over the field of concrete human history. These two elements fixed the character of all the post-Hegelian speculation in Germany as to what, in last analysis, is meant by the term state. Out of the metaphysical and psychological phases of the speculation developed the dogma that the state must be conceived as essentially a person. From a similar source arose the doctrine that the state must be regarded as an organism. Both the theory of personality and the

[1] *Supra*, chap. iv, sec. 4.

organismic theory, permeated as they were with the idea of life and growth, promoted the historical approach to the realities of political phenomena. History, just taking scientific form through Ranke and his school, became of such importance as to figure not only as an instrument in discovering the foundations of the state, but even as a determining element in the concept. The historical theory of the state took its place by the side of the transcendental and the organismic, and played a part with them in shaping the conceptions of nationalism.

The practical politics of Central Europe operated to determine the concept of the state as it did to influence the theory of the constitution.[1] Monarchy, though not absolute, had to be regarded as the historically indicated, if not the logically indispensable, form of government for the modern state. Prince and people were in the body politic as head and members. Monarchic theorists did not reject the idea that will was of the essence of the state. They denied, however, that the will of the state could take form or find expression through the aggregate of individuals known as the people (*Volk*). The state, as an embodiment of will, could properly be said to have personality; but this character could be manifested only in an actual physical person — the monarch. Thus the prince personified the state; and the theory had strong support that there could be no valid concept of the state as endowed with will or other attributes of personality unless its chief organ should be a living physical person.

[1] *Supra*, chap. vii, pp. 252 *et seq.*

This adaptation of the conception of the state as person to the special service of the monarchic party stimulated the liberals and republicans to the development of a doctrine more favorable to their cause. They held that the state in and of itself was person, quite without reference to the organ through which its will and power were manifested; that these attributes and all the others — feeling, purpose, conscience, *etc.* — that characterize a moral being were predicable immediately of an aggregation of human beings in the same sense as of a single human being. Since these attributes constitute personality, the state, it was argued, whatever the form of its government, is in the strict sense of the term a person.

The speculation and debate over such theories obviously involved extensive ramblings in the fields of metaphysics and psychology. Not less necessary, in course of time, became resort to the broad domain of objective history. "Person" had to be defined by the psychologist's analysis; *Volk* had to be traced to its germ by the investigations of the historian. More or less as a by-product of this double process in reaching the conception of the state as person, the idea of the nation forced its way irresistibly into the foreground of the discussion. Before taking up this idea for closer analysis, however, let us consider more concretely some of the conspicuous theories of state personality.

Hegel's striking doctrine as to the development of the state in history stressed, as we have seen,[1] the attribute of self-consciousness in the people (*Volk*).

[1] *Supra*, pp. 160, 164.

The idea received at the hands of Schleiermacher also an influential exposition.[1] A state, he held, was the form of a people's life, and came into existence when and so far as a consciousness of unity pervaded the multitude and rendered its social activities reasoned rather than instinctive. The normal succession of forms of government in history, as Schleiermacher saw it, was from monarchy through aristocracy to democracy — an order that illustrated the widening diffusion of political consciousness.

These views brought psychological analysis into close relation with the concept state and people, but still left the elements of personality in the individual members of the community rather than in the aggregate. Thinkers of a juristic habit of mind regarded the ancient device of a fictitious personality through which a corporation had legal life, as an adequate basis for the ascription of moral attributes to a people or a state. But the unmistakably predominant tendency of the time was away from every doctrine that made state or people the product of human creative power. Granting that a corporation was a creature of the human will, to compare the state to it would be to yield the whole claim of Rousseau and the revolution. Recourse was therefore increasingly had to theorizing that categorically assigned the characteristics of the individual person to a collection of individuals, and eventually so defined personality as to make it predicable indifferently of a monarch, of a people and of that which includes

[1] Schleiermacher, *Werke*, Band 32. *Cf.* Bluntschli, *Geschichte*, p. 668 *et seq.*

both, a state. When this was achieved, a broad highway was opened to those who, fearful of sovereignty in either prince or people, could proceed comfortably in the assurance that the dreaded power lay in the combination of the two, that is, the state.

The historical school of German political science contributed much to the development of the doctrine under consideration. Their special service was to define the concept "people" (*Volk*). Savigny, whose distinction and preëminence in historical jurisprudence covered half the nineteenth century,[1] made this concept the whole foundation of his philosophy of law. A people, as he defined it, is an aggregation of individuals living a definitely indicated kind of life and permeated by a common spirit (*geistigen Gemeinschaft*). This spirit (*Volksgeist*) lives and acts in every individual, but is distinct from the will and the right of the individual. The most obvious manifestation of the common spirit is the language of the people. Not less significant is its law (*Recht*). Chiefly by the transmission of the common language and law from one generation to another a people maintains its existence and its unity through the centuries. It tends always and irresistibly to reveal its inner and invisible spirit in outward and visible form, and this form is the state. In the state a people attains to true personality and the power to act. All the dogmas as to the creation of the state by and for the individual are baseless. According to nature the state

[1] Born 1779, died 1861. *Cf.* sketch in Bluntschli, *Geschichte*, p. 623.

has its origin in a people, through the people and for the people.[1]

Dahlmann, the equally distinguished and influential contemporary of Savigny, laid like stress on the historical development of a people, but conceived the state as a species of physical and spiritual personality that might be something more than the mere form of a people. A people often became merged into a population (*Bevölkerung*), but the state did not therefore cease to exist.[2]

This same tendency to give the state an independent personality appeared in the work of Georg Waitz, another famous historical scholar of the mid-nineteenth century. The climax of this movement of speculation, however, was exhibited in the philosophy of F. J. Stahl (1802–1861) and especially that of J. K. Bluntschli (1808–1881).

Stahl's system as a whole was in the spirit of the old dogmatic theology, often obscurantist in trend, but manifesting at many points notable force and acuteness.[3] The state he classes at the outset as one species of what he calls the ethical realm (*das sittliche Reich*). By this term he means conscious, unified government, directed by moral and intelligent purpose, over conscious

[1] ". . . der Staat ursprünglich und naturgemäss in einem Volk, durch das Volk, und für das Volk entsteht." — *System des Römischen Rechts*, Buch I, Kap. ii, sec. 10. Savigny here points out that the idea that the state originates in the will of the individual is due in part to the confusion of various senses of the word *Volk*.

[2] Dahlmann, *Die Politik*, secs. 6, 7.

[3] His systematic and exhaustive work is the *Rechts- und Staatslehre auf der Grundlage christlicher Weltanschauung*, in two vols. The *Staatslehre* is in the second volume, of which the third edition appeared in 1856.

and freely-obeying beings, who by this government are made a spiritual unity. Such is the authority that is manifested in the kingdom of God; and such is the civil order among men. In authority so conceived Stahl sees the dominion of personal character, and the state becomes thus to him a realm of personality. That is to say, the government (*Herrschaft*) is self-conscious, self-controlled and possessed of real power over men. The social-ethical world-order is not, as in Fichte and Kant, a rule or law to which personalities conform, but is itself a personality that comprehends and unifies them all.[1]

When Stahl emerges from the cloudland of his metaphysics his state, with all its halo of ethical personality, assumes the familiar form of the German constitutional monarchy. It is the union of a people under a governing authority (*Obrigkeit*), the natural but not necessary form of which is a physical person. The end of this union is to fulfil the life-purpose of the community, not of the individual; and to realize, so far as can be done by the ways of law (*Recht*), the social-ethical (*sittlich*) ideas inherent in the people. The common moral consciousness of the community (*sittliche Gemeingesinnung*) is the basis on which the legal and political institutions rest. The will of the people (*Volkswille*) may rightly be said to determine the existence of the state; but this is true only if by the will of the people is understood, not any product of individual wills, but an original spiritual (*Geistliche*) element that permeates all the individuals and determines their wills.[2]

[1] *Op. cit.*, Band II, Einleitung.

[2] A single formidable sentence sums up well Stahl's ideas as to

The vague and mystical element in Stahl's thought, as illustrated by this conception of the will of the people, has little if any place in the doctrine of Bluntschli. Whether for better or for worse this latter philosopher makes his idea of the personality of the state unmistakably clear and comprehensive. His point of view is juristic rather than metaphysical, *rechtlich* rather than *geistlich.* Law, right and rights, as all expressed in the single word *Recht,* he asserts to pertain only to self-conscious and self-motivated (*selbstthätige*) beings. But self-consciousness and determining volition are the distinctive characteristics of a person, as set off from an animal or a mere thing. Therefore, to be *Rechtsfähig* or *Rechtssubjekt* — to be capable of participating in relations involving law, right and rights — is to have personality, to be a person. A human being is a person because such relations constitute the core of his life (*Lebensordnung*). But a multitude of human beings

the importance and inner significance of the state: "Die Einigung der Menge zu Einer geordneten Gemeinexistence — die Aufrichtung einer sittlichen Autorität und Macht mit ihrer Erhabenheit und Majestät und der Hingebung der Unterthanen — die Lebensbefriedigung, die nicht den Menschen vereinzelt, sondern der Nation und den Menschen nur in der Nation gewährt wird, namentlich das Bewusstzein und das hebende Gefühl, diesem geordneten Gemeinwesen und dieser Nation mit ihrer geistigen Bedeutsamkeit anzugehören — das eigenthümliche Ethos, das nicht im sittlichen Leben, in Erfüllung des Gebotes, sondern in sittlicher Herrschaft, in Einsetzung und Handhabung des Gebotes, in Verwirklichung der sittlichen Herrscherideen, der Macht, der Weisheit, der Gerechtigkeit besteht — das sind die Charaktere die das innerste Wesen des Staates ausmachen und die ihren Grund und ihre Bedeutung nicht im Einzelleben, sondern nur im menschlichen Gesammtdasein haben." — *Op. cit.*, II, p. 134.

The implications of this passage throw a rather interesting light on Stahl's disparagement of Hegel, and especially of the later Hegelians, for having promoted the apotheosis of the state. P. 140.

may fall literally in the same category; the order of its existence may be exclusively determined by relations of law, right and rights. Such is the case when the multitude is so organized and coherent as to form a state. It then possesses self-consciousness, intelligence and will, and is a person in precisely the same sense in which the individual is a person.[1]

Bluntschli takes the utmost pains to make it clear that the collective person (*Gesammtperson*) is not a legal fiction or a figure of speech.[2] A people, he maintains, has a self-conscious spirit and will that is something distinct from either the sum or the majority of the wills of its component individuals. It has further, in its institutions, a body (*Körper*) that confirms its existence and manifests its will. Thus the spirit of a people, taken in combination with its political institu-

[1] The fullest exposition of Bluntschli's views on these subjects is in various essays in his *Kleine Schriften*, especially the first volume, "Aufsätze über Recht und Stat."

In translating the word *Recht*, in the text above, I have deliberately used the clumsy expression "law, right and rights" because Bluntschli employs the term without discrimination to designate what is meant in English by any one, any two, or all three of those words. A shotgun rendering is most likely to hit his meaning.

[2] As a picture is something more than a collection of oil and colors, and a poem something more than a collection of verses, and a country something more than the sum of certain areas of land and water, and a tree something more than an aggregate of plant cells, so a people is something more than a multitude of human beings. *Kleine Schriften*, I, 297.

This species of analogical argument is repeatedly employed with much effect by Bluntschli in support of his doctrine as to the relation of the unit and the aggregate. He apparently ignores altogether the important fact that, while a human being is self-conscious and in some measure at least self-determining, a plant-cell or a poet's verse is not. Such a difference may conceivably vitiate the analogy between the aggregates.

tions, constitutes an entity in which the elements of personality are in the strictest sense real.[1]

The discovery and scientific development of this truth, that the state is a real person, Bluntschli considered one of the great services of the Germans. The Romans, themselves no mean politicians, had, he said, a dim uncertain perception of the truth, but lacked the scientific insight to ferret out its full significance. To round out the concept to completeness Bluntschli proceeded to ascribe to the state as person even the attribute of sex.[2] If the state, he reasoned, has truly the characteristic attributes of the human person, we cannot blink the primary classification of human beings into male and female, and we must find in which of these classes the state-person belongs. The conclusion reached, through processes strangely fantastic for a writer who was merciless toward "ideologues," was that the state is the male, while the qualities distinctive of the female are to be found in the other great aggregate-person of human society, the church.

This grotesque extension of the personality doctrine brought much ridicule upon Bluntschli and sensibly impaired the influence of his general political theory. He held tenaciously to his fanciful idea, however, and

[1] "In dem Volke waltet und ist lebendig ein Gemeingeist und ein bestimmter Gesammtcharakter, und das Volk hat in seinen Institutionen sich auch einen Körper geschaffen, welcher sein Wesen bethätigt, und seinen Willen offenbart. Das Gesetz, die Politik des States, die Verwaltung, die Rechtspflege sind alle nur zu verstehen aus diesem Volksgeist und Statskörper, nur aus der Persönlichkeit des Stats." — *Kleine Schriften*, I, 99.

[2] *Ibid.*, the essay entitled "Der Stat ist der Mann," esp. pp. 283 *et seq.*

left it in place in his last revision of his great systematic work.[1] With due allowance for the perversion, however, his exposition of the concept of the state as person was as lucid and cogent as any ever published. While he did not always make it clear whether personality was an attribute primarily of people or of state, he never left a doubt that it was an attribute of a people that had become a state. His ultimate formula for the concept of the state was this: "An aggregation of men united, as government and subjects on a definite territory, into a social-ethical, organic, masculine personality."[2]

With the idea that the state or people was a person developed *pari passu* the broader conception of an organic life expressed in every social group. This particular doctrine, while manifest in the speculation of Bluntschli and others as to the state, received its chief development in the philosophy of society and in the sociological treatment of politics. The doctrine of group personality, on the other hand, continued to have much influence on those who viewed the state from the point of view of public law.[3] In both kinds of specula-

[1] See his *Allgemeine Staatslehre*, 5te Auflage, 1875, Buch I, Kap. i, 7.

[2] ". . . eine Gesamtheit von Menschen, in der Form von Regierung und Regierten auf einem bestimmten Gebiete verbunden zu einer sittlich-organischen, männlichen Persönlichkeit. Oder kürzer ausgedrückt: Der Staat ist die politisch organisierte Volksperson eines bestimmten Landes." — *Ibid.* It is noteworthy that in the first of these two forms the thought seems to attach personality to the state, while in the second the person is rather the people (*Volksperson*).

[3] Jellinek, for example, pointed out that in the material world a collection of molecules becomes a unit — an individual thing — only when man thinks of it as involving purpose or end (*Zweck*).

tion the centre of interest was the people as a group rather than any individual person, whether monarch or subject. Such was the situation in the field of theory when the exciting events of practical politics in the third quarter of the nineteenth century demanded close attention to the relation of people and state to the concept of nationality.

3. *The Nation as a Unit of Race and Language*

The term "nation" was in use in all West-European languages from the days of Rome; but the importance of fixing its meaning with precision as a term of political science became obvious only in the revolution time of the late eighteenth century. Ordinary usage made no nice discrimination between "nation" and "people." When circumstances brought into practice the dogma that political authority had its source exclusively in the people, it was a pressing necessity to determine what was meant by the people. Likewise when, as a consequence of the wars precipitated all over Europe by the revolution, a reconstruction of governments to correspond to national needs was demanded, the concept nation had to be considered with care.

All through the history of political theory we have seen distinctions of race presented as the causes and

A brick is a unit only by virtue of our perception of the end for which that aggregate of particles exists. Likewise a collection of men is a unit in the same sense through the ascription to it of a definite end or purpose, by which every individual in it is determined. Such a unity is a person just as soon as it possesses an organ for the expression of its will. There is in this idea of person no fiction, no mystery, but merely the application of the ordinary teleological process of human thinking. *Gesetz und Verordnung*, 193 *et seq.*

sufficient explanations of distinctions in institutions and power. The Greeks, the Romans, the Teutons all left copious records of their conviction that their respective achievements were due to the qualities inherent in a peculiarly gifted blood. After the passing of Rome the partition of the civilized world between Christian and Mohammedan found a similar explanation in the genealogies of the patriarchs that figured in the sacred writings of both creeds. When the medieval monarchies began to appear on the soil of the Carolingian empire their virtues were laboriously imputed by myth and legend to the heroic stock from which rulers or people or both had sprung.[1] From feudal times this racial explanation of political phenomena was transmitted to the modern era. A nation was thought of as a population of substantially a common blood.

The eighteenth century, however, was too sophisticated to accept the idea literally. The mixture of races in every people of Europe was one of the most familiar facts of history. A more acceptable criterion of identity as a nation was accordingly found in language. On the basis of sameness or diversity of speech, it was held, nations were distinguishable as nature itself had divided them, quite without reference to the will of man.

A systematic and powerful expression of this species of doctrine was embodied by Fichte in his famous *Addresses to the German Nation.*[2] In maintaining that

[1] For the French derivation from the Trojans see *Political Theories, Ancient and Medieval*, p. 225. A similar ancestry for the English is the theme of Geoffrey of Monmouth and Layamon.

[2] *Supra*, p. 145.

the Germans were superior to the other branches of the Teutonic stock he laid much weight on the purity of their language as compared with those that had been blended with the Celtic and Latin. Men, he argued, are shaped by language more than language by men. The spiritual development (*Geistesbildung*) of a group loses both unity and force when alien elements, of unfamiliar connotation, enter freely into its speech.[1] Particularly destructive of a truly national life is the incorporation of a dead language into the usage of a people. Words and idioms that have ceased to represent the thoughts of living men will inevitably introduce a morbid element into the spirit (*Geist*) of those that restore them to service. Fichte finds in this doctrine the ground of his conviction that the Germans are of a sounder national life than the Latinized peoples of Europe.

Language, however, while of high significance in the concept of the nation, was not, in Fichte's analysis, the essence of the matter. For this he had recourse to his idealizing philosophy. Human life means but the development of the primordial (*Ursprünglich*) and divine. This process is various in its manifestation. Where a society of men reveals in its natural and spiritual life the progressive development of the divine in accordance with some special law, there is a nation (*Volk*).[2] The common participation in this special

[1] *Humanität* and *Popularität*, for example, he says mean nothing at first sight to the uncultivated German, and the meaning they eventually acquire has in it something alien, distorted and uncongenial to the German character. But *Menschenfreundlichkeit* and *Leutseligkeit* would make at once an identical appeal to all Germans.

[2] Fichte's formal definition of *Volk* is this: "das Ganze der in

law is what, in last analysis, unites the individuals into a natural whole. The content of this law defines the national character. A nation, thus, is in Fichte's view a mode in the manifestation of the primordial, the divine, the eternal, — The Absolute.

That there was little in this conception to inspire men to fight for independence was not concealed from the philosopher. He united with his abstractions, therefore, a more practical appeal, though not one that could be called frivolous. Only the noble-minded (*edeldenkende*) among men, he declared, are of concern in the political life; and it is peculiarly characteristic of the noble-minded to long for immortality. To incorporate their personalities by word or deed in the eternal (*Ewig*) is a controlling desire of their lives. Hence their devotion to the social and spiritual order in which their lives are lived; for the nation, in which this order is expressed, is the realization and the guarantee of the immortality they crave. Patriotism (*Vaterlandsliebe*) is not possible in those who are not animated by the longing for immortality, and by the feeling that it is attainable through identification with the nation.

Fichte's conception of the nation exhibits thus two of the conspicuous features that appeared in other phases of his political theory. The intense individualism of his revolutionary fervor[1] recurs in the idea that

Gesellschaft miteinander fortlebenden und sich aus sich selbst immerfort natürlich und geistig erzeugenden Menschen, das insgesamt unter einem gewissen besondern Gesetze der Entwicklung des Göttlichen aus ihm steht." — Rede VIII, in *Werke*, Vol. VII, p. 381.

[1] *Supra*, p. 138.

the attachment of men to a concrete nation is determined fundamentally by their longing for immortality. Self-interest of this particular type he makes the indispensable condition of national life. From a diametrically opposite point of view the complementary, if not contradictory, dogma appears that the nation, quite irrespective of the individual, is an element in the unfolding and realization of pure abstract idea. To conceive the nation in this latter aspect is possible, the philosopher holds, to such intelligences only as grasp the notion of the eternal and the divine. Men so limited or so barbarous as not to believe in this or to look upon human life as a development of this primordial principle cannot be in the real sense a nation or possess a national character. But where, as in the German people, the true ideal is apprehended, the nation, Fichte declares, is far above the state and the common social order. The state, in maintaining internal peace, order and well-being, is but an instrument for the promotion of the nation's end. These conditions, with liberty itself, must be sacrificed when necessary that the nation may achieve its purpose — the realization and development eternally of the divine principle embodied in it.

A comparison of this doctrine of Fichte's with that which Savigny began to propound a few years later[1] shows that the basic philosophy is the same in both. A definite social aggregate of human beings owes its life and its identity to the part it has in a transcendental scheme of universal existence. This aggregate (*Volk*)

[1] *Supra*, p. 304.

Savigny holds to be most perfectly apprehended by human intelligence as state (*Staat*), while Fichte holds its character to be best expressed as nation (*Nation*). Language gives to Fichte a sufficiently clear indication of the outlines of the entity; Savigny finds an additional revelation of the inner reality in the people's law. What both philosophers agree upon with perfect harmony is, that the true substance of the national character is never determined by, or revealed in, the conscious acts or volitions of any single individual or any single generation.

4. *The Nation as a Geographic Unit*

The course of theory on the relation between nation and geography is closely analogous to that of the relation of nation to race. Through Bodin and Montesquieu, as we have seen,[1] the determination of governmental institutions by the geographical situs was made an important feature of scientific politics. In this early speculation attention was given chiefly to the influence of physical environment in its large aspects — latitude, altitude, climate, relation to the oceans — just as the characteristics of race were at first treated as applicable only to the largest aggregates of men. But later, in the one case as in the other, the deterministic principle was carried over to the detailed conditions of lesser units. As the kind of physical facts that had been held to explain the distinction between Semitic and Japhetic peoples in general were resorted to in explaining the difference between particular peoples of either stock,

[1] *Political Theories from Luther to Montesquieu*, pp. 112, 418.

so it was sought to find in such physical conditions as had differentiated dwellers in different zones a basis for distinction between communities dwelling side by side in the same zone. The search received a practical stimulus from the wars for territory that prevailed in Europe in the name of the balance of power. In line with the whole manner of eighteenth-century thinking [1] it became the formula for the demand of each power that it should have its "natural boundaries." Thus again the idea developed that there were geographic facts inherently identified with the existence of any given nation.

The more serious philosophy did not seize with special avidity the suggestion that a particular territory was an essential element of concrete nationality. Conservatives were naturally suspicious of the idea, though their devotion to the old dynastic order led them often to use it to support the adjustments made in the interest of that order. Edmund Burke was of course disinclined to put emphasis on anything but the social and political institutions of a people as determining its character. "Our country," he said in his *Appeal from the New to the Old Whigs,* "is not a thing of mere physical locality. It consists, in great measure, in the ancient order into which we are born. We may have the same geographical situation, but another country; as we may have the same country in another soil." [2]

Fichte vacillated in respect to the part played by the geographical factor. In his ideal of a closed commercial

[1] *Supra,* p. 46. [2] *Works,* IV, 167.

state he adopted, as we have seen,[1] the theory of "natural boundaries," but interpreted the term in an economic rather than a military sense. This doctrine gave to physical environment great significance in the theory of the nation. In his *Addresses*, however, Fichte swung sharply away from such a conclusion and declared roundly that the abiding place (*Heimath*) of a people was much more the effect than the cause of its essential character.[2]

The wavering manifested by Fichte was reproduced in the speculation of many succeeding decades. It was involved in the uncertainty that prevailed as to the relation of nation, people and state. That some one, if not every one, of these entities was deeply affected by geographical facts was generally asserted. But the precise meaning and the interrelationship of these terms remained long undetermined. Schleiermacher propounded the dogma that a clearly defined geographic unit (*Bodeneinheit*) will be, in the nature of things, the abode of a *state*. Not that the geographical fact was the cause of the state. He denied this as well as the doctrine that community of blood or of language made the state. All that he held was that through some process of history the inhabitants of the region would sooner or later become a self-conscious political organism,[3] and the boundaries of the region would be the limits of the organism.

Much in the manner of Schleiermacher, Hegel, in his *Philosophy of History*, swept the whole surface of the

[1] *Supra*, p. 144. [2] Rede IV.
[3] *Werke*, Band 32, S. 11, 15.

earth in a grand survey to see where the abodes of states could be detected.[1] Rather more distinctly than Schleiermacher he suggested the deterministic influence of the physical facts on the political; yet he fell far short of making geography the creative force in the development of nations.

The net result of all the speculation that has been noticed was that some relation between geography and the nation was recognized, but the character of the relation was not made at all definite. And such remained the situation throughout the fierce controversies of the mid-century over the rights and wrongs of nations and of nationalities. For none of the concrete problems as to boundaries could a scientific formula furnish an acceptable solution. The mountains, deserts, seas, rivers and other features of the earth's surface that had seemed to be natural marks of separation for communities of men either were lacking where need for them was greatest, or, when present, actually furnished additional incentives to strife in the rivalry for occupation and control of them. Nor could the limits indicated by geography be made to coincide with the limits indicated by language. A Germany that fulfilled the glowing demand of Arndt for unity "*so weit die deutsche Zunge klingt*" would outrage every canon of geographic theory, and would present many points where geography could find nothing whatever to offer as a boundary. And there in the heart of Europe lay the Swiss—a stout and respected nation, defying every rule of both language and geography in its national life.

[1] Sibree's translation, Introduction, pp. 79 *et seq.*

No more in the facts of physical environment than in those of blood and language, therefore, did the political theory of the early nineteenth century find an objective criterion of nationality that would suffice to still the insistent clamor of the democratic liberalism for recognition of the human will as the paramount factor. Through the growing precision of geographic science as wrought out by Humboldt and Ritter, and through the rise of ethnology and anthropology and comparative philology, the influence of heredity, environment and speech on the evolution of human societies was more justly apportioned and balanced, and political science defined the nation in terms that gave due weight to each, while assigning to the will and feeling of living men a part that was far from the least.

5. *Nation and Nationality*

The task of tracing the growth of the dogmas of nationalism during the half-century following 1815 is made almost impossible by the confusion in the sense of the chief terms involved. In both scientific and popular usage, and in all languages alike, the meanings attached to "nation," "people" and "state" exhibited all degrees of diversity and contradictoriness. In English Bentham and Austin and Cornewall Lewis attempted to escape the difficulties by devising new and too often cumbrous terms and definitions;[1] but their labors received little recognition by anybody. In many cases where their suggestions were promising for clearness there was too much of pure utilitarian

[1] See especially Lewis's *Use and Abuse of Political Terms.*

implication to encourage acceptance, and in many other instances they refused recognition to ideas and distinctions that they regarded as savoring too much of silly German idealism, unsuited to the hard common sense of Englishmen. The French were too deeply immersed in the conflict between liberals and reactionaries for the control of the government to use terms in any sense save that which would inure to the advantage of the two parties respectively. Only in German speculation was there a serious effort to work out a precise political terminology, and even here no consensus was achieved.

As between nation (*Nation*) and people (*Volk*) the Germans tended clearly to use the former when the idea of race was to be stressed, and the latter when governmental institutions or functions were chiefly in mind. This was the precise reverse of the tendency in usage of the terms in English. As ethnology and anthropology and the new sociology revealed the errors and uncertainties of ancient ideas about race distinctions, German political science relegated *Nation* to these preliminary fields. For the concrete problem of German unity a more serviceable word was *Stamm*, which figured quite largely in the debates of the mid-century.[1] This made no appeal to European speculation at large; but another term made its way so rapidly into general use as to absorb all the connotation of

[1] The nearest to an equivalent of this term in English is probably "stock." It means a social aggregate consisting of families mostly of the same blood — a branch of a race. The Bavarians, *e.g.*, are a *Stamm* of the German *Nation* (in Fichte's sense of *Nation*). *Cf.* Mohl, *Encyklopaedie*, 2te Aufl., sec. 4 and note (1872).

political bearing in the word nation and thus to contribute to its displacement. This new term was "nationality" in the concrete sense — a nationality (*nationalité, Nationalität*).

Originating in the protests of various communities against the disposition made of them by the Congress of Vienna, this word nationality focussed both popular and scientific conceptions of political fundamentals, and in all languages alike. In the vocabulary of revolutionary agitation it designated any community in which or for which independent or autonomous government was insistently demanded. Czechs, Serbs and sundry other groups of Slavic people, Irish, Roumanians — each was recognized as a nationality when a claim to all that was implied in "nation" would have excited ridicule. The rights and wrongs of nationalities were the theme of Mazzini's solemn and splendid literary visions, but no one could discern any solid substance in his rhapsodizing, save anarchistic democracy. Louis Napoleon proclaimed his adhesion to the principle of nationalities; but for the sake of a deal with Bismarck for territory he would deny that the Belgians constituted a nationality.[1] Thus the new term was abused by the practical politicians and the agitators; in the analysis to which more scientific minds subjected it, important progress was revealed.

In the first place, the influence of blood and language steadily receded in relative significance through the decades in which the nationality was the centre of de-

[1] *Cf.* the excellent art. by Hauser, "Le principe des nationalités," in *Revue Politique Internationale*, No. 20 (1916).

bate. Other factors were recognized as playing a large part in the bond of social union. Religion, law, customs, morals, literature, art, the extent and kind of intercourse with neighboring societies — all these, as well as the physical environment, were seen to work for the consolidation and as well for the disintegration of peoples. As the growing social sciences brought to light the more subtle and obscure operations of these factors, history with its rapidly developing improvements in scope and accuracy brought prominently into view the fact that the resultant of all these forces varied greatly from age to age. Thus the idea gained ground that there was in nationality, either as a quality or as a concrete fact, little or nothing of the fixedness or finality that had been ascribed to it. The evolutionary philosophy which Darwin made so conspicuous in the physical world at the middle of the century had its inevitable effect on political science. It tended steadily to appear to thoughtful minds that, so far at least as concerned the unconscious elements in the concept, a nationality was but the expression of an existing combination of social forces that was doomed to pass as it had come.

Under this historical interpretation of the idea of nationality there could be presented a bewildering variety of objective conditions explaining the existence of different peoples at the same time and of the same people at different times. The modern English were assumed to be determined by unity of race, language, religion, geographical situation; the contemporary Swiss exhibited complete diversity on each of these matters; the Germans were unified as to some and diverse as to others. But the authentic history of a millennium showed in Great Britain and in Germany in past times hardly less diversity than Switzerland exhibits to-day, and drove from the field of rational politics the idea of any permanent form in which the identity of a people was expressed.

Out of the difficulties inherent in the earlier conceptions of nation and nationality arose the doctrine that the essence of the matter was to be found in the political institutions of a people. The transition to this theory is seen in the distinction that was devised between natural and political nationality.[1] Race and language were held to determine natural nationality, while the political species was that which prevailed where a lesser was absorbed by a greater people through the exertion of either moral or physical force. The people resulting from this blending process was held to have as good a claim to independence as one that based itself upon race and language.

The doctrine just noticed was prompted in large measure by practical issues arising out of the aspirations of France under Napoleon III for territorial aggrandizement at the expense of small states on its borders. The full development of the doctrine appeared in the theory as to the relation of nationality and state, which will be considered in the next section. A well-reasoned definition of nationality in the historical spirit, independently of the political elements, was presented in

[1] *Cf.* Zöpfl, *Grundsätze des gemeinen Deutschen Staatsrechts*, 5te Auflage (1863), Erster Abschnitt, sec. 13.

the fifties and sixties by Bluntschli,[1] whose Swiss nativity, South German university associations, liberal sympathies in current politics and broad historical scholarship constituted a peculiarly effective equipment for scientific speculation.

The formula in which he embodied his conception of a people (*Nation*) is this:

> A union of masses of men of different occupations and social strata in a hereditary society of common spirit, feeling and race, bound together especially by language and customs in a common civilization which gives them a sense of unity and distinction from all foreigners, quite apart from the bond of the state.[2]

In the exposition of this formula Bluntschli gave due weight to all the familiar factors in nationality — race, language, religion, geography and general physical environment, but he added and emphasized the psychological influences of common feeling and common spirit. This state of mind of the individuals he declared to be responsible for the initial impulse to unity. Objective conditions and the general course of history brought this impulse to fruition. The relative importance of the various conditions varied from age to age, and the character and manifestations of the national spirit varied accordingly; but the constant factor must be, so long as a people could be said to exist, a sense in the individuals of unity among themselves and differ-

[1] See especially his *Kleine Schriften*, Band II. The lecture on the development of national states (p. 70) is a fuller statement and discussion of the ideas contained in his *Allgemeine Staatslehre*, Buch 2, Kap. 1–4. This latter work appeared in six successive editions from 1852 to 1886, the last posthumous.

[2] *Theory of the State*, English translation, p. 90.

entiation from other groups. The feeling and spirit that are the essence of nationality might be and generally were unconscious in their origin and development; but they were none the less real. The concept of the nation could be understood only as a concept of historical civilization (*Cultur*).

Two features of Bluntschli's definition need to be especially noted. The first is the suggestion of Hegelian and Fichtean mysticism in the resort to a hazy and indefinable state of mind as the ultimate factor in nationality. The second is the care with which a people as thus defined (*Nation*, *Nationalität*) is distinguished from a people in the political sense (*Volk*). Bluntschli sets forth at length and with iteration the doctrine that a people may or may not constitute the basis of a state, but remains a people without regard to that. The criteria of the two entities are quite independent. In this reasoning he is on ground that was at the centre of the stirring politics of the mid-century, where, in the struggles for national existence and glory, the differences and conflicts of political theory were only less heated than the conflicts of statesmen and armies.

6. *The National State*

The conceptions of state and nation examined in the preceding sections were always more or less intimately blended in the systems concerned. Yet there was wide difference of doctrine as to the precise relationship of the two ideas. This was accentuated by the lack of uniformity in the usage of the terms, and by the general liberal and conservative leanings respectively of the philosophers. At the middle of the century, moreover, the intense conflicts over German and Italian unity and the movement for secession in the United States furnished decisive concrete foundations for divergencies in theory.

The state was, as has been shown, explained as ultimately expressed in the attributes of personality or of organism or both. Nationality was expressed in various historically developed facts and feelings pervading groups of human beings. It became an important question whether the facts and feelings that determined nationality were essential to the concept of the state. Was the lofty function in the scheme of human existence assigned by Hegel and Stahl and Bluntschli to the state, predicable of an aggregate of men that lacked the character of a nationality? In short, could there be a state without a people?

The distinction between a people and a population had been a commonplace of political theory from at least the time of Cicero.[1] Under the influence of Rome's far-flung and long-enduring dominion the idea of people had been in large measure submerged in that of population, and the identity of the state had been fixed by reference to the sovereign ruler quite without regard to the mass of the ruled. Bodin propounded the precise formula that determined this doctrine for modern times.[2] Hobbes and the English Utilitarians adopted it substantially intact. When Bentham and Austin made the "habit of obedience" the criterion of

[1] *Political Theories, Ancient and Medieval*, p. 120.
[2] *Political Theories, Luther to Montesquieu*, pp. 86, 96.

a political society or state, they left no room for considerations of nationality; but continental and American thinkers were not easily able to ignore it.

In German theory the imperial idea had some supporters. The unmistakable power of the Austrian monarchy made it awkward to deny to it the character of a state. Hence there continued to be reactionary thinkers who held that wherever and so far as a single sovereign authority was in control, there a state had its being. The racial, linguistic, historical or other likenesses or unlikenesses among the population had nothing to do with the matter.

Much more general, however, was the doctrine that "state," while not necessarily presupposing a people, had a special significance in connection with nationality. By acquiring the attributes of the state, a nationality (*Nationalität*) was held to become in the full sense a people (*Volk*). This was the particular doctrine of the historical school of thought in political science. Savigny declared that only after achieving personality as state could a people manifest the spirit that it embodied.[1] Waitz asserted that the nationality was a natural union, which was rounded out and perfected by the political union of the state.[2] To Stahl and Bluntschli, also, their respective conceptions of the state[3] were particularly if not exclusively valid as expressing a unity of organization for the maintenance of law and justice in a people already united by other bonds of nationality.

To the question whether there could be a state with-

[1] *Cf. supra*, p. 304. [2] *Grundzüge*, Kap. I. [3] *Supra*, pp. 305 *et seq.*

out a people, the philosophy of the mid-nineteenth century, therefore, was not uniform in its answer, but showed a strong leaning to the negative. What was the answer to the converse question: Could there be a people without a state? Was community of race or language or history or tradition, or a sense of such community regardless of the facts, sufficient to justify political science in ascribing significance to an aggregate of men in which unity of government and law was lacking? In this matter as in the preceding there was no complete consensus of doctrine. Speculative opinion varied much according to the sympathies of the philosophers in the practical issues of the time. There were those who held that a common sense of law and justice, expressed in political institutions, was but one of the attributes that defined a people and was in no way an indispensable one; that there could be a people without the state. There were those who held that the state was the necessary form of a people (*Volk*) and that only so far as manifested in this form could a people be said to exist. Finally, there were those who held that a stateless people, or nationality, must necessarily have in it the seeds of political consciousness, and must therefore be regarded scientifically as a potential and inchoate people destined certainly to assume the state form.[1]

[1] German discussion of these various ideas was particularly voluminous. See Savigny, *System des Römischen Rechts*, Buch I, Kap. ii, sec. 9; Dahlmann, *Politik*, sec. 6; Waitz, *Grundzüge*, Kap. I; Zachariä, *Vierzig Bücher*, Buch II, Hauptst. 2; Stahl, *Rechts- und Staatslehre*, II, S. 165. Not all these authorities are self-consistent, presenting different conceptions of people and state according to the needs of the particular topics under consideration. This is especially the case with Zachariä; with the reference above compare III, 5, 2, and XI, 4.

The doctrine that nationality and political independence were inseparable was basic in all the revolutionary agitation of the times. Mazzini's impassioned dreaming seemed almost rational now and then as he expounded the moral order of the world and revealed in it the law that every people in whom a consciousness of unity was expressed in its language, literature and history must have a governmental unity to correspond. Such a people, he held, embodied a particular spirit to which a part was assigned in the progress of the human race, and it was therefore an absolute right that the development and activity of that spirit should be unhampered.[1]

The Mazzinian philosophy of the national state was so blended and permeated with his demands for democracy in government as to lose much of the cogency that survived his rhapsodical form of expression. Substantially, however, his thought was that of the Germans who saw in nationality an element in the world order, entitled to free expression through the organism of the state. Americans on both sides in the Civil War of 1861–65 were more or less consciously under the influence of the same doctrine. Northerners and Southerners both proclaimed themselves the embodiments of a national world-mission, but they differed as to the relative weight of the factors that fixed the limits of a nationality.[2]

[1] See Mazzini's *Essays*, translated by Okey, esp. pp. 19, 154–5, 170–1.

[2] The North emphasized geographic continuity, while the South stressed uniformity of social institutions and especially the sentiment of unity among the people.

Speculation of the less fervid and revolutionary order tended to uphold a qualified but not absolute form of the dogma of the national state — to maintain that a people united by other bonds need not necessarily have also the form of the state, but would probably acquire it sooner or later. According to this view the peculiar function of a people in the life of humanity might be fully realized through its literature, language, religion or art, without the aid of political unity. Bluntschli, for example, was positive in rejecting the dogma that every people must be a state and every state a people. Experience and logic both convinced him that the two need not coincide. The state might embrace the whole or fragments of several nationalities; a people might be politically organized in several states. Not every people, he declared, was endowed with the capacity for exclusive state life. Nationality must be regarded as a cultural, not a political concept. The consciousness of unity that defines a people might exist as to various aspects of civilized life without extending to the governmental organism. Yet Bluntschli could not escape the conclusion that among the influences that operated to bring states into existence nationality had always been strong and in modern times had become clearly the strongest.[1]

This conception of the national state, assigning to it relative and transitional rather than absolute value, was well suited to the historical spirit that was dominating political theory. The progress of many small

[1] *Kleine Schriften*, II, 84 *et seq.* Also *Allgemeine Staatslehre*, Buch ii, Kap. 2–4.

nationalities in civilization and self-consciousness was a conspicuous fact of recent decades, and their aspirations for independent governments were duly justifiable by the doctrine. At the same time the right of existing national states to be was fully explicable. Beyond this there remained opportunity to foreshadow a future world-state, into which the national states would insensibly merge as the consciousness of unity progressed from and through nationality to humanity.[1]

The logical sufficiency of the reasoning on which the possibility of a world-state was based was generally conceded. If language, religion, law and the other elements of civilization should become uniform throughout mankind, a political system to correspond might be anticipated. The national state would be by the application of its own principle submerged in and superseded by the larger whole. This, however, was clearly an ideal for the remote future. Of immediate practical concern was the problem to what extent, if at all, recognition was due from the national state to a community within its bounds whose feeling of unity with its neighbors was qualified by aspirations for some measure of autonomy. This was the problem involved in the momentous discussions over what was called particularism in Germany, state-sovereignty in Switzer-

[1] *Cf.* Bluntschli, *Allgemeine Staatslehre*, p. 114: "Die Entwickelung der Menschheit setzt nicht bloss die freie Offenbarung und den Wettkampf der Nationen als Grundbedingung voraus, sondern sie verlangt hinwieder die Verbindung der Nationen zu höherer Einheit. . . . Die höchste Staatsidee ist menschlich."

Schleiermacher, in the earlier decades, rejected the idea of a world-state, but on practical rather than theoretical grounds. See his *Works*, Vol. 32, p. 31, esp. note.

land and the United States. The question was primarily one of politics and constitutional law, but the controversies over it led to the formulation of the most absolute dogmas concerning the national state, as well as to the most astute and subtle assaults on the validity of that conception. Two Americans were conspicuous in these achievements. John C. Calhoun, in his *Disquisition on Government* and other writings, propounded theories in 1850 that the European philosophers of the next generation gladly appropriated for the defence of the rights of the lesser communities. On the other side Elisha Mulford, in *The Nation*,[1] gave to the American people, after the Civil War, a version of German political theory, in the manner and with much of the substance of Stahl, skilfully adapting the doctrines to the demonstration that against the national state any form of self-assertion by a lesser community within it violates the moral order of the universe. To Mulford a homogeneous population on a continuous and well-defined geographic area was a divinely designated embodiment of sovereign political power; the social aggregates through whose coalescence this people was created retained only historical or administrative, never supreme governmental, significance. Where the conditions of nationality prevailed in these aggregates the union-state

[1] The word nation is used by the author for the express purpose of inculcating the idea of the national state; for he declares that he means by "nation" what is usually expressed in English by "state." To designate a state in the special sense of member of the United States he resorts to the typographical form "State," but prefers to substitute for it as a rule the term commonwealth. Preface, p. viii.

(*Bundesstaat*) became *ipso facto* the type of sovereign organization.[1]

The confederacy (*Staatenbund*), on the other hand, was found equally rational by Calhoun, and far more reconcilable with the facts of history and law. Most important from our present point of view was his stress on the continuing validity of the will of a community in fixing its political status. That the supremacy of this will could be set aside by the mere geographical proximity of other communities, or by association with them, even if they were of like nationality, was to him sheer nonsense. His doctrine illustrated the existence, throughout the heyday of the nationalistic theory, of an opposition to it based upon the idea that in last analysis the foundation of the state was laid not in objective conditions, historical or environmental, but in the volition of living men.

7. *Summary and Conclusion*

The seventh decade of the nineteenth century witnessed the unification of Italy, the United States and Germany. In the momentous events attending this achievement the principle of objectively determined nationality was exploited extensively in Italy and America and to a less degree in Germany. Race, language and geography happened to indicate bounds that corresponded fairly well with the purposes of the American and Italian nationalists, and this fact colored the emotional appeals of the war times. For the Germans, the conditions both external and internal im-

[1] *The Nation*, chaps. v and xvi.

posed serious qualifications upon the demand for boundaries fixed by race or geography.[1] But to whatever extent the idea of objectively determined nationality persisted in popular thought and emotional literature, it ceased by the end of the eighth decade of the century to have any important place in political theory.

The rational foundations of the idea were steadily undermined by both the facts and the philosophy of the age. Old ideas as to distinctions between races and languages were wholly transformed by the development of anthropology and ethnology.[2] The natural barriers by which geographic unities were determined were reduced to nullity by the marvels of intercommunication wrought by steam and electricity. Capitalistic industry and commerce created lines of union and of cleavage that crossed and endlessly confused the ancient lines of language and kindred. The historical and comparative methods in jurisprudence and philology destroyed on the one hand the myths of long-standing national solidarity and achievement, and proved on the other hand that institutions assumed to be the characteristic glory of certain peoples were as widespread as humanity itself.[3] Political science caught the full infection of the Darwinian spirit that ruled in the physical field, and the state was regarded as at any time merely a stage in an endless series of evolutionary transformations.

[1] *Supra*, pp. 298, 319.

[2] See the excellent monograph by J. L. Myres, "The Influence of Anthropology on the course of Political Science," in University of California Publications in History, Vol. IV, no. 1.

[3] *Cf.* Henry Sumner Maine, *Ancient Law;* E. A. Freeman, *Comparative Government.*

Under the influence of this philosophy there was a constant tendency of theory to ignore, or at least to reduce to insignificance, the objective elements in the conception of nationality. Correspondingly the importance of the popular will was increased. This movement was a concomitant of the steady growth of democratic ideas in all phases of social and political life. The policy of the Napoleonic empire in France gave ostentatious support to the principle that an expression of a people's will should take precedence of all other considerations in determining its allegiance, — that the plebiscite should be the supreme criterion of nationality. However grotesque were some aspects of this principle in practical application,[1] its theoretical foundations were in harmony with the times.

The unification of Germany by Prussia exhibited no application of the plebiscitary principle, nor, indeed, of the other principle of determining nationality. Brute force was all that operated when Prussia absorbed the Danes of Schleswig and the Germans of Hanover, and the new-made empire took over the French of Alsace-Lorraine. In America deference to the principle of the popular will was indicated by the use of the plebiscite in adopting the terms of the readjustment of relations between the victorious and the vanquished sections; but the form was illusory, and the substantial factor in the reconstruction was the military power of the North.[2]

[1] For example, in the annexation of Nice to France, and in the French establishment of Maximilian's empire in Mexico.

[2] The elections in the conquered states were under the direction

When, just at the end of our period, the Balkan question convulsed European opinion, and the problem of nationality had to be solved for Roumanians, Serbs, Bulgars, Turks and Greeks, there was a distinct reaction toward the principle of objective determination. Race, language, religion, historical tradition and myths were all duly paraded as grounds for the erection of Turkish provinces into national states. Geography, however, especially in Macedonia, failed to furnish unities that would correspond to those indicated by the other factors. In the contentions over boundaries the popular spirit and will rose to a prominent position in each of the new states, though the manifestation of this influence was more striking in hatred of one another than in internal cohesion and harmony.

Despite the adverse influence of the Balkan problems, the general trend of rational theory continued toward primary emphasis on feeling and will as the principle of nationality. This prevailing doctrine at the end of our period was skilfully and eloquently summed up by Renan in a discourse delivered at the Sorbonne in 1882.[1] He did not conceal the conscious relation of his argument to contemporary problems; he confessed his animosity toward those great states which take peoples by the throat and say, "You speak the same language that we do, therefore you belong to us." But this and other allusions to current aspects of Pan-German and Pan-Slavic policy do not affect the clarity and force of his scientific contentions.

and control of the army of the United States, enforcing rules prescribed by the conqueror as to who should vote.

[1] Published in his *Discours et Conférences*, 2me éd., p. 277.

Renan takes up in order all the different items in the list of objective facts that have been used to explain nationality. Race he finds without significance, because the term itself is ambiguous and obscure, and in the sense of blood kindred no race is pure.[1] Language is not conclusive, as is shown by the diversity in Switzerland, which is a nation, and the identity in Great Britain and the United States, which are not one nation. Community of interests makes not a nation, but at most a customs-union.[2] Geography — natural frontiers — is the most arbitrary of criteria and means only endless wars. History, when authentic, is more likely to divide than to consolidate a nation; only when preserved in erroneous form or forgotten altogether are the facts of its beginnings promotive of nationality.[3]

Having excluded thus all the external criteria, Renan finds the essence, the soul of a people to consist in two facts: First, that the community possesses a common heritage of memories, whether of achievement and glory or of sacrifice and suffering;[4] second, the actual consent, the positive desire of the individuals to live together and enjoy and transmit the heritage they have received.

[1] He refers with malicious joy to the Slavic admixture in the German, especially the Prussian population. "Pour tous il est bon de savoir oublier."

[2] ". . . un Zollverein n'est pas une patrie."

[3] "L'oubli, et je dirai même l'erreur historique, sont un facteur essentiel de la création d'une nation, et c'est ainsi que le progrès des études historiques est souvent pour la nationalité un danger."

[4] It is implied in the reasoning of the preceding note that the glory and sufferings involved may be mythical without impairment of their nation-making efficacy.

However unsatisfactory Renan's formula may be in final analysis, it expresses well the dominant thought of his day. The national state was coming to be explained in terms of human psychology.

SELECT REFERENCES

Bluntschli, Theory of the State, Book II, chaps. i–vi; *Kleine Schriften,* I, pp. 260–286; II, pp. 70–99. Calhoun, Disquisition on Government. Fichte, Addresses to the German Nation (translation), chaps. iv and viii. Hegel, Philosophy of History, Introduction. Lincoln, Inaugural Address, 1861, and Message to Congress, July 4, 1861. Mazzini, Essays, pp. 1–22, 137–176. Renan, "*Qu'est-ce qu'une Nation?*" in *Discours et Conférences,* p. 277. Rose, Nationality in Modern History. Savigny, *System des heutigen römischen Rechts,* Band I, secs. 7–10. Stahl, *Staatslehre,* pp. 1–20, 131–168. Davis, Political Thought of Heinrich von Treitschke, chaps. iv and vii.

CHAPTER IX

SOCIETARIAN POLITICAL THEORY

1. *The Rise of Socialism and of Sociology*

PARALLEL with the movement of doctrine concerning the constitutional and national developments of the nineteenth century a current of speculation took pretty well-defined form by the middle of the century under the names of socialism and sociology. Not that these two terms were synonymous; they designated, on the contrary, systems of thought that were quite distinct from each other in character and in purpose. Yet regarded from the point of view of the history of political theories they have this in common, that they have their origin and their end in the study rather of society than of state or government, but produce incidentally strictly political ideas of momentous import.

The rise of socialism was closely related to the economic conditions that characterized the various stages of the revolutionary movements in Europe from 1789 on. Sweeping confiscations of property such as were wrought upon the church and the nobility in France inevitably raised the general question as to the right of property, and the sufferings of the poor united with the intemperate logic of the intellectuals to bring about an abortive insurrection in Paris, headed by Babœuf and directed to the abolition of private ownership, particularly in land. This was in 1796.

From then to the end of the Napoleonic period France was too much engaged in other things to be concerned about socialistic or communistic theory or practice, though Fourier brought out in 1808 the first of his influential works.

When peace came in 1815 and the trying period of readjustment followed, a new factor in the general economic situation became at once predominant and England assumed the first place in the socialistic movement. The new element was the factory system of production. In England what is now known as the industrial revolution had been definitely accomplished. Steam power and machinery had given to the great textile and iron industries the form and organization that in substance they have to-day. Other industries were in process of the same transformation. Great shiftings of population were in progress, with the attendant tumult, suffering and general unrest. Wage earners in the large establishments found themselves, so far as their living was concerned, at the mercy of the owners, and found all efforts to better their condition thwarted by laws that were often antiquated, often brutal. Trade unions, strikes and other means for the maintenance of the workingmen's interests subjected those resorting to them to severe penalties. Yet the antithesis of capitalists and wage earners was rapidly hardening, and the strife of these two new social classes, though they were not yet wholly self-conscious, was a conspicuous feature in the life of the people.

For the ills of the times increase rather than alleviation was indicated in the teachings of the capitalistic philosophers. Malthus was suggesting, if not proving, that the forlorn condition of the working masses was permanent and inevitable. Ricardo was proving that the dominant right of the landowner and the capitalist in the products of industry was imbedded in the very nature of created things. James Mill was coldly formulating the rule of economic existence, summed up in pitiless competition, with the wall always for the weaker.

It was against the spirit of these doctrines, as well as against the conditions on which they were based, that the earliest systematic socialism took shape. Robert Owen, a practical factory owner, began as early as 1800 to determine the relations of employer and employed by coöperation rather than competition, and he and his followers preached for half a century the reordering of society so as to render impossible the poverty and wretchedness of the wage-earning classes. Between 1820 and 1840 the Owenites were an important element in the forces that brought about reforming legislation to improve the general situation. The laws that made trade unions criminal were repealed (1825), and in 1833 the first regulation of factories in the interest of the laborers was embodied in the statutes. These measures were part of the same large movement which resulted in the sweeping political reforms of the period. In spirit they were Whiggish, not radical, and were permeated with the characteristic Whig solicitude for the rights of property. In the heat of the agitation, however, there had appeared among the supporters of the laborers' cause systematic and well-argued denials of all just claim by landlords and capitalists to their rents and profits. This doctrine, put forth by William Thompson, John Gray, Thomas Hodgskin and others, made little permanent impression in England, but became fundamental in the later revolutionary socialism of the French and Germans.

The same decades in which Owenism most flourished in England witnessed the rise to prominence in France of the systems of Charles Fourier and Henri de Saint-Simon. The most influential works of both these philosophers appeared in the twenties, and the importance of their followers was most marked in the thirties and forties. Fourierism and Saint-Simonism approached social reform, not like Owenism from the practical side, but by the way of philosophic speculation. The purpose to get rid of the poverty and wretchedness that threatened society with disaster animated both Fourierists and Saint-Simonians. Only the latter,[1] however, found possessors of great wealth to be the chief obstacles to improvement and set up demands that the old ideas about the sacredness of their property should be discarded.

As the agitation about constitutional and nationalistic reform led up to the great convulsion of 1848, the various movements on the Continent for social improvement assumed definitely the character of political socialism. Owen, Saint-Simon, Fourier and others of their time had sought to effect the renovation of society

[1] For a distinction between Saint-Simon himself and the Saint-Simonians in this matter, see Menger, *Right to the Whole Produce of Labor*, p. 67.

through the voluntary adoption of their various remedial schemes by the convinced better classes. But landowners and capitalists manifested little disposition to abandon their rents and profits for the dim chances of social peace that the projects of the reformers offered. The laboring class found little improvement in the conditions of their life. Accordingly there appeared the demand for the overthrow of the existing system by whatever means were necessary, and the exaltation of the hitherto suppressed class to the first place in the political and economic organization of the nation. The good of the laborers must be made, it was held, the chief end of government, and society must take into its own hands the economic functions which landowners and capitalists had abused for their selfish ends.

In and about 1840 Louis Blanc and P. J. Proudhon promulgated doctrines that on different lines, but with like uncompromising directness, asserted the right of labor to the product of its effort regardless of the claims of idle landlords and capitalists. Blanc's teaching looked to a democracy that should supplant the capitalistic monarchy of Louis Philippe; Proudhon repudiated all forms of government alike and avowed himself an anarchist. The revolution of 1848 in France brought Louis Blanc and his projects into much prominence, but also to failure and exile.

Meanwhile the industrial conditions responsible for the English and French doctrines that have been noticed were extending to central Europe and producing eager and able German advocates of the doctrines. In January, 1848, on the eve of the revolutionary outbreak, Karl Marx and Frederick Engels formulated the famous Communist Manifesto, which may properly be regarded as marking the definitive entrance of revolutionary socialism into politics and political theory. The document contained no doctrine that had not been set forth before; but the form and sequence in which the principles were arranged were admirably adapted to the purposes of a political platform. Particularly effective was the portrayal of the antagonism, immovably fixed in the nature of things, between bourgeoisie and proletariat — the class war that would shape all social life till the final triumph of the proletariat should produce "an association in which the free development of each is the condition for the free development of all."

With the economic doctrine that was at the base of all the forms of socialistic theory it is not the purpose to deal in this place. The relation of this theory to the philosophy of government, however, will be examined in the following sections. At present it is necessary to turn to the development of sociology, which had begun to take shape at the very time when socialism was passing through its initial stages.

A distinction between society and state had pervaded the speculation of philosophers more or less consciously from the earliest times. The life of human aggregates had presented phases that were perceived to be remote from the field occupied by government and that were recognized at times to be more significant than the political phases. During the fifteenth, sixteenth and seventeenth centuries the state, as centred in the absolute monarch, dominated social philosophy. With the revolutionary eighteenth a reversal of the situation began. Vico, Montesquieu, the Physiocrats, Adam Smith and the economists, with also the jurists of the natural and the common law, brought into the foreground the non-governmental forces that operated in the life of the peoples. This was the field that was cultivated by Saint-Simon and the other founders of socialism. Sociology was their real subject; but the name itself and the application of it to a pretty clearly defined place among the sciences were due to Auguste Comte, a one-time disciple of Saint-Simon.

Comte's Positive Philosophy in its first general outline appeared in 1824 and became, with its full development, an influence of incalculable importance in the later thought of the century. He assigned to sociology, indeed, a sphere so all-embracing that its later votaries had to contract it materially; but the matter and method of the science were largely determined by his system. The terminology introduced by him is the current coin of social and political discussion to-day. Order and progress, social statics and social dynamics, military society and industrial society, egoism and altruism, — are all familiar pairs of antithetic terms that owe their vogue to Comte's unexcelled faculty for generalization. They suggest how successfully he combined in his great system the dogmatic and the historical method, and found a place in the evolution of humanity for both individualistic and socialistic doctrines and institutions.

Herbert Spencer, whose Synthetic Philosophy was substantially before the world at the end of our period, gave to sociology a content that was much narrower than that which Comte had given it, but made it correspondingly more definite and manageable. The indebtedness of Spencer to Comte, chiefly indirect and unconscious, is readily discernible, but there are at the same time even more obvious the strongly marked independent features of the later work. Evolution, recognized with balance and moderation by the Frenchman, was the whole spring of the Englishman's philosophy. Moreover, this evolution was affected by the biological principles that were so brilliantly demonstrated by Darwin in his epoch-making works of the fifties. The Darwinian influence contributed much to give to the Spencerian sociology a certain materialistic quality. This, with its vast research among the institutions of primitive societies and its bumptious though illogical individualism, set it off with great distinctness from the philosophy of Comte. Spencer's thought was, however, much more in harmony with the spirit of the time than the Frenchman's emotional and religious vagaries in his later days, and Spencer became the starting point of all further progress in social science. His significance in the philosophy of society was in marked contrast with the weakness of his influence on the theory of the state, wherein he tenaciously maintained an individualism that steadily lost ground before the rising tide of socialistic doctrine.

2. *Owen and Fourier*

When in the latter half of the nineteenth century the revolutionary dogmas of Marx and his school had become most conspicuous in the social movement, the earlier systems became known, by way of distinction, as Utopian Socialism. Under this term were included the doctrines and projects of Owen, Saint-Simon, Fourier and others.[1] The name was in some sense justified by the ideal societies that were advocated and put to a practical test by these thinkers and their followers. But while Plato and More and Campanella had constructed their fanciful commonwealths with no expectation of their being realized, the nineteenth century Utopians were profoundly convinced that their several systems were destined in no distant future to effect an entire transformation of social life.[2]

In the governmental reforms that were so much at issue in their time these philosophers had little or no interest. The political would disappear with the social evils when society should be reorganized on the proper principles. All the schools found in history evidence that the normal course of mankind in progress toward its goal had been checked and deflected by ignorance and error concerning the principles of group life; all held that a correct understanding of those principles would bring naturally the resumption of progress.

All agreed that an important, if not the most im-

[1] Cabet, Lamennais and the "Christian Socialists" might properly fall within this class.

[2] *Cf.* Owen, *Book of the New Moral World*, Preface and Introduction. Saint-Simon, *Œuvres*, t. 41, p. 121 *et seq.*

portant, source of the ills that afflicted mankind was poverty and its consequences. All agreed that the prevalence of poverty was due largely, if not exclusively, to the exaggerated recognition of self-interest as the mainspring of human action, and that the existing system of industry and commerce, based upon this principle and operating by unrestricted competition, must unendingly increase the misery of the race. All scored the injustice of unearned wealth as vehemently as they lamented the sufferings of undeserved poverty. All denounced the existing capitalistic system. Fourier, however, found capital indispensable, subject to the regulations imposed by his system; Owen maintained that when his simple rational laws for the creation of what is good for men should prevail, there would be no "useless private property"; but the Saint-Simonians announced as the most important means to the realization of social justice that the right to unearned property, so far as it depended on inheritance, must be abolished.

The error that has led men astray, so the Utopians all argued, has been the assumption that nature designed the individual rather than the group to be the basis of social existence. Society is not a deliberately created device of previously isolated men for the promotion of their several selfish interests; it springs from the feeling not from the reason of mankind. Sympathy — the sense of alikeness — brings men inevitably together; benevolence — willing the good of all — is the natural principle of association. These basic factors have been almost wholly lost sight of in the theory and practice of social life. Rivalry, competition, strife and war, with the endless exploitation of the weaker by the stronger, have become the accepted methods for determining the relations of individuals and of peoples to one another. To change all this and restore the reign of nature's peace and order to humanity, is the proclaimed purpose of all the Utopians.

The projects of the various schools for the achievement of this end had some things in common, but were for the most part widely divergent from one another. Owen and the Owenites devoted themselves chiefly to the improvement of conditions in the industrial world. Philanthropic devices for the benefit of the laborers were urged by precept and by example upon the obdurate British factory owners, and the legislation that was at last secured, against the bitter opposition of the *laissez-faire* economists, received hearty support from the Owenites. The most characteristic feature of their work, however, was the establishment among the working classes of coöperative societies for the supply of their needs. This form of voluntary association for the production and exchange of commodities attained great prominence and wide vogue in the twenties and thirties. Coöperation was hailed as the much-desired expedient for escaping the evils of the strife between capital and labor. The success of this device confirmed Owen in his belief that he had solved the problem of society in general, and he set forth with fanatical fervor his scheme of a reorganized world.[1]

[1] The scheme is embodied in a "Universal Code of Laws," which he says must supersede "the accumulation of nonsense and absurdity

The unit of this new order is to be a community of families numbering from 500 to 3000 persons, living on a tract of land large enough to support the members. The internal affairs of the community are to be directed by a council consisting of all the members from thirty to forty years of age; relations with other communities are in the charge of a like council of the members from forty to sixty years. Unions of these primary communities will be constituted under similar councils for larger areas. All the councils are to act in conformity to the code that Owen formulates, the basis of which is the fundamental law of nature that the individual's character is not formed by himself, but is the result of the circumstances and education to which he has been subjected. The chief prescriptions of the code are those that insure the "same general routine of education, domestic teaching and employment" to all children of both sexes, who are put from birth under the care of the community. Members who, despite their education, fail to act rationally are to be removed to the hospitals for physical, mental or moral invalids, where their cure is to be effected by the mildest possible treatment. If any directing council contravenes the fundamental laws of human nature it will be supplanted by a new one consisting of the members of the community between twenty and thirty or over sixty years of age. It is not explained how this substitution is to be effected, and there is nowhere in the scheme, save

in what are called *codes of law*, formerly or now in practice throughout the irrational-made nations of the world. . . ." — *Book of the New Moral World*, part vi, pp. 83–7.

in the clause referring to the hospitals, any suggestion of coercive government. What is to become of the existing political systems of the world is not discussed, but the thought is not obscure that they will fade imperceptibly away in the light of the new order.[1]

Fourier's project for escape from the evils of civilization took shape in that form of communal life which became famous as the "*phalange.*" His primary concern was with agricultural rather than industrial production, with the household rather than the factory. The true principles of association he worked out in an elaborate system wherein much acute and suggestive reflection was made useless by incoherent presentation and pedantic terminology.[2] The outstanding feature of his social philosophy was the doctrine of what he called "passional attraction" (*attraction passionelle*). According to this doctrine the passions or feelings of men, rather than their reason, must be considered the basis of every kind of association, and particularly of that coöperative union through which the primary needs of physical life are satisfied. Naturally all men dislike the incessant, monotonous labor that produces the necessities of life. Naturally every man finds relative if not absolute pleasure in some species of

[1] Owen's *Book of the New Moral World* is dedicated to King William IV, who, with other royal personages, displayed much interest in Owen till the reformer's unconventional views on religion and the relations of the sexes made further public interest inexpedient.

[2] For our purpose his *Théorie de l'unité universelle* is all that it is necessary to consult. All his important doctrine is there. The work was first published in 1822 under the title *L'Association domestique agricole.*

labor or in some alternation in species of labor. Ignorance or disregard of these basic facts accounts for the evils of social life whether in ancient or in modern times. Slavery, serfage and the wages system, with the governmental institutions that accompany and sustain them,[1] are but different forms of the distortion that results from the effort of certain classes, by deliberate association, to put all the repellent labor of social life upon others and retain the agreeable for themselves alone.

The way out is to transform the social organization in the light of the principles that Fourier has discovered. Labor must be made attractive, and therefore productive beyond all comparison with earlier ages. Every variety of taste, talent and other endowment must be recognized and utilized in the proportion that science shows to be requisite for the harmony of the whole and the happiness of the individual members. The typical association for this end is a group of five hundred families, fifteen to eighteen hundred persons, voluntarily united in a community which Fourier called a "phalanx."[2] It should include capitalists, laborers and persons of talent, each contributing as he is able to the productiveness and agreeableness of the community's life. Through the organization and specialization of the functions essential to the industries carried on, occupations suited to every taste would be avail-

[1] But Fourier makes very few references of any kind to political matters.

[2] The features of the phalanx are described repeatedly in all of Fourier's works. They may be found in the *Selections* by Franklin and Gide, especially p. 137, and in Brisbane's volume, *Theory of Social Organization*, part ii, pp. 81 *et seq.*

able, with the result that every member would labor with the zest of pleasure. "Passional attraction" rather than competitive greed for gain would rule the community's life. No wages should appear in the system. Every species of necessary labor must be performed by the members, participation of all in the generally repulsive kinds being stimulated in various ingenious ways. Every member of the community must be a shareholder, whose part in the profits shall be determined in accordance with a scale that assigns a fixed proportion to capital, to labor and to talent. But every member must be guaranteed a minimum return sufficient to free him from anxiety for himself or his family, and every member must possess the right to labor in such occupations as are adapted to his preference and his capacity.

With the establishment of such a system of social organization Fourier believes that poverty will disappear, true liberty will be assured to every individual, the real natural rights of man will be recognized, happiness and order will be universal, and consequently government, so far at least as its coercive activities are concerned — armies, scaffolds, prisons, courts of justice — will have no longer any cause for existence.[1] The trend of Fourier's thought is to anarchism.[2] There never appears in his writings, however, the slightest suggestion of revolutionary violence. His conviction is unfaltering that the great truths he has revealed will make their way by their own virtue.

[1] *Cf.* Brisbane, *op. cit.*, part i, p. 148.
[2] *Cf.* Gide, *op. cit.*, p. 22.

3. *Saint-Simonian Doctrine*

The chief writings of Henri de Saint-Simon on social reform were produced during the last ten years of his life, 1815–25. After his death a community of his disciples carried on at Paris an active agitation for the spread of his doctrines until 1831, when internal dissension and the action of the government terminated the formal existence of the school. Between the views actually enunciated by Saint-Simon and those formulated by his successors, of whom Enfantin was the recognized head, there is enough difference of form and substance to warrant the distinction usually made in the expression "Saint-Simon and the Saint-Simonians."[1]

The Saint-Simonian doctrine presents no scheme so concrete as that of Fourier or even that of Owen for the reformed organization of society. On the other hand it is far more profound and coherent in its underlying philosophy. It embodies a remarkable interpretation of history and displays extraordinary analytical power in the formulation of its dogmas.

Among the doctrines preached by Saint-Simon himself, the supreme significance of productive industry and those engaged in it, as compared with the non-productive or positively destructive (*i.e.*, military) activities and classes, was at the basis of all his thought.

[1] Most of the writings of Saint-Simon and many of those of his disciples, together with accounts of his life and the affairs of his followers, are collected in forty-seven volumes under the title, *Œuvres de Saint-Simon et d'Enfantin*. The additional literature concerning Saint-Simonism is extensive. For our particular point of view the little volume by Janet, *Saint-Simon et le Saint-Simonisme*, is most useful.

He never wearied of exalting the workers and disparaging the idlers of society. A celebrated *jeu d'esprit*, that came to be known as Saint-Simon's "Parable," gravely calculated the relative effects on the nation that would result from the loss, in the first case, of the three thousand leading men of science, art and industry, and in the other case, of all the near relatives of the king, all the chief executive, military and judicial officials, and the ten thousand wealthiest men of leisure. The conclusion was that in the first case France would for at least a generation have no important place among the civilized peoples of the earth, while in the second case there would be no effect at all beyond a widespread regret at the disappearance of so many Frenchmen.[1]

Saint-Simon proved to his own satisfaction that the industrial class was the one useful class in society; that this must eventually become the only class; and that the sole criterion of excellence in legislative and administrative measures of the government was their favorable effect on industry.[2] The progress of social welfare depended on the advancement of science, the fine arts and the useful arts and to this advancement the contribution of the idle classes was less than nothing; for by their influence in the government they saddled

[1] *Œuvres*, Vol. XX, p. 17. Saint-Simon was prosecuted for this essay, but was acquitted (1820). For the same distinction between the *travailleurs* and the *oisifs* that was developed at the same time by Auguste Comte and Ch. Dunoyer, see Janet, *op. cit.*, p. 28. Janet properly notes the important fact that this distinction between workers and idlers was not at all a distinction between labor and capital. Bankers and manufacturers were among the workers; *rentiers* and great landowners were among the idlers.

[2] *Œuvres*, XIX, 74.

themselves on the nation and diverted to their support the earnings and the energies of the producing classes — the men of science, of art and of industry (*les savants, les artistes et les artisans*). With the government thus in the hands not of the producing but of the non-producing class, society presented to the reflecting mind the spectacle of a world upside down.

The new social order must rest on the political leadership of the useful class. Capacity rather than possessions must become the qualification for control of the public service. The producers must supplant the mere consumers — the bees the drones — in political authority. For the realization of which end in France Saint-Simon sketched out the reorganized political system. Without requiring the abolition of the monarchy, he called for a government with supreme power in a new species of parliament. This body should include, first, a house of invention, consisting of civil engineers, poets (*ou autres inventeurs en littérature*), painters, sculptors, architects and musicians; second, a house of examination, consisting of physicists and mathematicians; and third, a house of execution, consisting of captains of industry (*chefs des maisons d'industrie*), unsalaried, and duly apportioned among the various kinds of business. The first house would present projects of law, the second would examine and pass upon them, and the third would adopt them.

Saint-Simon readily admitted that this scheme would be called fantastic and utopian, but he submitted in its defence a highly suggestive historical argument, in which appeared many anticipations of economic, socialistic and sociological theory that have since become commonplace.[1]

Various expansions and modifications of this political program were formulated by Saint-Simon, but he never ceased to manifest his feeling that both political and economic considerations must be supplemented and controlled by those of a purely spiritual character if social reform was to be assured. The full expression of this feeling was given in the *New Christianity*, written in the year before his death.[2] This brilliant essay embodied a bitter and eloquent attack on both Catholics and Protestants for having lost sight of the fundamental principle of Christianity and of religion itself. The new church must stand, he holds, on the dogma that the end of religion is to ameliorate as rapidly as possible the condition of the poor — the most numerous class of society. Social righteousness can be attained only through a social organization that is adapted to this end.

[1] *Œuvres*, XX, especially pp. 50 *et seq.* This volume consists of the periodical called *L'Organisateur*, conducted with many vicissitudes by Saint-Simon and his disciples in 1819–20. The reader will not fail to see much in this volume that suggests the philosophy of Comte and the history that was produced by Niebuhr, Thierry and their school in the first half of the century, with a strong leaning to economic and social interest and interpretations. Comte and Thierry were both Saint-Simonians.

[2] Saint-Simon died in 1825. The *Nouveau Christianisme* is in *Œuvres*, XXIII, 99. It was written apparently to carry out a purpose announced in his critical preface to the contribution of Auguste Comte to the "Catéchisme des Industriels." Saint-Simon says of his disciple's work: ". . . notre élève n'a traité que la partie scientifique de notre système, mais . . . il n'a point exposé sa partie sentimentale et religieuse. . . . Nous remédierons autant qu'il nous sera possible à cet inconvénient. . . ."—*Op. cit.*, XXXVIII, 4.

It was this doctrine of the master that determined the course of his disciples after his death. They constituted themselves into a society for the practice and promulgation of the Saint-Simonian religion, and for six years, until dissolved by the police, this society was a conspicuous centre of radical agitation. Its leaders gave to their master's doctrines an exposition that is superior to his own in coherence and clarity, and they developed some of his ideas into dogmas that were more in the line of the later socialism than anything distinctly enunciated by himself. Their system was substantially as follows.[1]

History shows mankind passing alternately through social conditions that may be designated as respectively organic and critical. The pagan world to the time of Socrates and the Christian world to the time of Luther were organic; the post-Socratic period was critical till Catholic Christianity brought a new organic era, which was destroyed in turn by the Lutheran reform and the revolution. It is time for the reordering of society in the organic kind, and Saint-Simon has revealed the way.

Through this succession of epochs humanity has been making its way, however blindly, to a single goal — the association of all men in all their relations for the peaceful exploitation of the material world for the satisfaction of their needs. In past ages, both the organic and the critical, there has ever been the exploitation of man rather than of nature, and the principle of an-

[1] The exposition of this system, chiefly by Bazard, with some contributions by Enfantin, is to be found in *Œuvres*, XLI and XLII.

tagonism has operated to thwart the prevalence of association. Pagan society was based on the exploitation of man by man through slavery, and for the sake of slaves war was general. Mediæval society practised the same exploitation through serfdom, and war for the dominion over the land that the serfs cultivated was general. The revolution has abolished the last vestige of serfdom, but the new industrial system has brought into play the old propensity, and those who have retained the property rights developed in feudal times are enabled to exploit the propertyless classes through the wage system. To remedy this particular wrong the Saint-Simonians look to a complete transformation of the idea of property, the first step in the process being the abolition of the right of inheritance.[1] Society must soon become an association of workers (*travailleurs*) and the control of the means of production must go to those who can use them, not to any who claim them by mere right of birth.

This conception of the future of property is but one feature, however, of the new social structure that Saint-Simonism is to introduce. The complete evolution (for no violent overthrow of existing institutions is to be for a moment thought of) will show a world society based upon three factors that dominate the life of mankind. These are religion, science and industry, corresponding to the principles of love, wisdom and power, and thus to the spiritual, the intellectual and the industrial qualities (*capacités*) of the individual. In every community the three classes of the population

[1] *Œuvres*, XLI, 238 *et seq.* and *passim.*

determined by the predominance of these three qualities respectively will carry on in harmony the activities requisite to the perfect life. Under such a condition society will be "organized" — will be a true association instead of a confused mass of struggling and hostile groups and individuals. The intolerable conditions in the critical period that is ending have been due to the exaltation of the principle of individualism and to the general prevalence of competition, especially in the industrial field. For this will now be substituted a régime of coöperation for the ends of society as a whole. Industry and science will work harmoniously together for the best employment of the instruments of production, which society alone must control. Religion, finally, will be the supreme coördinating and directing force in the system.

The Saint-Simonian community was thus in a sense a theocracy; at all events it was ruled by an absolute priesthood. Religion, however, meant to the Saint-Simonians something quite different from what it meant to the Christian. It comprehended the whole realm of the feelings or emotions as distinct from the intellect. It was manifest particularly in love and sympathy. But love and sympathy, rather than reason and force, were held to be the real bond of human society.[1] From this the conclusion followed that the government of a properly constituted association fell necessarily to the class in whom the feelings were most developed. The functions of this governing body were

[1] This doctrine is worked out pretty fully in *op. cit.*, XLII, 338 *et seq.*, 413 *et seq.*

strongly suggestive of those assigned by Plato to his philosopher guardians. The end kept in view and conditioning all their activity was expressed in terms that embodied the Saint-Simonians' most famous formula: "to realize and maintain the *association* of all the men on the surface of the globe, in which each shall be placed according to the capacity that he shall have received from God, and rewarded according to his works."[1]

4. *The Beginnings of Anarchism*

The utopian systems that have been examined in the last two sections were on the whole authoritarian rather than libertarian in their political outlook. To use words of later vogue, these systems were socialistic rather than individualistic. They contemplated the disappearance of the coercive functioning of government, but they retained, especially Saint-Simonism, the thought of a rational or spiritual control exercised by preëminently endowed individuals or classes. As distinct from this kind of thinking there appeared at the same time a development of the strictest individualism into the formal theory of anarchy. The Frenchman Proudhon, in 1840, was apparently the first to assume formally the name of anarchist. The substance of the doctrine that justified the name, however, had been pretty fully set forth half a century before by the Englishman William Godwin, in his *Political Justice*.

Godwin assumes that the happiness of individuals is the end of all social institutions, that government

[1] *Œuvres*, XLII, 348.

contributes to this end only because the errors and perversities of some few render control in some form inevitable, that these errors and perversities result not from will but from weakness and ignorance, and that as weakness and ignorance diminish government will pass to its euthanasia.[1] "Each man," Godwin says, "should be wise enough to govern himself, without the intervention of any compulsory restraint; and since government, even in its best estate, is an evil, . . . we should have as little of it as the general peace of human society will permit."[2]

In the line of these doctrines Godwin directs a vigorous polemic against monarchic and aristocratic governments in particular, and in general against those democracies that dominate through majority rule over the individual. Moreover, such ends of governmental policy as national wealth, national prosperity and national glory, he holds to be deceitful formulas through which greedy and ambitious men lure the masses into debasement and poverty. War for such spurious purposes is the antipodes of justice. It involves repression of the individual to the maximum degree. All that government can legitimately do is to suppress injustice to individuals within its community, and defend the community against invasion from without.

In the existing condition of ignorance and weakness among men Godwin conceives that some measure of governmental authority is necessary. Its limit should be, however, (1) local associations (*e.g.*, in parishes) for dealing with offenders, who, he maintains, could

[1] *Political Justice*, Vol. I, p. 238. [2] *Ibid.*, p. 246.

never defy the sober judgment of the mass of their neighbors; and (2) for the settlement of difficulties between parishes and for general defence against invasion, a central assembly meeting either only when an emergency arises or at most for one day in each year. These bodies, both local and central, would at first act by command and force, but eventually expostulation and persuasion would effect their ends, and thus would follow "the dissolution of political government, of that brute engine which has been the only perennial cause of the vices of mankind."[1]

The existing system of private property is in Godwin's view no less irrational than political authority. Under the natural principle of the equality of men one man's claim to what he needs or wants is as valid as any other man's. From this dogma Godwin deduces the conclusion that the unequal distribution of wealth is unjust and must pass away. Not that the end should be attained by compulsory action of either government or individuals. Godwin stands firmly on his ground that compulsion, whether by one man or by a group, is baneful. Persuasion, not force, must remove the evil of property as of government.

Godwin's treatment of this subject[2] presents an interesting combination of the old speculations of Plato and More in their utopias with the theories of the eighteenth-century exponents of natural law and natural rights. He adds, however, considerations that were suggested by the English industrial conditions of his

[1] For this whole subject see *Polit. Just.*, Book v, chaps. 22–24.
[2] Book viii, in Vol. II, p. 420.

own time and that were to assume great importance in the socialistic philosophy of succeeding generations.[1] The influence of these ideas is traceable clearly enough in the works of the Saint-Simonians and others, but they received particular development and prominence in the speculations of the first avowed anarchist, Pierre Joseph Proudhon.

The whole substance of Proudhon's doctrine, so far as it concerns our subject, is to be found in his early and most famous work, *What is Property?* published in 1840.[2] He assumes the natural equality of men in rights, and the right of every man to the product of his own labor, and to nothing else. From this it follows that the wage-laborer retains, even after receiving his wages, a natural property right in the product. It is a violation of this right for the landowner and the capitalist to take any part of the product. Hence the retention of such part under the name of rent and interest is without warrant, and it is to wealth accumulated by such a process that he applies the well-known dictum, "Property is robbery."

Proudhon fully concurs in the distinction made by the Saint-Simonians between workers and idlers, but he

[1] See especially the second chapter of his Book viii, where he distinguishes three degrees of property: 1. the means of subsistence; 2. the fruits of labor; and 3. the produce of the labor of others.

[2] His complete works have been published in twenty-six volumes. The *What is Property?* has been translated into English by Benj. R. Tucker. Other writings of Proudhon that contain various aspects and elaborations of his political philosophy, for the most part less clearly and simply presented, are: La Guerre et la Paix, *Œuvres*, t. 13, 14; L'Ordre dans l'Humanité, *Œuvres*, t. 3; La Justice, *Œuvres*, t. 21–26; Solution du Problème social, *Œuvres*, t. 6.

gives a strictly economic turn to the discussion by identifying the idlers with landowners and capitalists. Thus the problem becomes one wholly within the field of industry rather than one of which industry is merely an element.[1] Proudhon combats further the Saint-Simonians by maintaining, against their rule that each must be rewarded according to his capacity, the dogma that in society equal sharing of the product of joint effort is the only just rule. Superiority in productive power, like superiority in talent or genius, may assure a degree of satisfaction and distinction to its possessor, but to society as a whole it is but part of one man's contribution to the total needs and deserves therefore but one man's equal pay.[2]

As to society and government Proudhon develops Godwin's doctrine with a refinement of analysis and a play of paradox that are far beyond the powers of the earlier writer. Man is social by nature, as Aristotle asserted. Sociability is manifested in three degrees, corresponding to successive stages in the development of intelligence. The first is sympathy or pity, "a sort of magnetism awakened in us by the contemplation of a being similar to ourselves"; the second is justice, "the recognition of the equality between another's personality and our own"; the third is social proportionality (*équité, humanitas*), which arises from the differences in strength, skill or courage among men, and is exhibited in the generosity and self-sacrifice of the superior and the gratitude and honor accorded by the

[1] *Cf. supra*, pp. 360–1.
[2] *What is Property?* Tucker's trans., pp. 129, 133–4.

inferior. All these degrees and aspects of the social instinct are essential in rational society, but justice has in fact been excluded from the life of humanity by the institution of property, and property has been chiefly responsible for the existence of government.[1]

Rousseau's account of the origin of inequality is suggested very strongly by the history of property and government as stated by Proudhon. The latter is, however, the more acute in his metaphysics. Primitive man, he holds, lived in the state of "negative communism," the sympathetic aspect of the social instinct dominating his life.[2] As the other aspects, justice and equity, developed, the superior man, freely receiving the respect and esteem of his fellows, took also by his power a larger share of material comforts. Thus property arose by force alone and was manifested in slavery, feudal services, taxes, rent, etc. Later the principal manifestation was in various forms of artifice, producing "the profits of manufactures, commerce and banking . . . and finally all sorts of social inequalities."

Along with these deplorable effects of property follows the worst of all, government. No matter what form it takes — monarchic, oligarchic, democratic, it is illegitimate and absurd; and Proudhon asserts flatly his own attitude toward all of them: "Although a firm friend of order, I am (in the full force of the term)

[1] For the whole theory of Proudhon on this topic, see *What is Property?* 1st memoir, chap. v (Tucker's trans., p. 219).

[2] In connection with this discussion Proudhon takes occasion to denounce communism as severely as he denounces property. "Property is the exploitation of the weak by the strong. Communism is the exploitation of the strong by the weak." *Op. cit.*, p. 250.

an anarchist."[1] The perversion through which the strong man in primitive times usurps control over material things enables him to usurp control of his fellow-men. It is natural for a group to look for guidance to its oldest or its wisest man; but when it begins to look to its strongest, despotism has supervened. His will becomes the rule for all and this remains the principle when the monarch gives way to the narrow group of oligarchs and to the majority rule of democracy.

Proudhon fortifies his *a priori* demonstration, which is not always cogent, that property and government are illegitimate in origin, with a rather clever manipulation of history to show that they have moved and will continue to move together to disappearance. Authority of the human will, he says, has already decreased before the growth of habits and customs that have become restraining laws. The function of the government is now executive rather than legislative. With the growth of science man comes to understand that

> political truth, or the science of politics, exists quite independently of the will of sovereigns, the opinion of majorities and popular beliefs, — that kings, ministers, magistrates and nations, as wills, have no connection with science; . . . that the function of the legislator is reduced, in the last analysis, to the methodical search for truth.

Thus, just as property is giving way to the advance of justice, *i.e.*, of equality, sovereignty of the will is giving way to the sovereignty of reason. "As man seeks justice in equality, so society seeks order in anarchy."

> Anarchy, — the absence of a master, of a sovereign, — such is the form of government to which we are every day approxi-

[1] *What is Property?* trans., p. 260.

mating, and which our accustomed habit of taking man for our rule and his will for law, leads us to regard as the height of disorder and the expression of chaos.[1]

In this proper order of society the truths of exact science rather than any human choice or volition will guide the social life.

Every question of domestic politics must be decided by departmental statistics; every question of foreign politics is a question of international statistics. The science of government rightly belongs to one of the sections of the Academy of Sciences, whose permanent secretary is necessarily prime minister; and since every citizen may address a memoir to the Academy, every citizen is a legislator. But as the opinion of no one is of any value until its truth has been proven, nobody can substitute his will for reason — nobody is king.[2]

Law, Proudhon continues, is merely a conclusion of reason. Legality, like justice, is as independent of human approval as mathematical truth. A human legislator does not *make* law: he merely states it. "He is the proclaimer, not the inventor."[3] Any one may announce a truth of political or social existence; it is law only when it is recognized by the nation; ". . . the nation is the executive power." Hence the claim by any individual that his will is law in any sense is destructive of social life. Humanity can be saved only by ruthless suppression of such claims and therefore by the overthrow of the property-owner (*propriétaire*), the bandit and the monarch, who are all in the same class.

[1] *Op. cit.*, pp. 263–4. [2] *Op. cit.*, p. 265.
[3] Godwin preached this doctrine.

The only just and true form of society, Proudhon concludes, is "free association, liberty — whose sole function is to maintain equality in the means of production and equivalence in the exchanges." "Politics is the science of liberty. The government of man by man . . . is oppression. Society finds its highest perfection in the union of order with anarchy."

The character of Proudhon's constructive proposals would warrant his classification with the utopian socialists as justly as with the anarchists. His forecast of the social and political future is as vague and incoherent as that of the Saint-Simonians and quite as fantastic as that of Fourier. On the other hand there is an aggressive and revolutionary quality in Proudhon's attack on the principle of government in general that is lacking in the earlier writers. His adoption, moreover, of the term anarchy as expressing the nature of his goal has a serious significance in distinguishing him from his immediate predecessors. Finally the part he took in the agitation that culminated in the great disturbances of 1848 and the succeeding years stamps him as belonging to a school of his own. He remained to the end of his life in 1865, amid a variety of experiences of prosecution and exile, a vigorous and independent exponent of a peculiar social and economic philosophy, maintained with a prolific output of the distorted erudition and paradoxical dialectic that were at once the strength and weakness of his style. His followers, however, were few. His force was primarily critical and destructive, and the trend of the time, among the assailants of the existing social order, was distinctly toward that species of doctrine that began to look to the leadership of the rising German socialism and its ablest representative, Karl Marx.

5. *Marxist Doctrine*

One of the most spectacular episodes of the revolutionary upheaval of 1848 was the experiment at Paris with national workshops. This was a practical application, in a crude and imperfect manner, of the socialistic dogma with which Louis Blanc had been conspicuously identified, that of the right to labor. We have seen that such a right had been among the natural endowments ascribed to all men by the French constitution of 1793.[1] When unemployment and poverty assumed distressing proportions in France through the rise of factories, this right was made the foundation of the demand that the government should guarantee to the citizens the opportunity to earn a livelihood. Blanc's plan was to insure to workingmen the equipment for coöperative production, so as to be independent of the capitalists. What was actually done by the revolutionary government in 1848 was to offer employment to practically all comers under the direction of the government itself. The undertaking ended in disaster and insurrection, but it stood as a sign of the transition of the socialistic movement from mild humanitarianism to political revolutionism.

The platform of principle on which the new socialism was destined to stand took form in the celebrated

[1] *Supra*, p. 122.

Communist Manifesto,[1] prepared by Karl Marx and Friedrich Engels in January, 1848. In this is embodied the whole substance of the doctrine, so far as concerns political theory, that dominated the socialistic movement till at least the death of Marx in 1883.

The basic idea is that the general social order at any given time is fixed by the existing system of production and exchange of the commodities required for the satisfaction of human needs. These economic facts determine the forms of political life. History shows governmental institutions changing with the changes in industry and commerce. But these industrial and commercial changes are reflected primarily in the transformed relationships of social classes. Here is found the clue to all history; for, in the words of the *Manifesto*, "the history of all hitherto existing society is the history of class struggles."

But the battling classes shown to Marx are not those so much discussed by the Saint-Simonians. Not the workers and the idlers, but the bourgeoisie and the proletariat, are the elements whose strife is the substance of contemporary social life. The odium that is loaded upon the idlers by the utopian-socialist literature is by the *Manifesto* assigned with increased measure to the bourgeoisie. This class, having, as the Third Estate, wrested social prestige and political power from the feudal privileged classes, is now, as tyrannic

[1] The *Manifesto*, printed originally in German and secretly circulated, is now available in many forms and in most modern languages. I have used the edition published by Charles H. Kerr & Co., of Chicago, probably in 1911, and described on the title page as the "Authorized English Translation."

capital, to be overthrown by the oppressed and exploited proletariat. Modern economic conditions render it inevitable that all lesser social groups shall be absorbed in one or the other of these two classes. Political, religious and scientific interests will become the servile tools of the capitalists, resisting individuals being crushed down into the ranks of the proletariat. Warring nationalities will forget their antagonisms and will all alike, by the pressure of world-wide commercial and industrial conditions, be divided into the parties of capital and labor.

The reciprocal antagonism of these two parties is unceasingly intensified by the operation of the same influences that created them. Under the law of its being the bourgeoisie moves remorselessly on from exploitation to exploitation, forcing ever new masses of its victims down into the ranks of the proletariat. Its own relative numbers correspondingly diminish and world society assumes ever more clearly the aspect of a small group of immensely wealthy capitalists dominating despotically, through their control of the means of production, the whole of the human race.

To Marx the end of this process is no less plain than its development. The masses of the proletariat, educated by their experience and conscious of their strength, will overwhelm their oppressors as the bourgeoisie overwhelmed the feudal classes. The political revolution will be succeeded and paralleled by the social revolution. All the instrumentalities of production, now monopolized by the few under the name of capital, will be taken over by the masses for the general good.

The political control that goes with this economic power will be assumed by the community, to whom it belongs. Such result is a necessary consequence of the forces at work in the progress of modern civilization. It is foreordained in accordance with the materialistic interpretation of history that is set forth with such power and plausibility in the *Manifesto*. It rests upon the relations between the physical constitution of the earth and the mental and physical attributes of man.

In strict logic the demonstration that the social revolution is inevitable would render unnecessary any deliberate action by men to bring it about. But Marx was as indisposed as any earlier or later determinist to let nature take its course unaided. From his youth he was active in the promotion of practical revolution. The *Manifesto* was designed as a program of action for the Communists, and it embodied therefore the announcement of concrete projects. These, if not always in entire harmony with the philosophy of the movement, constitute an important revelation of its practical spirit.

The immediate aim of the Communists is declared to be the formation of the proletariat into a self-conscious class, which shall overthrow the bourgeosie and appropriate to itself the political power of the vanquished. Then will follow, as steps in the regeneration of society, the wresting of all capital from the bourgeoisie; the centralizing of all instruments of production in the hands of the state, "*i.e.*, of the proletariat organized as the ruling class"; and the most rapid possible increase of productive forces. Credit will be centralized in the hands of the state, manufacturing and agriculture will be developed under the same auspices, the liability to labor will be imposed upon all, and education in public schools will be free for all.

None of these proposals was new in the history of socialism. The novel note was in the uncompromising demand that they should be realized by a revolution that should insure the supremacy of the wage-earning masses. The authors of the *Manifesto* were quite aware that they were proposing, not the abolition of class rule, but the transfer of absolute power from one class to another. And they defined political power as "merely the organized power of one class for oppressing another." But the proletariat, they explained, was organized as a class merely as an incident of the struggle with the enemy and for the purpose of effecting the revolution. When the new authority shall have swept away by force the old conditions of production, there will no longer exist any basis for classes and class antagonisms; the proletariat will have abolished its own supremacy as a class, and society will be, not a group of warring classes, but "an association in which the free development of each [individual?] is the condition for the free development of all."

This somewhat jaunty evasion of a serious dilemma is out of tone with Marxist doctrine in general and suggests the vagueness of the Utopians in respect to what is to follow the realization of the reforms that are aimed at. The idea that a millennial calm is to prevail after the triumph of the proletariat is in shrieking contradiction of all the implications of the *Manifesto* and other

Marxist productions. Conflict and struggle appear as normal and necessary concomitants of the social evolution, and Marx found great satisfaction in likening this to the biological evolution that Darwin was just bringing into consciousness.[1] But Darwin never suggested that the process would cease just as soon as man became finally rid of the characteristics of the *Pithecanthropus*.

Marx's own energies were employed throughout his life in developing and buttressing with abstruse economic theory the doctrine of bourgeois tyranny and the class struggle, and promoting all possible revolutionary enterprises for the overthrow of existing social institutions. His ideas and his influence were at the maximum of their importance in the sixties and the seventies. In these decades the International Workingmen's Association, of which he was the leading spirit, expressed in a peculiarly satisfactory way the policy that he approved for the promotion of the proletarian revolution. With the dissolution of the International, however, the leadership in practical movements for socialistic ends passed to those who adopted, without Marx's approval, the method of action through national political parties. Various modifications of Marxist principles gained acceptance in these parties, but the general doctrine of the *Communist Manifesto* remained dominant in the socialistic movement to the end of our period.

[1] Marx is reported to have said once: "Nothing ever gives me greater pleasure than to have my name thus linked onto Darwin's. His wonderful work makes my own absolutely impregnable. Darwin may not know it, but he belongs to the social revolution." — Spargo, *Karl Marx*, p. 200. *Cf.* also pp. 323 *et seq.*

6. *Lorenz von Stein*

A broad and in many respects most profound societarian philosophy of the middle nineteenth century was that of Lorenz von Stein. This made a deep impression in its time, but for various reasons passed soon into neglect and almost oblivion.[1] It is noteworthy in our survey, however, for its scientific synthesis of the earlier German dogmatic idealism with the historical materialism that was preached by Marx. It exhibited admirably the common ground in which socialism and sociology had their roots.

Stein's first work, published in 1844, was a history and analysis of French (utopian) socialism, leading to a prediction of impending social revolution. The general European convulsion of 1848 naturally led him to further reflection on the general subject and to the production of a larger work, which he prefaced with an introduction entitled "The Concept of Society."[2] This introduction presents the theory that is the subject of our consideration.

Stein's fundamental dogmas are suggestive at once of Haller and of Marx. Human association (*Gemeinschaft*), he holds, depends inevitably in structure and in function on the relation of the two classes — the haves and the have-nots. The potential or actual

[1] One important reason for this was the transfer of Stein's chief interest from social science to law and administration. For some particulars of his personality and career see Simkhovitch, *Marxism versus Socialism*, 174 *et seq.;* Bluntschli, *Geschichte*, 731; Spargo, *Karl Marx*, 67.

[2] The title of the work in full is this: *Der Begriff der Gesellschaft und die sociale Geschichte der französischen Revolution bis zum Jahre 1830*. The date is 1849. I have used the second edition, 1855.

subjection of the one to the other is determined by the continuous seeking for "goods," that is, for the satisfaction of desire, whether material or spiritual. This striving after "goods" is the substance of life in general, both individual and social; and all life is manifested in the action and reaction of two elements, the personal and the non-personal — conscious intelligence and blind force, man and nature.[1] In the social life of man these conflicting elements serve to distinguish what we call state from what we call society. The substance of the life of the human race is a ceaseless struggle between these two.

In the state is expressed the principle of free, self-determining personality. Its organization and action are directed to the development of every individual to the fullest liberty, to the fullest personal perfection. Society, on the other hand, expresses the principle of blind, unintelligent, instinctive self-interest — the purpose to make all external things, including persons, contributory to special needs and satisfactions. While the state operates to make every one free to achieve the satisfaction of his desires by his own intelligent efforts, society tends always to promote the ends of some individuals through the subjection of others.

Having thus connected his primary dogmas with the conceptions of state and society, Stein interprets familiar history in accordance with his theory. He finds the salient feature in the career of every community

[1] Stein explains his meaning by saying that the complete absorption of the non-personal by the personal is God, while at the other limit the absorption of the personal in the non-personal is death. Human life ranges between these limits. *Op. cit.*, p. xxx.

to be the conflict of classes — the effort of special interests to promote their respective good at the expense of their rivals. In pursuance of this object the immediate aim of each class is to control for its particular ends the power of the state. This means, in Stein's theory, that the struggle is fundamentally one between social forces and political forces — between society and the state. Where history records the prestige and power of gilds, monopolies and privileged classes, the record is that of the triumph of the social over the political principle. Where the system of caste prevails, this triumph is complete: the state is dissipated and destroyed in the class distinctions and the community exhibits what Stein calls "absolute society."[1]

A strong trend of humanity toward such supremacy of the social principle is found by Stein to be manifested in the career of every community. The domination of class, with the resulting condition of unfreedom (*Unfreiheit*), shows the universal power of natural forces. Only by a mighty exertion of conscious intelligence is the balance ever restored in favor of the state and of the personality and freedom which it expresses. But a perfect realization of freedom through the state is impossible, since men must live in society, and society implies some measure of unfreedom.[2] All that can be looked for is the overthrow of any class that at a given time has the power of the state in its hands. To that extent freedom will be obtained.

[1] *Op. cit.*, p. lix.

[2] Stein explains that this was the thought of Rousseau when he said that a perfect republic was possible only for the gods. *Op. cit.*, p. lxvi. *Cf. supra*, p. 31.

It is obvious that Stein contemplates as the normal mode of community life the same class struggle which appears in the *Communist Manifesto*. His exposition of the process through which the transition from unfreedom is effected shows a less uncompromising spirit than that of Marx.[1] Stein recognizes reform as well as revolution to be a logical and customary way to the end. The movement must begin, he holds, in society rather than in the state. The transformation of the social order always precedes and determines the shaping of the political order. This doctrine is the basis of Stein's contention that reform rather than revolution is the normal method of developing the régime of liberty. Here begins his divergence from the dogma of Marx.

For breaking the dominion of one social class over the rest the absolute prerequisite, Stein declares, is the acquisition by the subject classes of social "goods." Marxian doctrine concurs with this, but largely ignores all but material goods, that is, wealth. Stein, on the contrary, stresses the primary importance of spiritual goods. The independent personality that constitutes liberty rests more upon the spiritual than upon the material. An individual is free only when he possesses spiritual goods, and such possession connotes knowledge and capacity, or in short culture (*Bildung*).[2]

[1] As to the possible influence of Stein's first work on Marx, see Spargo and Simkhovitch, *loc. cit.*

[2] The difficulty of rendering *Bildung* by any single English word is well known. "Education" is in some cases satisfactory, but is likely to suggest a process rather than a result. "Culture" as a translation has obvious weaknesses, but seems fairly useful here.

A subject class takes the first step toward independence, therefore, only when it begins a cultural advance. From that time the struggle with the ruling class is continuous.

While the initial impulse comes thus from the spiritual side, material goods soon assume equal importance in the movement and the conflict. The demand for culture and the demand for wealth go hand in hand and give each other reciprocal support. Stein acutely indicates, however, an important distinction in this matter. Culture — spiritual goods — may always be acquired to an indefinite extent by those who lack it, without diminishing in any degree the possessions of those who have it; as to material goods this is far from universally true. In this distinction lies a reason for the greater bitterness of the class conflict when the issue has reached its full development on the economic side.

There are indeed three stages distinguishable in the process through which the subject class rises to power. First it acquires social goods — culture and property — and the justice of such acquisition becomes generally recognized. Second, by political reform or revolution the government is so transformed as to express this new sense of right in the constitution and law of the community. These two stages have been achieved in Western Europe. Before it lies the further and by far the most serious stage of the advance.[1]

The difficulty in this situation is explained by Stein through the application of his basic philosophy to the

[1] Stein, *op. cit.*, pp. xcviii *et seq.*

relation of capital to labor. It was relatively easy, he asserts, for the subject class under the old régime to acquire a share in social goods, especially property, since the superiority of the ruling class rested merely on passive possession. But the ruling class of the later day, the industrial capitalists, hold their position by laborious acquisition. They labor as truly as do the wage-earners and they maintain their social power by so using their capital as to increase it constantly and as constantly to exclude the wage-earners from any share in it. In industrial society the class that is without industrial capital is almost wholly at the mercy of the other: there is the utmost disparity, Stein holds, between the combatants when laboring possession is opposed to possessionless labor.[1]

The only way out is here, as in the earlier stage of the eternal struggle for liberty, through the acquisition first of spiritual goods by the subject class — through the attainment of knowledge and capacity by education. However impassable the barrier maintained by the dominant economic class against the acquisition of material goods by the wage-earners, the aspiration to culture can never be suppressed. There is no power in the world able to prevent the spread of knowledge and capacity. This is as true in a society based on industry as in any other. In this truth, Stein holds, is the key to the existing agitation in Europe. The civilized world confronts, not political cataclysm, but social reform or revolution. Such is the end portended by the rise of communism, socialism and the idea of social democracy.[2]

[1] Stein, *op. cit.*, p. civ. [2] *Ibid.*, p. cvi.

Under these three heads Stein classes the various theories and practical projects of social reorganization that were current. The terms "communism" and "socialism" he uses in a way that exactly transposes the meanings attached to them in the *Communist Manifesto*, but corresponds to the usage that later became universal. By communism he means the sort of doctrine set forth by the Saint-Simonians and Fourier; by socialism he indicates the ideas of Marx and his followers.[1]

The basis of all these subversive movements is, according to Stein, the instinctive craving for liberty and equality. Liberty means self-dependence and a free field for the development of the individual personality; it is the characteristic aspiration of the self-conscious man. Equality is an idea that is deduced from that of liberty, but takes in practical matters a crude and illogical, though highly influential, form, namely, the demand for an equal participation by all individuals in material goods. Communism, as showing favor to this idea, is severely condemned by Stein. In denying property to the individual and vesting it all in the community, it does not exalt the laboring class, but merely gives to the community or the state the position of superiority formerly possessed by individuals.

Socialism, on the other hand, gives labor as a class the control of the other class, that is, of capital. Socialism, Stein says, is based upon labor and thus upon the

[1] *Ibid.*, pp. cvii *et seq.* *Cf. Communist Manifesto*, pp. 47 *et seq.* Also Spargo, *Karl Marx*, p. 89 (concerning Weitling, whom Stein refers to as a particularly obnoxious communist) and p. 97.

idea of individual personality, which is peculiarly expressed in free labor. It does not, like communism, seek to obliterate all distinctions between individuals and so destroy all social organization. Its goal is a society based upon the division and organization of labor for production, without reference to questions of possession. To realize its ends Stein believes that the laboring class must get into its hands the power that is necessary to overcome the opposing class, and that power is the state.[1]

Logically the socialistic idea is closely connected with the idea of political democracy. Both rest upon the concept of personality independent of material goods. Because of this, Stein shows, there arises in the general social movement a natural union of the two elements. Political democracy works in the field of the constitution and the law; socialism works in the field of governmental administration and policy. This combination constitutes the idea of social democracy, as distinguished from socialism. The aim of the social democracy is to establish universal suffrage by the constitution, and to insure a governmental policy directed to the social emancipation of the laboring class.

The general principle that all the forms of current social agitation seek to establish is personal liberty — the control of the individual over external things for his own interest. This Stein recognizes to be a legitimate and an inevitable aspiration of men having any attainment of intelligence. The concrete object of contemporary demand is the control of capital — the

[1] Stein, *op. cit.*, pp. cxii *et seq.*

instruments of production — by those who have it not. The two methods variously advocated for achieving the end are social revolution and social reform. The way of revolution Stein holds to be delusive and futile. There would be no more liberty where labor lorded it over capital than there is where capital lords it over labor. Moreover, the dictatorship of the proletariat would rest on no such superiority of either physical or moral and intellectual force as to insure its continuance.

Reform rather than revolution is the method by which Stein would deal with the great crisis that he sees impending. He would avoid all such utopian aims as the realization of general equality or the abolition of poverty. All that will avail is the gradual and systematic establishment, by legislation and administration, of conditions that shall open to every possessor of the power to labor the opportunity to become the possessor of capital.[1] For in industrial society capital is the expression and realization of that control over external things that is the essence of liberty. Where liberty in this sense does not exist the social order stands in opposition to the idea of free personality and therefore cannot endure.[2]

Stein's philosophy is interesting as the doctrine of a conservative who is convinced that the radical social movement of his time is founded in justice and must be sympathetically handled by the ruling powers.

[1] "Die Bestimmung der persönlichen Freiheit in dieser [Erwerbs-] Gesellschaft liegt mithin darin, dass die letzte Arbeitskraft die Fähigkeit habe, zum Kapitalbesitze zu gelangen." — *Ibid.*, p. cxxviii.

[2] *Ibid.*, pp. cxxviii *et seq.*

Politically he is opposed to the revolutionary party. He believes that of all the forms of the state monarchy has shown itself in European history the purest embodiment of the principle of liberty. It has systematically sustained the interests of the oppressed classes against their oppressors and has thus played the proper part in the perennial conflict of state and society.[1] But whatever the type of organization, the constitution and the administration must conform to the economic and social principles that he has expounded. Stein is no less certain than the authors of the *Communist Manifesto* that the gentle humanitarianism and private experimenting of Saint-Simonism, Fourierism and the rest are obsolete, and that the industrial class war and the social revolution must be the central issues of serious political theory and serious political practice.

Stein's philosophy is important in another respect. It shows clearly the sociological trend of political theory. His distinction between society and the state and his elaboration of the social as distinct from the political form and function were highly significant. Sociology was in process of differentiation from political theory when Stein wrote. It already had a name as a distinct science. Within another generation it would become a definitely integrated body of knowledge and would be imposing upon political philosophy new and important types of dogma.

[1] Stein, *op. cit.*, p. xxxvii. See *supra*, p. 379.

7. *Auguste Comte*

The speculation of Stein shows numerous indications of Saint-Simonian influence, with Hegelian modifications. Probably the Saint-Simonian tinge was received indirectly through Auguste Comte; for when Stein began to write, Comte's *Philosophie Positive* had just been completed,[1] giving him a commanding position in the world of thought, and Comte built his system on Saint-Simonism. Moreover, when the structure had been completed in the distinctive manner of his own superior genius, he decorated it with an exaggeration of the Saint-Simonian religious futility.

Sociology was the name invented by Comte to designate the science that is concerned with the phenomena of the organic as distinguished from the inorganic world. More narrowly sociology means the science of humanity, excluding thus the other forms of organic life. In the first sense it includes biology; in the second sense it follows biology in the hierarchy of the sciences.[2] The working out of his famous grouping of the sciences was an incident of Comte's extensive speculation in the methodology of intellectual progress. The wonderful system embodied in his comprehensive *Positive Philosophy* was built up as indispensable to a sound theory of social life, and the search for such a theory had a definite origin in the Saint-Simonian effort at reconstruction after the Napoleonic wars. As a devoted follower of Saint-Simon, Comte produced, at the mature age of twenty-four, an essay in which the

[1] The work in six volumes was published in the years 1826–42.

[2] *Positive Polity*, II, 352–357.

philosophy was outlined that received its full development in the great works of his later years.[1] The title of the essay, *Système de Politique Positive,* and the essentials of its doctrine were the same as those of the four-volume work which, completed in 1854, rounded out with amazing fulness and richness the philosophy of Positivism.[2]

Like all the other Saint-Simonians Comte maintained that a wholly new method was indispensable in order to reach a scientific solution of social problems. The theories that had played the largest part in the revolution and the restoration were alike absurd. Natural rights, social contract, written constitutions and separation of powers — the mainstays of the revolutionary cause — were, he declared, devices of imaginative *littérateurs* and narrow-minded legists, useful for destruction of the old, but worthless for progress in the new order. Much more absurd were the feudal-theological dogmas of the régime that was overthrown and of the Holy Alliance that was trying to restore it. These reactionary dogmas Comte held to be as incompatible with the facts of the present as the revolutionary dogmas were with its principles. Of the three stages through which, by the very nature of the human mind, theory in every branch of knowledge is bound to pass, the

[1] The essay was published as the third part of Saint-Simon's Catéchism des Industriels. *Œuvres de Saint-Simon*, t. 38.

[2] The four volumes have been translated into English by disciples of Comte under the title: *System of Positive Polity, or Treatise on Sociology, instituting the Religion of Humanity.* Most important for our purpose is volume two, containing "Social Statics, or the Abstract Theory of Human Order," and translated by Frederic Harrison.

doctrine of divine right exhibits the theological, that of social contract and individual rights the metaphysical. The time appeared ripe to Comte for the emergence of political theory into the third stage — the scientific or positive.[1]

On this idea, then, rests the Comtian philosophy of society and government. It must be developed, Comte holds, by the method that has achieved such magnificent results in the physical sciences. It must be raised to a level with the other sciences of observation. It must cease to concern itself with theological myths and metaphysical abstractions, and confine itself to actual facts determined by observation and history. The institutions of government will be judged not by their conformity to the assumed will of God or to any ideal of speculative philosophy, but by their relation to the civilization and general social conditions amid which they are set up. To seek a system of government that shall be absolutely the best, without reference to these conditions, is precisely analogous, Comte says, to seeking in medicine a method of treatment that shall be universally applicable without reference to the disease or the patient. The absolute must be avoided in political science particularly; for the absolute in theory leads necessarily to the arbitrary in practice. Absolute law means arbitrary law-maker, and whether such law-maker be one or many, society suffers.

Comte's line of approach to the problems of political

[1] This famous doctrine of the three stages was concisely formulated in Comte's first essay on Positive Polity. See *Œuvres de Saint-Simon*, t. 38, p. 75.

science places him, thus, in the inductive and historical school that we have seen exemplified by Aristotle, Machiavelli, Bodin and Montesquieu.[1] He himself refers particularly to Montesquieu and Condorcet as having approximated to the principles of Positivism, Montesquieu in having based his conception of law on facts rather than dogma, and Condorcet in having made progress the general law of mankind's social life.[2] The one was sound in the importance attributed by him to the influence of physical facts, though he exaggerated, Comte believed, the effects of climate; the other was sound in disclosing for the past and predicting for the future a steady advance in the welfare of humanity, but erred grossly, in Comte's judgment, as to the stages through which this advance had proceeded and would proceed.[3]

In these criticisms of his predecessors Comte indicates very well the character of his positive political science. It involves first a philosophy of history, based on physical as well as moral and intellectual facts, and furnishing the scientific law of social growth; and second, an analysis of existing conditions in all aspects of social life, from which the stage of advancement already reached may be precisely determined. With the law of progress known and the existing stage also known, it will be as easy in social science as in astronomy to foretell what the next movement will be. Nor shall the charge of deadening fatalism have a

[1] See preceding volumes of this history under those names.

[2] *Supra*, pp. 108 *et seq.*

[3] *Œuvres de Saint-Simon*, t. 38, p. 148.

ground in this program. The law of progress is indeed fixed, so far as direction is concerned, beyond any human power to control; but the rate of the advance is subject to modification by physical and by moral causes that may be measured, and among the latter are political combinations (*combinaisons politiques*).

The science that results from the twofold process described above was at first named by Comte "social physiology" or "social physics."[1] Later he invented the name "sociology." The two branches constitute social statics and social dynamics, corresponding respectively to the great conceptions, Order and Progress, that sum up, in Comte's phrase, the life of civilized society. The principles of social statics, he says, received systematic organization by Aristotle, and philosophy since his time has confined itself too closely to this side of the matter. With dynamics united to it through a sound theory of progress, the positive science of society is complete. The great underlying principle of this science Comte expressed in the maxim: "Progress is the development of Order."[2]

What, then, is "Order"? It is the harmonious organization of social forces for the exercise of social functions. But every true social force is collective, and involves the "grouping of several individuals for a greater or less period of time around one pre-eminent

[1] ". . . il faut regarder la science politique comme une physique particulière, fondée sur l'observation directe des phénomènes relatifs au développement collectif de l'espèce humaine. . . . Cette physique sociale est, évidemment, aussi positive qu'aucune autre science d'observation." *Ibid.*, pp. 193–4.

[2] *System of Positive Polity*, II, p. 152.

individuality." This means, Comte holds, that the idea of government is implied in the idea of society, and conversely.[1] The principles of organization are two: distribution of functions and combination of efforts. In human societies the varying capacities of men produce the varieties in their functioning, and the combination of their energies, in the presence of individual ambitions, requires the cohesive force of government.

Comte's reply to the current doctrine that government was unnecessary was in every sense positive. He laid it down flatly that "force is the basis of every human society." Hobbes he approved of as right in this doctrine. To look for an adequate principle of social cohesion in the intellect or the feeling he considered absurd. "Social science would remain forever in the cloudland of metaphysics if we hesitated to adopt the principle of force as the basis of government." And by force here he meant physical, material power.[2]

Beyond this and other incidental dogmas as to the basic principles of political philosophy proper, Comte does not concern himself with the discussion of government. His interest is in other phases of the social order — in society rather than the state. Even while he insists so strongly on the physical force that underlies the existence of government, he hastens to point out the equal importance of intellectual, moral and religious forces in its functioning. The capstone of his system proves to be a church and a priesthood in which are centred all the ultimate elements of social control. In the more or less mystical vagaries of these last phases

[1] *System of Positive Polity*, II, p. 223. [2] *Ibid.*, p. 247.

of Positivism Comte exhibited a singular recurrence to the tendencies that prevailed in Saint-Simonism, toward which he had manifested in his prime, after he had broken with it, a not wholly becoming contempt.

Comte's influence was probably more important and more permanent through his social dynamics than through the social statics. The philosophy of history that is embodied in his work ranks with the greatest achievements of the human mind in generalizing from the past the elements of progress in civilization. His doctrine of the three stages through which the development had proceeded and must proceed remains very influential to the present day. Scarcely less so is his teaching as to the method and the utility of history.

The three stages through which, as Comte maintains, humanity advances are to be discerned in both the material and the spiritual characteristics of the successive periods and in both their general and their specific features. So far as concerns the matters of political import the marks of the three stages are as follows:

1. In the theological and military stage social relations are determined, both in general and in particular, by force. Conquest is the guiding aim of society. Industry exists only for the production of the necessities of physical life, and slavery is the status of the producers.

2. In the metaphysical and legalistic stage the military spirit still predominates, but industrial conditions are making themselves felt. Slavery gradually gives way to serfage and then to civil, though not political, liberty for the individual. The growth of industry

is pronounced, but its end is chiefly to promote military ends. Eventually it becomes itself the most important cause of war. As a whole this stage is transitional and indeterminate.

3. In the scientific and industrial stage industry has become dominant. It is the first influence in the relations of individuals to one another, and it tends to control all the relations of society. Social activity as a whole becomes directed to the sole end of production, *i.e.*, to the adaptation of nature to the needs of man, and in this is the essence of civilization.

This scheme of human progress, outlined in Comte's first essay, is developed in great detail in the third volume of his *System of Positive Polity*. It permeates, indeed, all his philosophy. A very slight knowledge of the works of the Saint-Simonians enables one to perceive how much Comte owed to the ideas that prevailed in their speculation. Of his independent contributions perhaps the most striking is the consistent reinforcement of his moral and political exposition by the analogies of the physical sciences, especially biology. The relation of sociology and biology he formally describes as that of two branches of a single science: the evolutionary process of humanity is systematically compared to that of individual man, and the characteristics of organic life are attributed to society almost as freely as to the human being.[1] Nothing more need be said to suggest the kinship of Comte's sociology to the system that immediately followed his — the Synthetic Philosophy of Herbert Spencer.

[1] See Coker, *Organismic Theories of the State*, chap. iv.

8. *Herbert Spencer*

By the middle of the nineteenth century, when Spencer began to write, the idea of transformation, development, growth, as characteristic of society and all its institutions, had become ingrained in social science. Moreover the direction of the flow of things was almost universally conceived to be progressive — toward a condition that on one ground or another was held to be better than what was passing away. Spencer shared fully in the prevailing fashion in social speculation, and by his remarkable gifts of thought and expression shaped forth, as the explanation of all social as well as other life, the theory of evolution. The elements of his theory had appeared in antecedent philosophy, but he combined them with a precision and power that left no doubt as to his own contribution, and he so candidly acknowledged his entire ignorance of his predecessors that his claim to originality cannot be disputed.[1]

Primarily he finds the principle of evolution exhibited in material phenomena. It appears in the transforma-

[1] The origin and development of his system of philosophy are set forth in much detail and with resolute fidelity to what he believes to be the truth in Spencer's *Autobiography*. The leading features of his system recur frequently in his voluminous writings on multifarious subjects from 1850 on. In 1860 he announced a series of volumes that should present the whole of the Synthetic Philosophy. The series was not entirely completed at his death, but many of the volumes had appeared in several editions, with significant modifications. For the present purpose the important works are *First Principles*, *Principles of Sociology*, *Data of Ethics*, and *Justice*. I have used the last revisions of these, together with the edition of *Social Statics and the Man versus the State* that was published in 1892 as a sort of tailpiece to the great system of which the original edition of the *Social Statics* was the beginning. The American edition of the works has been used throughout.

tion of matter from "an indefinite, incoherent homogeneity to a definite, coherent heterogeneity," as in the development of the earth from a uniform liquid mass to the diversified form and structure that we see. Further, the same principle pervades the organic universe and appears in the series of vegetable and animal species from the simplest to the most complex — from protozoa to man. Finally the law of evolution is equally clear to view in the life and development of society. The life history of the social group of men shows the same process of development as the life history of the human animal. Spencer sets forth with a very special interest the operation of the law by virtue of which the simple incoherent society of primitive men grows into the coherent and highly complex structure of modern civilized society in the same way in which the anthropoid ape grew into the *homo sapiens*, and the same way in which the fœtus becomes the philosopher. This constitutes the essence of the Spencerian sociology.[1]

The development of the science is presented through the classification of social phenomena under the heads of domestic, ceremonial, political, ecclesiastical, professional and industrial institutions. Each class is exhaustively and systematically treated in the light of the evolutionary principle and process. It is in the part on political institutions that we are particularly interested.[2]

[1] This name Spencer deliberately adopted from Comte. On the other hand the title "Social Statics," which Spencer gave to his first important book, was chosen in ignorance of the fact that Comte had already given that name to one part of his sociology. See Spencer, *Autobiography*, I, 414.

[2] *Principles of Sociology*, II, p. 229.

Society has already been defined by Spencer as an organism — as essentially in the same class with physical beings having life.[1] His exposition of the structure and life of society is expressed almost wholly in terms of the physical structure and life of human or other animals. Of all the philosophers who have throughout the ages marked the likeness of the social group to the individual none has exhibited more ingenuity or more plausible an appearance of scientific precision than Spencer.[2] Political institutions share the character and development of the larger entity of which they are an element, and therefore the organization and activity of government are interpreted by the same analogies of organic life.

It is to be borne in mind that Spencer, like the Utilitarians with whom he was in close relations, had no distinction in thought between state and government. Or better, he recognized no such entity as the state, in the sense in which we have previously used it, but considered society and government as together embodying all that was involved in the fundamental categories of political science.

Government, then, was to him the sum of the institutions of society concerned with that conscious and involuntary coöperation of individuals, which, along with their spontaneous and voluntary coöperation, must be regarded as essential to life in association with one another. The relative scope and intensity of these

[1] *Principles of Sociology*, I, pp. 447 *et seq.*

[2] For a good account of this sort of political theorizing in the nineteenth century, see Coker, *Organismic Theories of the State*, New York, Longmans, 1910. The account of Spencer is at p. 124.

two species of coöperation vary, he points out, with the circumstances of the particular society. The clear predominance of the one or the other species is the criterion of distinction between the two great types of society, the militant and the industrial. The comparison of these types, with the conclusion that the industrial is the higher and the goal of social evolution, furnishes us with Spencer's version of the idealism that appeared in the visions of Saint-Simon and Comte.

Spencer reaches his conclusion through a brave array of physiological and biological parallels and analogies; and he sustains his views by extensive references to history, especially the history of primitive and uncivilized peoples. The methodology of strictly inductive science is scrupulously respected. What results, so far as political theory is concerned, is a series of doctrines that are substantially identical with those propounded *a priori* by Spencer, long before his philosophy of evolution had taken shape. In essence these doctrines constitute an extreme individualism, verging on anarchism, and based on the philosophy of natural law and natural rights that dominated the era of revolution. At several points the maintenance of the individualistic thesis strains and distorts the sociological system, in general a model of symmetry and consistency. His social ethics, among the last of his systematic writings, reveals very clearly that the connection between evolution and individualism as he puts it is unreal and illogical.[1]

[1] The demonstration of this has been a frequent exercise of Spencer's critics. *Cf.* Barker, *Political Thought from Spencer to the*

Spencer maintains and defends the conceptions of natural rights and natural law so far as the essence of the ideas is concerned, though he wholly rejects the method by which earlier philosophy reached and defended them. He accepts the social contract as a theoretical, though not a historical, basis of political authority and institutions.[1] The free enjoyment of his natural rights by the individual becomes therefore in the familiar way a limit upon the governmental authority. Spencer's ethics by a happy coincidence produces conclusions that confirm this doctrine; for he finds that the evolution of all organic life, from jelly-fish to man, manifests the principle that good (*i.e.*, the preservation of the species) is attained when each individual receives the benefits and the evils of its own nature and its consequent conduct. In human life this means that each individual must receive justice; justice means that "every man shall be free to do what he wills, provided he infringes not the equal freedom of any other man"; and this freedom means that every man shall enjoy his natural rights.[2]

Present Day, chap. iv; *Political Science Quarterly*, Vol. VIII, p. 182. This last reference is to a review of Spencer's volume on *Justice* written by myself twenty-eight years ago. As a re-reading of Spencer has confirmed the opinions therein expressed, I have ventured to incorporate some parts of the article in the following paragraphs.

[1] In *The Man versus the State*, published in 1884. In *Social Statics* (1850) he assails the social contract idea, on the ground that the social organism must result from unconscious development rather than conscious will. The inconsistency here is rather in expression than in thought; for his characteristic contention is that society grows but the state (government) is made.

[2] This doctrine appears in the fullest and most systematic form in the *Data of Ethics* and *Justice*, but pervades many others of Spencer's works.

As to the content of this natural liberty, Spencer's wide ranging among the lower animals and primitive men brings to light no rights not already discovered by the eighteenth-century philosophers with much less effort. Life, liberty and the pursuit of happiness would sum up Spencer's list; and he steadfastly insists that the whole function of the state consistent with right and justice is to insure these ends to the individuals within it. The state as such has no life and personality the perfection of which can be a topic of ethical doctrine.[1] Right and wrong cannot be predicated of the acts in which its existence is preserved. Nor, on the other hand, can the termination of that existence be viewed with any other feeling than that with which one records the disappearance of a toe or a tail or other organ in the course of development of some animal species.

For Spencer reads the doom of the state (government) in the law of evolution that governs the life of society. The militant type will steadily decline with the decline of war, and the industrial type will prevail; the régime of status will give way to the régime of contract. The system exemplified by the Bodo, the Dhimals, the Pueblos, the Todas and the peaceful Arafuras will supersede that which is embodied in the record of Sparta,

[1] Spencer's use of terms in this matter is confusing. He speaks of the state as "the society in its corporate capacity," but denies to the state characteristics that he ascribes to the society. While the society is clearly an organism, the state apparently is not. The state is not an ethical entity, but it has duties; society is without sentiency, but exercises will. Much of the confusion involved in such statements would probably be avoided if Spencer had consistently used "government" instead of "state," and had refrained from identifying either with "society."

Rome, Russia and Germany.[1] England and the United States are nearest to the social and political system toward which the evolution of the race is moving. Representative ideas in government will prove increasingly necessary as society becomes peaceful and industrial. The executive will become elective rather than hereditary. Party antagonisms will pass away; for they express in general the conflict of the militant and the industrial systems, and as the industrial comes to prevail the party differences will disappear. Individualism will thus assert itself freely; and under the same influences decentralization and local self-government will prevail. The institutions and functions of political authority will decrease and will be limited to what is required for the maintenance of justice.

While Spencer refrains from any positive forecasting of actual society without government, the suggestion of such an idea frequently appears in his thought. His ethical doctrine contemplates the development of altruism to such a point that coercion will no longer be necessary for the maintenance of the natural rights of the individual, *i.e.*, justice. The inference is unavoidable that government will be unnecessary: voluntary will have wholly supplanted compulsory coöperation.

Again, he asserts that war, which is to him the chief cause of compulsory coöperation, has exhausted its utility in the evolution of man. It has peopled the earth with powerful and intelligent races; and integration of such groups has proceeded "as far as seems either

[1] *Principles of Sociology*, part v, chaps. xvii-xviii, in Vol. II.

practicable or desirable."[1] It has developed in men a stupendous power of continuous application, which industrial effort and competition may be depended on adequately to maintain. Hence, with the disappearance of war, the mainstay of political institutions is bound to disappear.

There is implicit thus in the Spencerian philosophy the conception of an absolute end in social evolution that is good and desirable in itself. To reconcile this conception with the first principle of evolution as the law of life is a problem without a solution. For life in general is regarded as a process of never-ending change, while in the life of the human social organism change is to cease when conditions are reached that realize justice.[2]

9. *General Influence of Societarian Theory*

In a general way the relation of the doctrine described in this chapter to the contemporary doctrine of constitutionalism and of nationalism was as follows. Assuming the distinction between society, state and government, constitutionalism tended to ignore the state and stress government, while societarian theory put both state and government in the background and concentrated attention on society. The relation to nationalistic theory was less simple. Both socialism

[1] *Principles of Sociology*, II, 664.

[2] Spencer seeks to evade this inconsistency by distinguishing the social organism from the individual organism as "discrete" and "concrete" respectively, and by denying to the one certain of the attributes assigned to the other. These devices create more inconsistencies than they remove. *Principles of Sociology*, I, 460 *et seq.* *Cf.* Barker, *op. cit.*, p. 118.

and sociology gave support to the conception of nationality by the emphasis they laid on the appeal to history and to sentiment. The utopian socialists based their doctrines on the past and present conditions of their respective fatherlands; the unit of Stein's and Comte's sociology was in large measure France or Germany or England. But Marxian socialism and Spencerian sociology cut across the nationalistic idea by emphasizing mankind in general. Both found the classes and the interests that were common to many or all communities a sounder basis of social and political theory than any merely national or merely constitutional class or interest or institution.

Another obvious tendency of the societarian doctrines was to renew with special features the eternal debate as to the identity and characteristics of "the people." While constitutionalism and nationalism were in general content with a "people" that was the triumphant Third Estate of the revolution, socialism and sociology reclassified the population, chiefly according to economic principle, and erected a new conception of "people" on the result. The Saint-Simonians, while admitting to a place in society only active producers of social goods, retained among these as leaders the intellectual class. Marx and his followers went to the limit in the direction of leadership by a single class, and assigned the dominant rôle in the life of society to the proletariat — a pitiless and uncompromising democracy of mere numbers. A somewhat similar distinction appeared in a comparison of the sociology of Comte with that of Spencer, — the one looking to the natural and pacific leadership of the spiritually gifted class, the other to a ceaseless struggle for existence between shifting groups, the source and limit of whose activity should be the rights and interest of the individual man.

So far as the organization of government is considered at all by the societarian philosophers, their inclination is for the most part toward representative institutions. The basis of the system they suggest usually shows a curious reversion to the mediæval type. Economic and social groups and interests are preferred to units of population or territory as the things to be represented. Such an idea expresses the reaction against the dogmas of revolutionary democracy as embodied in the institutions of the bourgeoisie; but it is startling to find in socialism the conceptions that were so conspicuous in the conservatism of Burke and the more extreme defenders of the *ancien régime*.

As to the source and scope of the authority to be exercised by governmental organs the systems considered in this chapter offer the extremes of divergence. We may designate as the socialistic type that doctrine which ascribes to society, through its political organs, unlimited power to shape the lives of its individual members to its needs, and as the anarchistic type that doctrine which tends to deny the need of any power whatever by society over the lives of its members. On this basis the Saint-Simonians, Comte and the Marxians are sharply distinguished from Godwin, Proudhon and Spencer. The one group regards regulation and direction indispensable to the existence of a society, whether the requisite power to regulate and direct results from the peaceful acquiescence of the less in the sway of the more intelligent, or in the submission of the less to the greater number through the pressure of brute force. The other group regards constraint upon individuals in the name of state, society or government as evil *per se* — as without warrant in the nature of man or of things in general. To this latter group man is indeed a social being, irresistibly drawn into life in communion with his kind; but the root of the impulse is held to be sympathy, fellow feeling, the sense of likeness and equality, not self-interest, inequality and the craving for mastery. Institutions that express the latter motives are considered perversions of humanity, and in this category fall what are called state and government. For these terms, together with "society" itself, signify to the anarchists nothing more than coöperating groups of individual men, and in the actions of these groups no attribute, motive or standard of right and wrong is involved save those of the component individuals.[1]

The ancestry of the doctrines discussed in this chapter is easily traceable. They derive from the law of nature and the rights of man that were exploited in the eighteenth century and its revolutions. Socialism

[1] The inclusion of Spencer with Godwin and Proudhon in the anarchistic class may seem unreasonable. His organismic doctrine suggests a marked distinction. Yet he drops the idea of organism whenever he deals with the sphere of government, and the reconciliation of his doctrines on these two points is impossible. It is fair to judge him, therefore, on the one alone, that is, the scope of state power. As to this, it cannot be questioned that he is, if not all the way over to the anarchists, at least nearer to them than to the socialists.

took up for development the dogmas of liberty and equality that Locke, Rousseau and Jefferson had propounded. Sociology, in contrast, developed the principles and method of Montesquieu and Ferguson and Haller. Of the natural rights that figured in the lists of the revolution, that of private property became the centre of societarian interest. To find in "nature" both the equality of all men and the inequality incident to property right, had been an embarrassing problem for the revolutionary parties and a prolific occasion for jeers from the conservatives. Socialism took its stand on equality and rejected any conception of property that conflicted with it. What the revolution did to landed property by confiscation in the name of the nation and political right, socialism aimed to do to capitalistic property in the name of society and social right. The relation, thus, to the theories of the generation immediately preceding was close, but equally obvious were the remoter relationships to the speculations of Plato, More, Campanella and others, who had seen in property the bane of humanity.

Sociology also, as well as socialism, endorsed in the main the dogmas of the revolution. Comte and Spencer reached in their respective methods conclusions in harmony with those of the eighteenth-century philosophy. As to property, they both found it an institution inseparably wrought into the fabric of human society from its beginnings. Whatever evils might be due to the capitalistic form developed in recent times Comte made mitigable by the infinite wisdom of his governing priesthood. Spencer, having in 1850 pronounced against the sanctity of property in land, reached in the full development of his system the conclusion that property was no less immovably fixed in nature than any other of the rights of man.

As to the posterity of the doctrines of the chapter, the subject is not strictly within the scope of this history. It may be briefly noted, however, that both socialism and sociology have waxed mightily in importance during the generation since 1880. Their methods and their dogmas have at times superseded in interest and influence the older systems of constitutional and nationalistic reflection. General political theory has been greatly modified by this development. An illustration of the way in which this has taken place appears in the theory of the state that was put forth just at the close of our period by Ludwig Gumplowicz, the Austrian publicist.[1] He blends the sociological dogma of endless evolutionary change under the operation of the laws of physical nature with the socialistic dogma of class war, expanded to include the conflicts of ethnic, religious and other as well as economic classes. Society he considers a group of classes, each struggling for the promotion of its particular interest, and the state the organization through which the class whose interest is dominant controls the rest. The implications of such doctrine need not be dwelt upon. They suggest to any reflecting spirit the importance of societarian speculation in the history of political theory.

[1] For a full and excellent exposition of the thought of Gumplowicz see the article by Dr. H. E. Barnes in the *Journal of Race Development*, Vol. IX, no. 4 (April, 1919). *Cf.* also *Political Science Quarterly*, IX, 140.

SELECT REFERENCES

Barker, Political Thought in England, chap. iv. The Communist Manifesto. Comte, Positive Polity, IV, pp. 527–586. Fourier, Gide's Introduction to Selections. Godwin, Political Justice, Book V, chaps. 22–24; Book VIII, chaps. 1, 2. Janet, *Saint-Simon et le Saint-Simonisme*. Menger, Right to the Whole Produce of Labor, sec. i, and Foxwell's Introduction. John Morley, Miscellanies, III, p. 337 (Comte). Owen, Book of the New Moral World, Part VI. Proudhon, What is Property? (translation), especially chaps. ii, iii and v. Saint-Simon, *Œuvres*, XXIII (*Le Nouveau Christianisme*); XLI, pp. 34–58. Simkhovitch, Marxism versus Socialism, chaps. ii, iii, viii and ix. Spencer, The Man versus the State, especially Part IV. Stein, *Der Begriff der Gesellschaft*, pp. xxix–xliv.

CHAPTER X

THE GENERAL COURSE OF POLITICAL THEORY

In the three volumes of which this is the last we have ranged from the days of Socrates to those of Herbert Spencer. From Socrates to Spencer was a lapse of twenty-three centuries. A history covering that period must record the acts and the thoughts of some seventy generations of men. Seventy times self-conscious reflection on matters of political theory received its impress from a different set of minds. To enlarge on the diversity of the environment, material and spiritual, in which these various generations lived would be but commonplace and tedious. It is appropriate here, however, having concluded our review of the changes in doctrine during this long period, to consider the general effects of the process on political theory. Comparing the fourth century B.C. with the nineteenth century A.D., do we find the principles and the problems of speculative politics essentially different or essentially the same? If they are substantially different, is the later condition the culmination of a progressive change in a uniform direction? or is it merely a stage in a series of haphazard and never-ending transformations?

The actual existence of government — of societies characterized by the control of man by man — was a fact of unbroken experience throughout those ages. Speculation on the subject fell chiefly under two heads: first, the organization and institutions through which this control should be exercised; second, and more fundamental, the source, origin and rational justification of governmental authority in any form. Let us review the course of doctrinal development on each of these topics.

I

When we consider the forms and agencies in and through which control of man by man should be exercised, we find some evidence of progressive modification in theory in the twenty-three centuries. A conspicuous instance is offered by the institution of domestic slavery. While a social and economic rather than a strictly political institution, it presented the extreme case of authority in man over man. Greek theory justified it by the dogma that nature made men unequal; Roman theory by the compact of vanquished and victor in war; mediæval Christian theory by the doctrine of God's penalty for sin; modern theory by all the foregoing, together with the dogmas of race inequality and social expediency. Against all these various doctrines was urged from the beginning the contention that by the decree of nature and of God men were free and equal, and that, whatever the basis for the subjection of the individual to society or the state, there was none for his subjection to another individual. This view, held by but few thinking men in the fourth century B.C., became in the nineteenth century A.D. generally prevalent, and was a concomitant of the widespread individualism of the time.

In respect to the broad forms of organization in which political authority may be manifested, the history of theory shows little variation throughout the twenty-three centuries. The Greeks differentiated monarchy, aristocracy and democracy, and the classification remained without much modification thereafter. In Roman days, but chiefly through the influence of the Greek Polybius, the "mixed" form was added to the original three, and it continued to play a large part to the end. This expressed, however, no novel element of primary principle. In modern theory was manifest the same lack of precision as in the ancient respecting the basis of the classification. Aristotle pointed out that aristocracy and oligarchy were distinguished from democracy sometimes by reference to the number of the ruling body, sometimes by reference to birth or wealth or intelligence. Modern thought exhibited the same inconsistency; and it followed earlier generations also in emphasizing the rôle of the aristocracy of intelligence, illustrating thus the class interest of the philosophers.

After Bodin made clear the distinction between state and government he applied the original threefold classification to both state and government, but rejected the mixed form in respect to the state. With the rise of the popular-sovereignty doctrine through Locke and Rousseau it became the prevailing idea that the state was in all cases the same — that is, that the community as a whole was always the depositary of the supreme authority, while the terms monarchic, aristocratic, democratic and mixed all applied only to the organization of the government. This distinction was not fully and consciously developed in earlier political theory. The ancients thought of the three forms as designating the exercise of both supreme and subordinate governmental authority by either an individual or one social class, in a society that included several classes. The ruling class was both state and government. The doctrine of Marx, Gumplowicz and other societarian theorists that class rule is normal and inevitable was a conscious reversion to the ancient way of thinking.

Along with the classification of polities arose the effort of the ancient thinkers to determine a normal order in which the different forms were bound to appear and succeed one another in the same community. Speculation on this subject remained characteristic of political theory from beginning to end of the period of our history. The motives that impelled the philosophers were as various as the methods employed and the results they reached. In the moderns appeared a basis of historical information that was longer in time, broader in space, and more accurate in detail, and an interest that was centred more in social than in distinctively political phenomena. Yet when one compares the *a priori* and fanciful teachings of Plato with those of Rousseau and the Saint-Simonians concerning the rise and progress of political organizations among men, and the more sober and scientific treatment of the same subject by Aristotle and Polybius with that by Vico and Comte, it will require much hardihood to pronounce that the moderns manifest a great progress in the philosophy of government.

One species of polity that was unknown and unconceived in the fourth century B.C. became familiar first in the nineteenth century A.D. This was the republic, in the sense of representative democracy. Representation, as a principle, does not appear in political theory until the later centuries of Rome, when the Prince was regarded as the representative of the Roman people taken collectively. With some modification the idea played a rôle in the constitutional politics of the mediæval Empire. In the fourteenth century, in connection with the conciliar movement in the church, the theory that a body of delegates, apportioned among constituencies that comprehended the whole people, was the only logical representative of the people, was formulated by Marsiglio and Ockam. It achieved little recognition in either ecclesiastical or secular politics. Only in the seventeenth century did the doctrine of representation come prominently into discussion, and then mainly in connection with that English conception of the people which took cognizance merely of existing and ancient groups of persons in historical corporations and counties. Delegates chosen by these constituencies formed one element in the Parliament that, with the King, embodied the supreme authority.

Finally, through the American and the French revolutions, theory and practice in the nineteenth century united to produce the representative democracy as the typical republic. In this the chief organ of state and government alike is to be an assembly of representatives chosen by constituencies that are geographically compact and numerically equal. The implication of democratic equality in this conception of a republic is sufficiently obvious; yet there has never failed to be manifest the idea, carried to its extreme by Rousseau, that a real democracy must involve some recognition of an authority in the unorganized, spontaneously acting "people" against which no act of any body of representatives can be valid. This idea preserves the conception of democratic government as contrasted with the more modern idea of the republic.

Two other features of modern political theory may plausibly be adduced as evidence of progress in the field. These are first, the distinction worked out between state and society, and second, the development of the doctrine of sovereignty. As to this latter it is to be said that the concept of sovereignty is implicit in every controversy over the conflicting claims of two or more systems of authority. It was at the bottom of the Hellenic struggles between the many and the few, of the Roman struggles between patricians and plebeians, senate and assemblies, of the mediæval struggle between secular and ecclesiastical powers, and of the modern struggles between monarchs and estates or parliaments. The mediæval and modern incidents produced conceptions and definitions of sovereignty that far excel in clearness and precision anything extant in the records of antiquity. To this extent, therefore, there was advance in political speculation.

As to the distinction between state and society, it is undoubtedly a useful contribution of recent speculation to political science. It is closely related to the general conditions that produce at first sight the impression of a very great difference between ancient and modern thinking on social subjects. For obviously political theory has been much reduced in scope by the expansion, classification and precise delimitation of the various kinds of human knowledge. Doctrine that was in Aristotle political has since his time been definitively assigned to theology, to ethics, to jurisprudence, to economics and to sociology. This fact gives no basis for judgment on the substance of the doctrine, but is a matter of names only. Every one of the special sciences mentioned goes back to ancient philosophies for substantial elements of its dogma propounded under the name and in the categories of politics. The field of this early speculation was in fact what we think of to-day as social science in general. That the name given to the ensemble of ideas about social man was "politics" was due to preoccupation of the Greeks with their particular social unit, the city-state or "polis."

The polis was to them primarily a society and only subsidiarily a state. It was ethical, furnishing the norm of right and duty. It was juristic, embodying in its institutions the foundations of law. It was economic, determining the conditions of material prosperity. It was sociological, revealing the principles that produced not only the best men, but also the best form of association among men. It finally was political, solving the problem of authority and liberty — of the control of one human will by another.

This last is the characteristic that has remained

through all the transformations of the ages ultimate and essential in theory deemed specifically political. Whatever institutions and relations have been thought of as the subject matter of any other science, those concerned with the regulation and control of one man or group of men in associated life by another man or group of men have been undeviatingly the subject matter of politics. And the fundamental problem of political theory has been constantly to determine on what principles the relation of authority and submission can be explained and justified. A review of the solutions accepted by the successive generations covered by our history will reveal to what extent there has been progress in this phase of speculation.

II

Greek thought on this problem in the fourth and third centuries before Christ included substantially all the solutions ever suggested. Most prevalent in the time of the great Socratics, Plato and Aristotle, was the doctrine that for enlightened peoples like the Greeks the submission of man to the authority of man was irrational. In a community that was political, that is, one that had developed the polis, or city-state, authority was in the polis and submission was to the polis. For peoples that had not developed this political form of society submission to the dominion of man — slavery — expressed the rule of undeveloped "nature," *viz.* inequality of power and control by the stronger. In the political community the life lived by the individual might appear at different times to be determined by the oligarchy or by the common people (*demos*) or by the tyrant; but the real and ultimate authority voiced by each of these was that of the polis as a society, and not that of any one or more individuals in it. Likewise when the regulation took the form of law, whether human (*nomos*) or divine (*themis*), it was the decree of the polis either through the custom of the community, or through some lawgiver deputed by it, or through the gods that were identified with its life. Nor was there conceived to be any aspect of the citizen's life to which the beneficent regulating authority of the polis did not extend.

Other conceptions of authority quite antagonistic to this did not fail of agitation by the acute Hellenic intelligence. The Cynics paved the way for Stoicism and the Cyrenaics for Epicureanism. Both these systems disparaged the pretensions of the polis to original and absolute authority. Above the social organization the Stoics set the cosmos — universal nature and her law. Before any social organization, polis or other, the Epicureans set, as its maker and controller, the individual man. Not, however, till Rome became by conquest the master of the civilized world did the influence of these ideas contribute to supplant by other conceptions the long regnant dogma of the city-state.

Rome's additions to the theory of authority were made primarily through the concrete practical operation of her constitution and her law. As a conquering power she was to her victims force pure and simple, as void of theoretical basis as the earthquake or the tornado. As an administering power the concepts of her public and private law profoundly affected general political theory. Her history and traditions abounded in suggestions of an absolute authority in the city-state, and at the same time left everywhere the impression of restraints upon its exercise. At the centre of the Roman system was the concept of the imperium, which was authority unlimited in scope, but assigned to determinate officials, conferred by the community in a prescribed manner, and subject in exercise to definite limits of space and time. Their *ius civile*, prescribing the rules of life for Romans, was centred about a formal code, supplemented by custom and by formally enacted statutes (*lex*). Their *ius gentium*, or law of the subject peoples, took eventually the form of a code, the prætorian edict. Behind both these systems of law, whatever their immediate source and limitations, was always conceived to lie the unlimited authority of the Roman commonwealth (*res publica*), or, more concretely, the Roman people (*populus Romanus*).

In the first two centuries of the Principate a new conception was incorporated into political theory among the Romans. Their jurists took over from Greek philosophy, particularly Stoicism, the idea of the *ius naturale,* according to which authority transcending all of human origin was ascribed to nature. The development of this idea tended clearly to an issue between the rule of universal nature and that of the Roman imperium as embodied in the Imperator-Princeps. The hard-headed practicality of the Romans availed to prevent concrete manifestations of this issue. Nature was too ill-defined an entity to be substituted for the commonwealth as incarnate in the Emperor. His will and power remained supreme in the practice of government, but in theory the authority of nature gained general recognition as superior to the authority of Rome. Indeed, the antithesis was declared between nature and all human authority whatever; for it was proclaimed by the Roman jurists themselves that under nature's law all men were free and equal.

Then came Christianity upon the scene. As this faith rose to influence and power its teachings transformed political as well as other philosophy. God and his scheme of creation gradually became recognized as the first cause of man and all human affairs. The divine will fixed the character and operation of social institutions. If the Roman People, now coterminous with the population of the civilized world, still conferred the imperium on the Emperor, it was by God's will that Emperor, imperium and Roman People itself existed. If nature governed human relations, God ruled nature — nature was God. Every social or political hierarchy or authority was but an incident in the working out of the divine scheme of creation. That there were rulers and ruled in human society was by God's command; not elsewhere could justification be found for the fact that a particular man was ruler and another was ruled. Nor was the authority of any law to be explained in any other way. Whatever the source and whatever the force of enacted human law, or customary law, or the law of nature itself, — all must rest for their justification ultimately upon the law of God.

The codification of this supreme law, so far as it was revealed to man, was in the Holy Scriptures and the interpreter of it was the church.

Such was the theory as to the basis of political authority during a thousand years of West-European life. Two distinct systems of regulation for mankind were recognized, the temporal and the spiritual, but the distinction between them, like the institutions embodied in them, resulted from the command of God. In both systems the subjection of man to man was characteristic, but the ruler's rule was valid only so far as it could be traced to the will of God. In both systems the subjection of the individual to the authority of a social aggregate, the church and the state respectively, was fundamental; but church and state, like Pope and Emperor and kings, had their authority only from God. There could be enquiry and debate as to demarcation of the spheres of the two systems and as to the details of the operation of each; but there could be no questioning by God's creatures as to His purpose in establishing the systems, or as to the righteousness of the principle expressed in them that authority had its origin in the will of a Supreme Being. All mediæval culture manifests the influence of this idea, — finds the warrant for government in the right of the ruler rather than in any consent of the ruled.

In the fourteenth century a movement away from this doctrine makes its appearance. It starts with questionings as to the interpretation of the law of God and develops through questionings as to the interpreter. In the fifteenth century nature and its law begin to assume again the importance that had been lost to them with the development of Christianity and its omnipotent God. Nature is learned to have declared, through the Roman jurist, that all men are free and equal. Nature must speak the will of God; hence it must be God's way that authority, under Him, shall be not in any man alleged to be superior, but in the people. This was the doctrine preached by Marsiglio in the fourteenth century, by Cusanus in the fifteenth and by a great throng of thinkers, Protestant and Catholic, in the sixteenth.

During the next two centuries the idea of God as the direct and immediate source of political sovereignty fell steadily away into the background. In the multitude of creeds that disintegrated Christianity the Scriptures ceased to afford any certain guide to the knowledge of the divine will. Nature, however, interpreted by reason, still persisted as a power operating uniformly throughout mankind, and indeed throughout the universe. In nature, therefore, and its law the political theory of the eighteenth century, like that of the third century, but more unreservedly, placed the foundation of social government and authority.

In this modern conception of the law of nature particular stress was from the outset laid on the limitations to which the control of man by man was subject. Nature's voice in the matter of liberty became of absorbing interest — of more concern than her voice as to authority. Individualism came into the foreground. The same nature that ascribed supreme power to the people as an aggregate was found to have set limits to that power in reference to the people as individuals. A sphere was conceived wherein no authority external to the individual could intrude. This theory of natural rights was by some thinkers expanded to its limit; the sphere free from intrusion was made to include the whole field of action, and authority over rational man was denied as irrational. Anarchy was thus proclaimed as nature's law.

Political theory during the nineteenth century was devoted largely to the task of adjusting the conceptions of authority and liberty so as to escape the dilemma of the anarchists. Nature was dropped out of consideration as God had been before, and other concepts were brought forward as fetters for the individual will. Reason, righteousness, history, especially as embodied in constitutional formulas, were variously adduced as the source of authority and the limit of liberty. The nation, a political organism independent of control by the individual, was set up as the source of control over him. Finally society, as an entity comprehending the whole range of human relationships, was declared to be the holder and distributor of authority over all.

These dogmas, with endless varieties of shading and detail, were in conflict in the philosophy of the nineteenth century, and the conflict is still in progress. Greek history shows that they were in like conflict, with different degrees of relative strength, in the fourth century B.C. Anarchistic individualism was preached by Sophists and Cynics; constitutionalism by Aristotle and the other conservative upholders of the *nomoi;* nationalism is but the theory of the city-state writ large; societarianism has never been more completely formulated than by Plato. In twenty-three centuries the movement of thought has but swung full circle. Such is the general lesson of the history of political theories. It is not different from the lesson of history in respect to all the other varieties of theory by which men have sought to solve the basic problems of their earthly existence.

BIBLIOGRAPHY

I. TEXTS AND EDITIONS OF WRITERS CONSIDERED

Austin, John.

Lectures on Jurisprudence. Fourth edition. Edited by Robert Campbell. Two volumes. London, 1873.

Bayet et Albert.

See Écrivains politiques.

Beccaria, Cesare.

Dei Delitti e delle Pene. Livorno, 1824.

An Essay on Crimes and Punishments. Translated. With a Commentary attributed to Voltaire. Dublin, 1767.

Bentham, Jeremy.

Works. Edited by John Bowring. 10 vols. Edinburgh, 1843. Especially Vols. I and II.

A Fragment on Government. Edited, with an Introduction, by F. C. Montague. Oxford, 1891.

Blackstone, Sir William.

Commentaries on the Laws of England, in Four Books. 4 vols. 13th ed. London, 1800.

Bluntschli, J. C.

Lehre vom modernen Staat. 3 Bde. I. Allgemeine Staatslehre. II. Allgemeine Staatsrecht. III. Politik. 6te Auflage. Durchgesehen von E. Loening. Stuttgart, 1886.

Theory of the State. Authorized English translation. Second edition. Oxford, 1892.

Gesammelte Kleine Schriften. 2 Bde. Nördlingen, 1879.

Bonald, M. de.

Œuvres. 11 tomes. 2me édition. Paris, 1817.

Burke, Edmund.
Works. 12 vols. 8th ed. Boston, 1884. Esp. Vols. III and IV.

Calhoun, John Caldwell.
Disquisition on Government. Edited by R. K. Crallé. Columbia, S. C., 1851.

Comte, Auguste.
Cours de Philosophie Positive. 6 tomes. Paris, 1829-1842.
System of Positive Polity. 4 vols. Translated by a group of collaborators. Vol. II, Social Statics, translated by Frederic Harrison. Vol. III, Social Dynamics, edited by E. S. Beesly.

Condorcet, Marquis de.
Œuvres. 12 tomes. Paris, 1847–49. Espec. Tome XII.
Outlines of an Historical View of the Human Mind. Translated from the French. London, 1795.

Constant de Rebecque, Benjamin.
Cours de Politique Constitutionelle. Avec Introduction et des notes par Édouard Laboulaye. 2 tomes. 2me éd. Paris, 1872.

Constitutions of France.
See Hélie, in part ii of this bibliography.

Constitutions, American.
Constitutions of the Several Independent States of America. Published by order of Congress. Philadelphia, 1781.
Federal and State Constitutions, Charters and other Organic Laws of the United States. Edited by B. P. Poore. 2 vols. 2d edition. Washington, 1878.

Dahlmann, Friedrich Christoph.
Die Politik auf den Grund der gegebenen Zustände zurückgeführt. 2te Ausgabe. Leipzig, 1847.

De Lolme, J. L.
The Constitution of England. New edition, with life and notes, by John MacGregor. London, 1853.

Écrivains politiques du XVIII siècle.
Extracts, avec une introduction et des notes, par Albert Bayet et François Albert. Paris, 1904.

Ferguson, Adam.

Essay on the History of Civil Society. 7th ed. Boston, 1809.

Principles of Moral and Political Science. 2 vols. Edinburgh, 1792.

Fichte, Johann Gottlieb.

Sämmtliche Werke. Herausgegeben von J. H. Fichte. 8 Bände. Berlin, 1845. Esp. Bde 3, 4, 7.

Filangieri, Gaetano.

La Scienza della Legislazione. 6 vols. Milano, 1822.

Fourier, Charles.

Œuvres complètes. 6 tomes. Paris, 1841–46.

Godwin, William.

Enquiry concerning Political Justice and its influence on Morals and Happiness. 2 vols. 3d ed. London, 1798.

Guizot, François P.

The History of Representative Government in Europe. Translated by Andrew R. Scoble. [Bohn] London, 1861.

Haller, Carl Ludwig von.

Restauration der Staats-Wissenschaft. 2te vermehrte und verbesserte Auflage. 6 Bände. Winterthur, 1820–34.

Hegel, G. W. F.

Werke. Herausgegeben von Dr. Eduard Gans. 2te Auflage. Berlin, 1840. Band VIII: Grundlinien der Philosophie des Rechts; Band IX: Vorlesungen über die Philosophie der Geschichte.

The Philosophy of History. With Prefaces by Charles Hegel and the translator, J. Sibree. New York, 1900.

The Philosophy of Right. Translated by S. W. Dyde. London, 1896.

The Philosophy of Mind. Translated, with five introductory essays, by William Wallace. Oxford, 1894.

Helvetius, Claud Arian.

De l'Esprit, or Essay on the Mind and its Several Faculties. Translated from the French. London, 1810.

A Treatise on Man. Translated from the French, with notes, by W. Hooper. 2 vols. London, 1810.

Holbach, Baron d'.

Système Social. 2 tomes. Paris, 1822.

Humboldt, Wilhelm von.

Ideen zu einem Versuch die Gränzen der Wirksamkeit des Staates zu bestimmen. Einleitung von Dr. Eduard Cauer. Breslau, 1850.

Sphere and Duties of Government. Translated by Joseph Coulthard. London, 1854.

Kant, Immanuel.

Metaphysische Anfangsgründe der Rechtslehre. 2te Auflage. Königsberg, 1798.

The Philosophy of Law. Translated by W. Hastie. Edinburgh, 1887.

Zum ewigen Frieden. Edited by C. Vogt. Bern, 1867.

Project for a Perpetual Peace. Translated. London, 1796.

Mably, G. B. de.

Œuvres complètes. 12 vols. Lyon, 1796.

Maistre, Comte Joseph de.

Œuvres. Publiées par M. l'Abbé Migne. Paris, 1841.

Marx, Karl, and Engels, Frederick.

Manifesto of the Communist Party. Authorized English Translation. Chicago, n. d.

Mazzini, Joseph.

Essays, translated by Thomas Okey, edited by Bolton King. London, 1894.

Mill, James.

Essays on Government, Jurisprudence, Liberty of the Press, and Law of Nations. Written for the Encyclopædia Britannica. London, n. d. [1820].

Mill, John Stuart.

On Liberty. London, n. d. [The New Universal Library].

Considerations on Representative Government. New York, 1875.

Morelly.

Code de la Nature. Avec l'analyse raisonnée du système social de Morelly, par Villegardelle. Paris, 1841.

Owen, Robert.

The Book of the New Moral World. London, 1842.

Paine, Thomas.

Writings of. Collected and Edited by Moncure D. Conway. 4 vols. New York, 1894.

Physiocrates.

Quesnay, Dupont de Nemours, Mercier de la Rivière, l'Abbé Badeau, Le Trosne. [Their writings] avec une Introduction, des Commentaires et des Notices historiques, par Eugène Daire. 2 Parties. Paris, 1846.

Proudhon, Pierre Joseph.

Œuvres complètes. 26 tomes. Bruxelles, 1868–76.

What is Property? Translated by Benj. R. Tucker. Two vols. in one. London, n. d.

Rousseau, Jean Jacques.

Collection complète des Œuvres de. 12 tomes. Geneva, 1782.

Political Writings, edited, with Introductions and Notes, by C. E. Vaughn. 2 vols. Cambridge, 1915.

Du Contrat Social. Le texte définitif et les versions primitives. Introduction et des notes par Edmond Dreyfus-Brissac. Paris, 1896.

The Social Contract. Translated, with Introduction and Notes, by Henry J. Tozer. Preface by Bernard Bosanquet. London, 1895.

Saint-Simon et Enfantin.

Œuvres de. 47 tomes. Paris, 1865–78.

Savigny, Friedrich Karl von.

Of the Vocation of our Age for Legislation and Jurisprudence. Translated by Abraham Hayward. London, n. d.

System des heutigen Römischen Rechts. 5 Bände. Berlin, 1840.

Schleiermacher, Friedrich.
Sämmtliche Werke. 33 Bände. Berlin, 1835–64. Ueber die verschiedenen Begriffe der Staatsformen is in Band 26. Die Lehre vom Staat is in Band 32.

Siéyès, Emmanuel.
Qu'est-ce que le Tiers État? Précédé de l'Essai sur les Privilèges. Édition critique avec une introduction par Edme Champion. Paris, 1888.

Smith, Adam.
Lectures on Justice, Police, Revenue and Arms. Edited by Edwin Cannan. Oxford, 1896.
The Wealth of Nations. Edited by J. R. M'Cullough. Edinburgh, 1872.

Spencer, Herbert.
An Autobiography. 2 vols. New York, 1904.
Social Statics, together with The Man *versus* The State. New York, 1892.
First Principles. New York, 1882.
Principles of Sociology. 3 vols. New York, 1892.
Justice. New York, 1892.

Stahl, Friedrich Julius.
Rechts- und Staatslehre auf der Grundlage christlicher Weltanschauung. 2 Bde. Heidelberg, 1854–56.
Die Revolution und die constitutionelle Monarchie. Eine Reihe ineinandergreifender Abhandlungen. 2te Auflage. Berlin, 1849.

Stein, Lorenz von.
Der Begriff der Gesellschaft und die sociale Geschichte der französischen Revolution bis zum Jahre 1830. 2te Ausgabe. 2 Bände. Leipzig, 1855.

Tocqueville, Alexis de.
Democracy in America. Translated by Henry Reeve. Edited with notes by Francis Bowen. 2 vols. 2d ed. Cambridge [Mass.], 1863.

Waitz, George.
Grundzüge der Politik, nebst einzelnen Ausführungen. Kiel, 1862.

Zachariä, Karl Salomo.
Vierzig Bücher vom Staat. Heidelberg, 1839–43.

II. HISTORICAL, CRITICAL AND DESCRIPTIVE WORKS

Adamson, Robert.
Fichte. Edinburgh, 1881.

Atger, Frédéric.
Essai sur l'histoire des doctrines du contrat social. Paris, 1906.

Barker, Ernest.
Political Thought in England from Herbert Spencer to the Present Day. New York, (1914?).

Barni, Jules.
Histoire des idées morales et politiques en France au 18me siècle. 2 tomes. Paris, 1865–67.

Baudrillart, Henri Joseph Léon.
Études de philosophie morale et d'économie politique. 2 tomes. Paris, 1858.

Beauverger, Edmond de.
Tableau historique des progrès de la philosophie politique. Paris, 1858.

Bluntschli, Johann Kaspar.
Geschichte der neueren Statswissenschaft, allgemeines Statsrecht und Politik. Dritte Auflage. München und Leipzig, 1881.

Bonar, James.
Philosophy and Political Economy in some of their historical relations. London, 1893.

Borgeaud, Charles.
Adoption and Amendment of Constitutions in Europe and America. Translated by C. D. Hazen. Introduction by J. M. Vincent. New York, 1895.

Bosanquet, Bernard.
The Philosophical Theory of the State. London, 1899.

Brie, Siegfried.
Theorie der Staatenverbindungen. Breslau, 1886.

Brisbane.
See Fourier.

Bryce, James.
Studies in History and Jurisprudence. New York and London, 1901.

Buchez, P. J. B., and Roux, P. C.
Histoire Parlementaire de la Révolution Française. 40 tomes. Paris, 1834–38.

Caird, Edward.
The Critical Philosophy of Immanuel Kant. 2 vols. New York, 1889.
Essays on Literature and Philosophy. 2 vols. New York, 1892.
The Social Philosophy and Religion of Comte. New York, 1885.

Coker, Francis W.
Organismic Theories of the State. New York, 1910.

Cushing, H. A.
History of the Transition from Provincial to Commonwealth Government in Massachusetts. New York, 1896.

Davis, H. W. C.
The Political Thought of Heinrich von Treitschke. London, 1914.

Deloche, Maximin.
Du principe des nationalités. Paris, 1860.

Dicey, A. V.
Lectures introductory to the study of the Law of the Constitution. London, 1885.

Faguet, Émile.
La Politique comparée de Montesquieu, Rousseau et Voltaire. Paris, 1902.
Politiques et Moralistes du dix-neuvième siècle. Première série. 3me édition. Paris, 1891.

Fourier, Charles.
Theory of Social Organization. [Translated, with Introduction and Notes] by Albert Brisbane. New York, 1876.
Selections from the Works of. With an Introduction by Charles Gide. Translated by Julia Franklin. London, 1901.

Franck, Ad.
Réformateurs et Publicistes de l'Europe. Dix-huitième siècle. Paris, 1893.

French Revolution.
See Buchez; also Legg.

Girardin, M.
Rousseau, sa vie et ses ouvrages. 2 tomes. Paris, 1875.

Hélie, Faustin-Adolphe.
Les Constitutions de la France. 2 tomes. Paris, 1875.

Higgs, Henry.
The Physiocrats. London and New York, 1897.

Jameson, John Alexander.
A Treatise on Constitutional Conventions. 4th ed. Chicago, 1887.

Janet, Paul.
Histoire de la science politique dans ses relations avec la morale. 3me éd. 2 tomes. Paris, 1887.
Les Origines du Socialisme. Paris, 1883.
Saint-Simon et le Saint-Simonisme. Paris, 1878.

Jellinek, Georg.
The Declaration of the Rights of Man and of Citizens. Translated by Max Farrand. New York, 1901.
Gesetz und Verordnung. Freiburg i. B., 1887.

Kent, C. B. Roylance.
The English Radicals. London, 1899.

Lafayette.
Mémoires, Correspondance et Manuscrits, publiés par G. W. Lafayette. 6 vols. Paris, 1837–38.

Laski, Harold J.
Authority in the Modern State. New Haven, 1919.

Legg, L. G. W.
Select Documents illustrative of the History of the French Revolution. 2 vols. Oxford, 1905.

Léon, Xavier.
La Philosophie de Fichte. Précédé d'une préface de Émile Boutroux. Paris, 1902.

Levkovits, Moritz.
Die Staatslehre auf kantischer Grundlage. Bern, 1899.

Lewis, Sir George Cornewall.
Remarks on the Use and Abuse of some Political Terms. Ed. by Thomas Raleigh. Oxford, 1898.

Liepmann, B. M.

Die Rechtsphilosophie de Jean Jacques Rousseau. Halle, 1898.

Lingley, C. R.

The Transition in Virginia from Colony to Commonwealth. New York, 1910.

Lowell, E. J.

The Eve of the French Revolution. Boston, 1892.

Maine, Henry Sumner.

Early History of Institutions. London, 1875.

Menger, Anton.

The Right to the Whole Produce of Labor. Translated by M. E. Tanner. With an Introduction and Bibliography by H. S. Foxwell. London, 1899.

Merriam, C. E.

History of the Theory of Sovereignty since Rousseau. New York, 1900.

A History of American Political Theories. New York. 1902.

Michel, Henri.

L'Idée de l'État. Essai critique sur l'histoire des théories sociales et politiques en France depuis la Révolution. 2me édition. Paris, 1896.

Mollat, Georg.

Reden und Redner des ersten deutschen Parlaments. Osterwieck — Harz, 1895. [Contains speeches of the leaders on the principal issues in the Frankfort Convention of 1848, and the drafts, first and final, of the constitution, all taken from the stenographic report of the sessions.]

Morley, John.

Rousseau. 2 vols. London, 1888.

Miscellanies. 3 vols. London, 1892.

Morris, George S.

Hegel's Philosophy of the State and of History. Chicago, 1887.

Mulford, E.

The Nation: the Foundations of Civil Order and Political Life in the United States. New York, 1871.

Müller, Wilhelm.
Political History of Recent Times. Translated by John P. Peters. New York, n. d. [1882].

Myres, John Linton.
The Influence of Anthropology on the course of Political Science. (University of California Publications in History, Vol. IV.) Berkeley, 1916.

Paulsen, Friedrich.
Immanuel Kant. Translated by J. E. Creighton and Albert Lefevre. New York, 1902.

Pfizer, P. A.
Ueber die Entwicklung des öffentlichen Rechts in Deutschland durch die Verfassung des Bundes. Stuttgart, 1835.

Rehm, Hermann.
Geschichte der Staatsrechtswissenschaft. Freiburg i. B., 1896.
Allgemeine Staatslehre. Freiburg i. B., 1899.
(Aus [Marquardsen's] Handbuch des Oeffentlichen Rechts: Einleitungsband.)

Ritchie, David G.
Darwin and Hegel with other philosophical studies. London, 1893.

Robinson, J. H., and Beard, C. A.
Readings in Modern European History. 2 vols. Boston, 1908.

Rose, J. Holland.
Nationality in Modern History. New York, 1916.

Rosenthal, Lewis.
America and France: the Influence of the United States on France in the XVIIIth Century. New York, 1882.

Scherger, George L.
The Evolution of Modern Liberty. New York, 1904.

Simkhovitch, V. G.
Marxism versus Socialism. New York, 1913.

Sombart, Werner.
Socialism and the Social Movement. Translated from the sixth German edition by M. Epstein. London and New York, 1909.

Sorel, Albert.
L'Europe et la Révolution Française. Première Partie. 4me édition. Paris, 1897.

Spargo, John.
Karl Marx: his Life and Work. New York, 1910.

Stephen, Sir Leslie.
History of English Thought in the Eighteenth Century. 2 vols. 3d ed. London, 1902.
The English Utilitarians. 3 vols. New York and London, 1900.

Tissot, J.
Turgot: sa vie, son administration, ses ouvrages. Paris, 1862.

Treitschke.
See Davis.

Veneday, Jakob.
Macchiavel, Montesquieu, Rousseau. 2 Bde in 1. Berlin, 1850.

Zoepfl, Heinrich Matthias.
Grundsätze des gemeinen deutschen Staatsrechts. Erster Theil. 2 Bde. 5te Auflage. Leipzig und Heidelberg, 1863.

Zweig, Egon.
Die Lehre vom Pouvoir Constituant. Tübingen, 1909.

INDEX

Printed in the United States of America.